BIENHAMER COLLEGE OF LAW

KT-437-313

JANE CLARKE

Yummy!

EVERY PARENT'S NUTRITION BIBLE

PHOTOGRAPHY BY VÉRONIQUE LEPLAT

THE LIBRARY
NORTH WEST KENT COLLEGE
DERING WAY, GRAVESEND

HODDER
MOBIUS

064459   641.5622
613.2083 CLA
Gravesend £16.99   -7 FEB 2011

This book is dedicated to Navin Poddar, aka Baba.
Maya and I owe you our life.

Copyright © 2006 by Jane Clarke

First published in Great Britain in 2006 by Hodder & Stoughton
A division of Hodder Headline

The right of Jane Clarke to be identified as the Author of
the Work has been asserted by her in accordance with the
Copyright, Designs and Patents Act 1988.

A Mobius Book

1

All rights reserved. No part of this publication may be
reproduced, stored in a retrieval system, or transmitted, in any
form or by any means without the prior written permission
of the publisher, nor be otherwise circulated in any form of binding
or cover other than that in which it is published and without a
similar condition being imposed on the subsequent purchaser.

A CIP catalogue record for this title is available from the British Library

Hardback ISBN 0 340 89879 8
Trade paperback ISBN 0 340 92382 2

Photography © Véronique Leplat
Photograph on p.196 © CatV
Illustration on p11 based on a diagram © British Nutrition Foundation
Recipe development and styling by Sarah Tildesley

Designed by Nicky Barneby @ Barneby Ltd
Typeset in 9.75/14pt Trade Gothic and ITC American Typewriter
Colour Reproduction by Dot Gradations Ltd, Wickford, Essex
Printed and bound by Butler and Tanner Ltd, Frome, Somerset

Hodder Headline's policy is to use papers that are
natural, renewable and recyclable products and made
from wood grown in sustainable forests. The logging and
manufacturing processes are expected to conform to the
environmental regulations of the country of origin.

Hodder & Stoughton Ltd
A division of Hodder Headline
338 Euston Road
London NW1 3BH

Yummy!

Contents

THE LIBRARY
NORTH WEST KENT COLLEGE
DERING WAY, GRAVESEND

Foreword

I was extremely excited to receive this book and after reading the first three pages I was hooked! Being an avid reader of Jane's columns, I was thrilled when I found out that she was writing a book about children's nutrition and wellbeing.

I've been a mum for nearly four years now, and what an adventure and journey it's been so far. I have two gorgeous little girls, aged three and four, who can be described in many words, the main ones being: cute, mischievous, complex, inquisitive, naughty, cheeky and happy . . . Usually they are one or two of these things at any time, but I've found that when they sit down to eat their dinner they are suddenly all of these things at once! Mealtimes can quite often be a fraught time in our house.

I do feel very proud of the way my husband and I have fed the girls – from the very beginning, with my breast milk, all the way through to the salmon and couscous that they are having for their tea tonight. However, it's not always been easy. It can be very hard to feel confident that what you are doing for your children is right and good for them. That concern relates to all aspects of their development, but none more so than the issue of feeding them. I always say to my friends who are fellow mums and dads that if we could just eliminate their three meals a day it would magically cut my stress levels in half! But it's important to get all the help and support we can, regarding this huge part of all of our lives. And that's where Jane comes in . . .

Although I have a very keen interest in healthy food, and nutrition in general, it was only recently that I discovered the existence of a very harmful ingredient called 'hydrogenated fat', which is found in a whole load of everyday food, from chocolates to biscuits to my one big vice – sachets of cappuccino. It's been linked to heart disease, but I hadn't even heard of it before. It makes me wonder how many other hidden evils are lurking in our food. I now find myself spending ages analysing the contents of everything I buy, especially food for the girls. I was, therefore, most intrigued to read in this book about all the 'veiled' additives that, as busy mums, we have no time to get informed about. Jane really has her finger on the pulse and brings us the most up-to-date information in a way that's really easy to understand.

Yummy! has been so clearly set out. It makes a change to read a book on a subject like this and not feel blinded by science, or have to grapple with long, unpronounceable words. I also loved Jane's references to her own daughter, Maya. Knowing that the author of a book is going through exactly the same things that you are trying to deal with makes it all that much more realistic and significant. Sometimes I just feel so inundated with constantly changing information about health, diets, food scares and all the rest, that I just can't keep up! One day something is meant to be good for you, the next it's bad . . .

I definitely related to the section about being obsessed by pasta as both my girls love it. Most days, from the moment they wake up, they ask if they're having pasta for tea. And God bless the days when they are, as I know we're in for a tantrum-free mealtime!

It's also great to finally find a book that offers you alternatives as a parent. By this I mean, for example, that Jane gives you loads of different healthy snack options for your children so that you don't have to resort to the same old sugar-infested biscuits all the time. I often spend hours browsing in my local health shop looking for decent, healthy snack alternatives, checking the backs of packets hoping to find 'No sugar, no additives', etc on the labels. It can be really tricky to find treats for the girls that aren't packed with sugar and things that are harmful. Which is why it's so good to finally read a book with nutritious recipes aimed at feeding children from the inside out. It's a refreshing change not to be expected to cut shapes out of their food or make ridiculous patterns with it just to get them to eat. After all, I believe that the best food you can give your children is food that you have cooked yourself, if you can. The recipe that I particularly love, and intend to make for the girls' birthdays, is the genius sugar-free cake idea on page 250. And, knowing Jane, the taste and flavour definitely will NOT be compromised!

For me, this is the best book I've come across in terms of everything a parent needs to know about nutrition, health and fantastic food for kids. It's simple, easy to understand and, most of all, damn interesting! I know that, having read it, I now feel very confident about trying out some of the recipes and putting the information into practice. There are lots of invaluable hints and tips throughout the book and I'm certain that, armed with this knowledge, we can all take our babies through to adulthood knowing that we are doing the best we can for them nutritionally.

Thanks, Jane!

Jools Oliver x

Introduction

'Children are our most valuable natural resource,' as Herbert Hoover said, and that sums up why I have written this book. As both a mum and a nutritionist I passionately believe that the food I feed my daughter has an enormous impact on her day-to-day health, the way her whole body develops, the way she concentrates in nursery, her ability to learn and to integrate into society. It's this passion that I want to pass on to parents, to inspire you to nourish your child's potential.

Although scientists have known for many years that food has an enormous impact on our health, it's only in the last half decade that the debate about which foods are best for our children has started hitting the headlines. I suspect this is because we in the wealthy west have only just woken up to the fact that we seem to have got things alarmingly wrong. We have more overweight children than ever before, more parents having to resort to putting their kids on behaviour-modifying drugs such as Ritalin, more very young kids showing signs of heart disease and Type 2 diabetes, something we never used to see in children. How have we let things get so bad?

Parents, schools, the food industry and government, along with large sections of society, have at last, thank goodness, realized that we've got to start sorting our kids' diets out. The first decade of a child's eating life can significantly influence whether or not that child develops a weight problem. How you feed your children can also affect whether they develop blocked coronary arteries, or problems regulating their blood sugar levels, and

hence develop heart disease and diabetes when they grow up. Get the food thing right and your children have a greater chance of avoiding the conditions and illnesses we parents dread – cancer, heart disease, arthritis, depression, dementia, etc. I know this sounds alarming, but it's true.

Although many healthcare professionals, dedicated school dinner ladies and headteachers have long been shouting from the sidelines at government, food manufacturers and schools, it's Jamie Oliver who has woken the nation up to how crucial it is for schools and parents to get food right. I worked with him on the *School Dinners* TV series and was as shocked as he was to see how bad things had got – we have literally been killing our kids. But as Jamie showed, with the right knowledge (and the money, the staff, the willingness to change), schools can positively influence the life of their pupils. It's now my turn, as a nutritionist, to get what I hope is an equally inspiring message out to parents – a little yummy-tasting knowledge can go a long way.

I decided to write this book as soon as I became a parent, which was two years ago when I adopted Maya, my utterly adorable minxy three-year-old. I've written *Yummy!* not only as a result of working with Jamie on *School Dinners*, which showed me that there's still some way to go before all parents, as well as schools, know what children should be eating, but also because until I was actually responsible for a child's wellbeing, 24/7, I hadn't quite realized how confusing the mixed messages about kids and food are. The (mis)information coming from the media, the power of TV advertising, not to mention the reach of the supermarkets, are all factors here. Parents are up

against a media machine that our parents didn't have to contend with when they were feeding us, and this media beast is very powerful at influencing food choices. The issues can seem pretty overwhelming, but in *Yummy!* I've set down what I think are the things you need to get right in your child's diet and some ways to make your task as easy as possible.

Another reason I've written *Yummy!* is that after fourteen years of running my nutritional practice, treating kids and their families for all sorts of food-related issues, and my experience more recently working as a journalist for *The Times*, receiving hundreds of letters each year from parents who are worried and unsure about how their children should be eating, I wanted to pass on what I've learned. You'll find here my treatments for everyday health concerns, from tummy-ache, to poor concentration at school, to dealing with a child who seems to be gaining too much weight. And perhaps more than anything, I've written *Yummy!* because when I and my friends entered the parenting stage of our lives, none of us could find a book to inspire us, one that was full of positive messages, not just scary what-not-to-do's (which just overwhelm me and stop me reading on). I wanted a positive, beautiful book with delicious, easy-to-make, nutritious recipes that didn't take an age to shop for or to cook. (Whoever has time to sculpt carrots into funny faces these days!)

Yummy! is for parents of children aged between two and eleven, as this is the time we have the biggest chance and need to get the food thing right. I've tried to keep things inspirational and informative, but brief and to the point, because if you're anything like me, having endless time to sit and read will be something that belongs to the past now that you're a parent (in my case it's been parked alongside lie-ins, uninterrupted conversations and an accurate memory – whatever happens to our brains?).

You'll see from my personal anecdotes about Maya that on many occasions I've ballsed it up. I shall never be allowed to forget the radioactive-looking shocking-pink birthday cake I embarrassingly had to serve at her second birthday party, for example. I dropped the top of the pink food colouring into the icing and had neither the time nor the energy to make any more! Thankfully, at Maya's third birthday party Sarah Tildesley, who helped me come up with the most delicious recipes you will ever find in a child's food book, rescued my reputation by creating a sugar-free but completely yummy birthday cake. My friends were so grateful for being able to take home children that weren't wired and horribly moody.

Like all parents, I've had to make some compromises and have by no means been given an easy ride. Right from the start, Maya has had very clear ideas about what she's going to do and eat (like mother, like daughter). If it was left to her, right now that would be cake, cake and more cake – maybe with the odd dish of pasta thrown in. We've had our battles, and I've had the 'You must be joking, I'm not eating THAT' look on many occasions, having slaved away for what seemed hours preparing something I knew she should be eating and thought she'd gobble up.

Until I became a mum, I hadn't realized how these food rejection moments can be the straw that breaks the camel's back, especially with the extra time and energy pressures that being a single working parent brings. But despite all this, food in our family is the centre of almost everything – luckily I have a daughter and friends around her who love eating, and allow me to indulge them with nutritious and delicious food. I hope my chapter on how to cope with a fussy eater (page 121) will help you work out a way to ride the waves.

I've divided the book into five parts, which, while they can be read consecutively, each work in their own right. Chapter 1 demystifies the nutritional basics – what your kid's body needs and where to get it. Chapter 2 gets straight into the practicalities – how to put a day's meals together, which nutrients you need to include in an energizing breakfast, what snacks to carry around with you during the day, which foods to put in a packed lunch or a picnic, which foods are guaranteed to replenish your kids at the end of the day and get them in the right zone for sleeping. (Don't be put off – it's not as hard as it sounds.)

Chapter 3 is all about key concerns that I have and that I've learnt worry parents during my years in practice and as a journalist, from what I call the baddies, such as additives, sugar, bad fats, genetically modified food and the premium costs of healthy eating, to the goodies – how we can best get our kids' bodies to absorb nutrients from food, whether it's worth paying the extra for organic, and more quirky issues like friendly bacteria and omega oils. Chapter 4 gives you the nutritional low-down on how to treat and manage everyday complaints, from colds and coughs, to manic behaviour, to food allergies and diabetes – which foods to eat and which to steer clear of.

Last but not at all least, Chapter 5 is all about looking after **you** – giving you ideas on how to eat to keep up with the kids, how to get your very tired body going in the morning, how to rediscover the body you used to have before you became a parent (which includes dads as well as mums, as I've seen many dads' bodies change, and not for the better!). After all, though I seem to forget this on a regular basis, I've realized that if I'm exhausted and feeling grouchy Maya picks up on this and runs with it big-time, and we end up in an unhappy, even more drained mess. So checking in with yourself, seeing what you're doing for yourself food-and-drink-wise as well as for your child, making a few tweaks (which can sometimes be all it takes), looking after YOU, is a crucial part of successful parenting.

And to bring it back to where it all started, in my kitchen, *Yummy!* contains fifty recipes, ranging from American-style pancakes with nut butter, to roast chicken with couscous and an easy lemon yoghurt sauce, to raisin and oatmeal shortbread biscuits (delicious with frozen banana, a secret you've yet to discover!) – all foods that the whole family, however big or small, can eat. I don't believe in children having separate kids' menus (do you hear me, restaurants?). I've included a few more exotic ideas to try, such as chai and crispy polenta wedges with creamy mushrooms, as it's good to be a bit more adventurous with children's cooking, and I've also 'borrowed' some ideas from friends and family – for which huge thanks.

Finally, I hope *Yummy!* boosts your knowledge, confidence and energy so that you can feed your child nutritious food and turn eating well into a central part of your lives. It really is to everyone's advantage!

Like all parents, I've had to make some compromises.

CHAPTER ONE

Nutrition for Kids: the Basics

The issue of feeding your child the right foods can seem a huge mountain to climb at the outset – so many books to read, so many products on the supermarket shelves, such a lot of advice dished out by every other parent, relative and neighbour. Everyone's experience is different, and tips and titbits will be useful over the years, but the first thing to structure into your child's diet are the basic food groups, the carbohydrates, proteins and fats, so that they can grow well, feel well, have enough (but not too much!) energy, and develop a strong immune system. Like adults, every day your child needs ideally to have food rich in each of these key groups. However, while adults can sometimes get away with cutting corners and missing things out, children should have something from each group for one simple reason – they're in an active growing phase of their lives, when their bodies need not only to cope with the demands of growth, but also to start laying down some good foundations and stores.

The Balance of Health diagram helps us see what groups of foods our children need. Actually, this is a model that applies to everyone over the age of five and can be gradually introduced for younger children, too. I'm not going to blind you with science, it's just useful to see which foods lie where in terms of importance and how they need to be balanced.

The two biggest segments are firstly, carbohydrates and fibre – bread, cereals, grains, rice, pasta, quinoa, millet, spelt, etc and secondly, fruit and vegetables. Roughly one third of our intake should be from the first carbohydrate group of starches and one third should be from the fruit and vegetable group. Of the remaining third, most of it should be from the protein groups of dairy and meat/fish and tofu etc. Less than one sixth of our diet should be made up from the fat- and sugar-containing group, and of course it is much better to eat good fats such as those found in oily fish, nuts and seeds and natural sugars such as fruit and honey. That said, cake is not evil, of course, so long as it's eaten in the right proportions! Bear in mind that it isn't necessary to follow the model at every meal, but rather over a day or two. You will see that some foods fall into more than one section, for example meat comes into both protein and fats.

CARBOHYDRATES

Carbohydrates that are grain-based, as opposed to fruits and vegetables, are broken down into complex and simple varieties. These should form a large part of your child's diet because they are the best source of the good energy they need in order to run around, feel well and grow. The more complex the grain, the less processing it's been exposed to; they're incredibly rich in nutrients and seem to give a child more consistent energy throughout the day and reduce the likelihood of them becoming crabby, which can be the case with more refined carbohydrate/sugary foods.

The great complex carbs are unsweetened mueslis, porridge oats, wholemeal and wholegrain breads, wholemeal muffins, pitta breads, yummy cornbread, brown rice, millet, spelt, barley and buckwheat noodles. I know some of these sound a bit hardcore, but bear with me. Simple carbohydrates are those that have had most of their fibre removed and may well have been bleached and refined – these are found in the white breads and pastas (and of course the biscuits and cakes) we see in the supermarket. We can and should include some of these simple carbohydrates in our children's diet – life would be sad without white pasta with olive oil and parmesan cheese, or fresh white toast

Fruit & veg

Breads, cereals,
potatoes

Meat & fish

Dairy

Fats & sugars

with butter and a yummy pure fruit spread – but we should try not to make them the only source of carbohydrate because in the processing most of the goodness has been removed along with the husk of the grain, so we don't find the minerals and vitamins that are naturally found in the complex carbohydrates. In Britain most white flour is fortified with calcium and niacin, and this can be good especially for kids who aren't able to tolerate or don't like dairy products, but if you can persuade your child to eat some wholemeal bread and complex carbohydrates as well, this is ideal.

Just as too much simple carbohydrate can mean kids don't feel satisfied enough after eating (it's the fibre within the husk in complex carbs that makes them feel full), and therefore eat too much and gain too much weight, it's also not good to fill them up with too many complex high-fibre carbs either. Too much wholegrain can be too bulky, can upset their gut, can mean they don't get enough energy from their food; so they may not grow as well as they should, may feel tired all the time, and in extreme situations (though I've only seen this a few times, with mums who tend to be overly obsessed with their child's health) can mean they don't absorb enough minerals such as iron and calcium from their diet, since lots of wholegrain can reduce the absorption of these essential minerals. In theory they could develop weak bones and iron deficiency anaemia, but this is rare.

It's about balance at the end of the day: I have a rule of thumb that kids up to the age of five should generally have roughly two-thirds white pasta, white bread, white rice – the simple but still good starchy foods – to one-third the more complex wholemeal bread, wholemeal pasta, brown rice, etc., and should then switch to two-thirds complex carbs and one-third simple carbs until they're teenagers. It really depends on how well your child is growing, what their gut health is like, whether they get constipated, etc., or if they are going through a voracious appetite stage and perhaps filling out in the waistline area (see page 139).

I tend to vary a bit whether I use all wholemeal flour in pastries or cakes, choose wholemeal or buckwheat pasta with a chunky vegetable sauce or a white pasta with a simple macaroni cheese. I just keep Maya away from the highly refined, sweet, overly processed cakes and biscuits, preferring her to have a slice of carrot cake or traybake fig bar (see my recipes on pages 212–259).

It's about balance, at the end of the day.

FIBRE

Fibre is something many kids are lacking in, which is why so many of them suffer from constipation (also down to lack of fluid) and obesity – it's the fibre-rich foods that make meals feel satisfying for a long time. Technically, fibre is needed to help keep their digestive system working efficiently, their hearts healthy, and it also helps balance their blood sugar levels – fibre slows down the digestion and absorption of carbohydrates (see glycaemic index, page 83), which impacts on energy levels, ability to concentrate and learn and reduces the chances of developing conditions such as diabetes.

Fibre is found in two main forms in our diets, soluble and insoluble, and kids need both. Soluble fibre is found mainly in fruits and vegetables and grains such as oats. Insoluble fibre is found in the husks of grains such as wheat and rye, so wholemeal rye bread, wholemeal bagels, etc. are rich in insoluble fibre, which tends to keep the gut moving well – soluble fibres can help with the gut, but they're more efficient at looking after blood sugar levels and the heart through their positive effects on cholesterol and other fats in the blood. To maximize the amount of fibre in your child's diet, it's best to keep the peel on fruits such as apples and pears and to include some wholegrain products, such as porridge for breakfast or wholemeal bread in their sandwiches. Children should get their fibre naturally from food rather than adding it in the form of bran or supplements (unless prescribed by your doctor) – and raw bran should not be used as it inhibits the absorption of essential growth minerals such as iron and calcium.

Fruits and vegetables are also classified as complex carbohydrates and they're great for kids and adults alike. By the time children get to the age of five they should be having five portions of fruit and veg a day, so that they get plenty of vitamins, minerals and fibre, especially plant chemicals such as phytonutrients – all of which are great for their hearts, guts and immune systems. Every cell in the body will benefit from the nutrients contained in fruits and vegetables. A portion of fruit is roughly equivalent to:

Remember the five-a-day mantra: by the age of five, children should be eating five portions of fruit and veg a day.

* about 40g (a handful) of dried fruits, such as apricots, prunes, dates, figs, sultanas, raisins, peaches, pears and mangoes
* 100g (about a cupful) of small fruits like strawberries, blueberries, raspberries, gooseberries, cherries, lychees and kumquats
* 2 medium-sized fruits – plums, greengages, peaches, apricots, nectarines, kiwi fruits and passion fruits, for instance
* 1 orange, apple, banana, pear, grapefruit or apple
* 100g (a large slice) of melon, mango, papaya, guava or pineapple
* 100ml of freshly squeezed fruit juice

And here are some examples of what constitutes a portion of vegetables:

* 70g of tiny vegetables, such as peas and sweetcorn
* 80g (cooked weight) of root vegetables, such as carrots and turnips
* 80g (cooked weight) of pulses, such as chickpeas and baked beans
* 80g of a cooked vegetable dish, like a vegetable casserole or ratatouille
* 90g (cooked weight) of green vegetables, such as spinach and cabbage
* 100g (raw weight) or 80g (cooked weight) of vegetables such as peppers, squashes, tomatoes and onions
* a large bowl of salad vegetables
* 100ml of vegetable juice

If your child is under five, gradually after weaning introduce more and more vegetables and fruits. They might take to puréed vegetables first, like pumpkin and sweet potato, and you can introduce them to crunchier textures and bigger pieces as they get older.

After the age of five, if you give them a glass of freshly squeezed juice for breakfast, a piece of fresh fruit later in the morning, a vegetable or salad something with their lunch, some fruit at teatime and vegetables with their supper, you'll have hit the five-portion target. It's good to vary the vegetables as much as possible because some are particularly rich in certain minerals and vitamins (spinach in iron and carrots in beta-carotene, for example) and having a variety will increase the range of health-giving nutrients the body receives. While exotic fruits like mango are great things for your child to experience, there's nothing wrong with a common or garden apple, orange or banana – every fruit, like every vegetable, has a place, and when you're not sure they'll even eat all of it, cutting a mango can be a costly exercise. I know it's not easy to get kids to eat a variety of fruit and vegetables, but later in the book you'll find lots of ideas for fussy eaters!

Some parents don't like their kids eating whole unpeeled fruits and become far too precious about cutting up and peeling them. This can make a lot of unnecessary work, and kids need to know that fruits don't grow ready-peeled – there's so much goodness just inside the peel. Kids can manage whole fruits – just make it clear to them that they need to sit down and be careful when eating, so they don't choke, and that the deal is they finish

THE LIBRARY
NORTH WEST KENT COLLEGE
DERING WAY, GRAVESEND

what they've taken. Don't let them just keep taking a bite out of every piece of fruit in the bowl!

Tinned, frozen, cooked and dried fruits and vegetables can surprisingly be as nutritious as fresh ones. If they've been heat-treated, tinned fruits and vegetables contain a little less vitamin C, but some manufacturers compensate for this by adding vitamin C to their products in supplement form. Opt for tinned fruits in natural fruit juice, not sugary syrup. Frozen fruits and vegetables are frozen soon after they have been picked, which means they are just as healthy as fresh. (I find frozen berries a particularly useful standby, and defrost them as and when I need them to use in smoothies, cereals, crumbles and compôtes.) Fresh, raw fruits and vegetables usually contain more vitamins and minerals than cooked ones, but they can sometimes play havoc with your child's digestive system, in which case cooked fruits, such as poached pears (in a juice such as orange juice, not in wine), or baked apples or peaches, and roasted and puréed vegetables, may suit them better.

Studies indicate that organic fruits and vegetables contain more vitamins and minerals than their non-organic counterparts and are furthermore free of the artificial pesticides, antibiotics and chemical residues to which non-organic produce is exposed, which can't be good for kids.

WHAT IF THEY DON'T LIKE FRUITS OR (MORE LIKELY) VEGETABLES?

It's unlikely that you won't be able to find a fruit they like, because they generally enjoy the sweetness – from clementines, mangoes, figs, kiwis, to apples and bananas. Try blending fruits into a smoothie or freezing pure fruit purées to make ice lollies or ice creams (see recipes on pages 254–255). You can also purée, cook and stuff fruits to make them more appealing to a fussy child. When it comes to vegetables, just try as hard as you can to serve them in different guises – roasted, puréed, stuffed. As long as they eat one or two types a day, they should get enough nutrients.

If they're going through a really bad patch and just won't touch vegetables, even when you disguise them in sauces, etc., you could give them a general multivitamin and mineral supplement to tide them over (see page 25). However, there's no replacement for real fresh food, so each week try to coax them back into having the real thing – they won't glean as much goodness from supplements as from real fresh foods. Try each new food 8–10 times before you finally write it off as a dislike, as kids are just like the weather – they change all the time!

Tinned, frozen, cooked and dried fruit and vegetables all count.

PROTEINS

Proteins are essential for growth, brain development and building and maintaining a healthy bone structure, and the amino acids which are the building blocks of proteins are also good for encouraging the production of happy hormones called endorphins. There are a total of twenty-two amino acids, eight of which are called essential because we can't make them in our body and must therefore get them from our food. Before going into greater detail about types of protein, a word of warning: some parents think the more protein their child eats, the stronger their muscles are and the more they grow – and in this high-protein-diet society I've also come across parents worried that carbohydrate foods will make their child put on too much weight, so they tend to base their child's diet mainly around protein. These attitudes aren't healthy for kids. Kids don't grow more if they eat more protein, and too much protein can cause their kidneys to be over-burdened by the acids that are the breakdown product of proteins – so moderation is the key.

Proteins are divided into two groups: animal-based and plant-based. Animal proteins are sometimes referred to as primary proteins, as they contain all eight essential amino acids, and are considered to be the most important ones for growth (but you can also be healthy being vegetarian – see page 112). In our western society the animal proteins are usually chicken, seafood, fish, red meat, white meat, eggs, milk, butter, yoghurt and cheese. Plant proteins are referred to as incomplete proteins because they don't contain all of the essential amino acids, so you need to give your child a combination of nuts, seeds and grains in order that they receive all they need. Plant foods rich in proteins are pulses, legumes, lentils, tofu and other soya products, and you can get some protein from cereal grains such as quinoa and from buckwheat and seaweed (which unless you're a big Japanese food fan doesn't tend to be a major source in kids' diets, although my pink sushi can be a hit – see page 229).

Every day you need to ensure your child has some protein along with the carbohydrate. (See page 20 for how to juggle the foods.) Although nuts and nut butters are great sources of protein, you should avoid whole nuts with kids under five and ensure that there isn't a possibility of a nut allergy (for example, if you have a history of this in your family).

FATS

Kids need their fats – it's essential to include some in their diet. They need fats for brain function, to help them learn, behave, concentrate, etc., to provide some insulation under their skin so they don't lose too much body heat, and to produce essential hormones to ensure healthy growth and development. Some fat is also needed to ensure good absorption of fat-soluble vitamins. However, many parents have become frightened of the fat issue, especially since low-fat products have infiltrated and dominated the supermarket shelves, and think low-fat products must be better than normal ones. Of course children shouldn't have too much fat because they'll become overweight, get clogged arteries, etc., but the majority of normal-weight children should be eating enough good fat and not tucking into low-fat foods, which can sometimes be high in sugar.

It's all about knowing which are the better fats for kids to eat. The omega-rich fatty foods such as mackerel, sardines, herrings, salmon, fresh tuna are goodies – ideally all kids should have a couple of portions (a portion being 140g) each week. Girls should stick to two portions (because of concerns over the build-up of toxins in the body which could harm babies born to them in the future), but boys can have up to four portions a week. With recent concerns over the mercury levels in tuna, however, I wouldn't go above a couple of portions of tuna a week for either boys or girls. The omega oils are fantastic for brain function, for hearts, joints, and virtually every part of the body. If your child doesn't like fish, or if you'd like non-fish sources of these magic oils, turn to oils such as hemp and flax (linseed), walnuts and their oil, and seeds such as sunflower and pumpkin (which are best ground up to aid absorption). I grind the seeds up and use them in porridge, in smoothies, or smuggled into Maya's breakfast cereal.

Other fats – from dairy produce such as butter, cheese, cream, yoghurt, milk – are fine to be included in kids' diets, as they also contribute calcium, magnesium and vitamins A and D. (See good and bad fats, page 75.)

Don't be frightened of fat. It's essential to include good fats in their diet.

GETTING THE BALANCE RIGHT

WHAT DOES A NUTRITIONALLY BALANCED MEAL LOOK LIKE?

Looking at the Balance of Health diagram on page 11, you'll see that your child's meals should contain some foods from each of the food groups – for Maya and me that means we start the day with a wholegrain or fruit-rich breakfast. This can be anything from a small glass of freshly squeezed juice, some wholemeal toast with either a little butter and pure fruit spread, or a little smooth peanut butter with a sliced banana on top, or a banana on its own with some natural yoghurt and grapes. Although I've always needed a substantial breakfast, Maya isn't much of an early-morning eater, so I'm happy for her to just try to eat any of the above, or a small bowl of porridge with honey and raisins, and then later on, when she's got going, have a bigger mid-morning snack. Some kids need to move around before they start feeling hungry. But whatever time it is, I do try to get some food into her in the morning, as it helps regulate her mood, her energy levels and her gut. At weekends we might have a more substantial brunchy-style meal (see my suggestions on page 39), but the words fibre, fruits, good healthy cereals are foremost in my mind.

For other meals I tend to cook a carbohydrate food like rice or pasta (wholemeal or white), with some chicken or fish, or a beany casserole, to supply the protein, along with some salad or a couple of vegetables of some sort, and use just a little fat, such as oil or butter, in cooking. I always try to serve at least two different fresh seasonal vegetables with each meal and to vary the proteins and carbohydrates, so that Maya gets a good spectrum of nutrients – if you eat seasonally, foods remain special, not always the same predictable veg, and of course seasonal food tends to be highest in nutrients, and cheapest and best value in the shops.

There are times when Maya will be so keen on a specific food that she wants to eat it all the time – at the moment she wakes up and asks for pasta for breakfast! I sometimes give in and try to incorporate her preferences (not pasta for breakfast, though!), but I always have the final say – keeping variety wide. Parents who always prepare what the child asks for can get into some really tricky power games – especially if the child asks for one thing and then refuses to eat it and asks for another. Try to stop yourself going down this road, as it can mean utter cooking misery and a very fussy manipulative little one. (See page 130 on fussy eating.)

I don't go much for fried fatty foods, because not only are they astronomically high in fat, but the fact that the fat is heated up to high temperatures means there is a likelihood that it will partially break down into trans fats, which are damaging for the heart (see page 75). A couple of times a week I try to get Maya to have some oily fish such as sardines on toast, although she can't eat salmon and tuna because I have a severe allergy to these. Instead I tend to incorporate the vegetarian sources of the omega-rich foods in our diet, using hemp oil on salads, grinding seeds up and putting them in her cereal (see page 248).

I usually end one of our daily meals with a slice of good healthy cake or a fruit crumble or fruit layer, and the other meal with yoghurt and fruit –

maybe just a plate of fresh fruit, a quick easy pudding. Commercial low-fat yoghurts, especially those designed to appeal to kids, can be astronomically high in sugar (see page 40), so I give Maya natural yoghurt and add a little fresh fruit or honey – both supply vitamins and minerals, and honey has good antibacterial properties.

HOW MANY MEALS A DAY?

It depends on your child. Some can manage on three meals a day and not much in between, but Maya, for instance, burns off so much energy that she tends to need little pit-stops – usually one snack mid-morning and one mid-afternoon. Little and often works for her. Like all kids, though, she goes through feast and famine periods, as I call them: some days she's not bothered and won't eat much, others she'll eat me out of house and home. As long as the not wanting to eat doesn't go on more than a couple of days at a time and she doesn't have any other signs of being unwell, I don't panic. I just make sure she drinks enough water to stay well hydrated, knowing she'll eat when she's hungry – and eventually she does.

I think routines and structure work well with children, so I base each day around two main meals and a breakfast. I am a big fan of breakfast for kids, as it gives them enough energy to get off to the best start. I try to make sure lunch includes proteins, fats and carbohydrates, and the same with the meal at the end of the day, with the main snacks being fruits. Parents who free-fall through the day, feeding their kids on demand, or not giving them much structure meal-wise, can find their child either becomes overweight or lacks fresh fruits, vegetables and proteins, as the easily available snack foods they tend to reach for are more likely to be refined and full of fats and sugars.

Timing-wise, I try to leave Maya a good hour to an hour and a half after her evening meal before she goes to bed, as this gives the food more time to go and stay down.

Try to establish a routine. Structure helps to encourage healthy eating.

VITAMINS AND MINERALS

If you are worried about your child not getting enough nutrients, you can give them a vitamin and mineral supplement. The ideal supplements are those made especially for kids, which list the dietary reference values (DRVs) for the nutrients. (See also maximizing nutrients, page 107.)

Fat-soluble vitamins

Vitamin A/beta-carotene

This is needed for healthy growth, skin, teeth; it protects against infections and is a powerful antioxidant, so helps prevent diseases such as heart disease and cancers. Best sources are cantaloupe melon, pumpkin, squash, carrots, peaches, apricots, red and orange peppers, tomatoes, liver, egg yolk, dairy produce, mackerel and herrings.

Vitamin D

This is needed for building and maintaining strong, healthy bones and teeth; it also helps muscle function. It works with vitamins A and C to boost your child's immune system and prevent colds. Vitamin D is mainly manufactured by the skin when it's exposed to sunlight, but the following foods are also good sources: sardines, herrings, salmon, tuna, dairy produce and eggs.

Vitamin E

This is needed for healthy skin, a good strong immune system, a healthy heart, and also helps reduce the amount of scarring kids get from bumps and grazes. It's found in all vegetable oils, avocados, broccoli, almonds, sunflower seeds,

eggs, soya and whole grains, which includes oatmeal, rye and brown rice.

Vitamin K

Great for building and maintaining healthy strong bones and essential for helping blood to clot properly – you may recall that babies are given an injection of Vitamin K straight after birth. But you need to top the supplies up as they grow. Vitamin K can be found in bio yoghurt, egg yolks, fish oils, dairy produce and green leafy vegetables, although kids also manufacture quite a lot of vitamin K in their gut – the good bacteria produce it.

Water-soluble vitamins

Vitamin B1

This vitamin is needed for energy production, carbohydrate digestion, heart function; helps children concentrate and their brains generally to function well. Found in wholegrain foods, such as good cereals and bread, oats, rye, millet, quinoa, legumes, pork and liver.

Vitamin B2

Like vitamin B1 this is needed for digestion of carbohydrates, but also of fats and proteins, and generally helps children's bodies derive enough energy from food. It's also needed for their hair, nails and the development of their sex organs. Best sources are bio yoghurt, fish, liver, milk, cottage cheese and green leafy vegetables like spinach.

Vitamin B3

Good for the sex hormones and other hormones connected to the digestive system, such as insulin, the hormone that regulates blood sugar levels in the body, and also for thyroxine, serotonin and other mood and brain hormones. We generally say that B3 is found in the same foods as B1 and B2.

Vitamin B5

This is needed for conversion of fats and carbohydrates into energy and also for supporting the adrenal glands, which regulate the stress response in the body. It also ensures a strong immune system. We find it in wholegrains, rye, barley, millet, nuts, chicken, egg yolks, liver and green leafy vegetables.

Vitamin B6

Children need vitamin B6 for a strong nervous system, for an equally robust immune system and to help repair the body when it gets injured. Found in poultry such as chicken and turkey, lean red meat, egg yolks, oily fish, dairy produce, cabbage, leeks and wheat germ.

Vitamin B12

The growth system, digestion and nerves need vitamin B12, as do the production of energy and healthy blood cell departments. Kids also need enough B12 in their diet to ensure they absorb enough iron. It's found in red meats such as beef, liver and pork, shellfish and other fish, eggs and dairy produce; for vegetarians, you can also find B12 in seaweed and spirulina.

Folic acid

This is perhaps most famous for its role in preventing neural defects during pregnancy, but it's also good for the immune system, energy production and preventing anaemia. Best sources are the good old dark green leafy vegetables like kale, spinach, egg yolks, carrots, apricots, pumpkins and squashes, melons (particularly the cantaloupe variety), whole-wheat and rye.

Biotin

Children need biotin for their hair and nails, skin and energy production. Found in brewer's yeast, brown rice, nuts, egg yolks and fruits.

Vitamin C

Vitamin C is needed for a strong immune system, a healthy heart, good skin, preventing diseases like heart disease and cancer in later life, and helping bumps, scratches and cuts to heal properly. Best sources are kiwi fruits, blueberries (in fact, all berries), pomegranate juice, citrus fruits, potatoes, pumpkins and squashes, sweet peppers, green leafy vegetables, cabbage, broccoli, cauliflower and spinach.

Minerals

Calcium
Calcium is essential for bones, teeth and heart, and is also needed to help kids' muscles work properly. It's found in dairy produce, small-boned fish like sardines, green leafy vegetables, soya products, almonds, sesame seeds (so tahini and hummus are great), sunflower seeds (which I roast and give Maya as a snack with sultanas and raisins) and dried fruits such as apricots.

Iron
Iron is important for growth and development and crucial in the production of healthy red blood cells, which carry oxygen around the body. It also works with other essential minerals such as calcium and the B vitamins. Found in liver, lean red meat, egg yolks, peaches, apricots, figs, nuts, bananas, spinach, watercress, broccoli, avocados and fresh herbs, particularly parsley. Vegetarian sources include dark green leafy vegetables like spinach and kale, seaweed (if you can get them to eat it!), figs, pot barley, baked beans in tomato sauce (always a good standby), nuts, oatmeal, avocados, apricots, prunes, broccoli, asparagus, lentils, sunflower seeds, fortified breakfast cereals, wholemeal bread and brown rice.

Magnesium
Magnesium helps the body deal with stress, generate enough energy and build strong healthy bones; it also helps with muscle work and the nervous system. It's found in citrus fruits, green vegetables such as broccoli, cabbage, nuts and seeds, dried fruits (especially figs and raisins), tomatoes, garlic, carrots, potatoes, aubergines, onions and sweetcorn.

Selenium
This mineral, which works alongside vitamin E in the body, is essential for the immune system and to build good skin. It's found in all fresh fruits and vegetables, shellfish, sesame seeds, wheat germ and bran (so healthy cereals are a good source), tomatoes, broccoli and, last but not least, brazil nuts – which can be ground into a delicious mix with seeds to sprinkle on cereals or in porridge.

Zinc
Most people know about zinc being involved in the immune system, but it's also good for sexual development, moods, nervous system and brain function. Sources are fish and shellfish, lean red meats, wholegrain, poultry, nuts and seeds, eggs, cauliflower, berries, dairy produce such as yoghurt, oats, rye, wheat germ, brown rice and buckwheat.

Vitamin and mineral chart

This chart shows how much of a vitamin or mineral a child requires at various stages, and the foods in which that amount can be found. In the food equivalent column, the first amount relates to the oldest age group and the smaller amounts in brackets to the two younger age groups respectively (if just one amount is given in brackets it relates to both younger groups). While I have tried to choose realistic foods that children would eat, in some cases you'll see that the portion size would be unrealistic for the age group. But you wouldn't just rely on one food to meet a DRV, as other foods in the diet would contribute as well. So by eating one rich source and other foods to make a balanced diet your child can glean the amount of the nutrient their body requires.

If you are worried about your child not getting enough vitamins and minerals you can give them a supplement designed for kids. It's best to aim to get them eating a really varied diet, though. That way they'll get everything they need.

	1–3 YEARS	4–6 YEARS	7–10 YEARS	FOOD EQUIVALENTS
Thiamin	0.5mg	0.7mg	0.7mg	50g pork fillet (30g) or 180g (1 medium) baked potato (150g)
Riboflavin	0.6 mg	0.8 mg	1mg	70g (2 bowls) Cheerios or 80g (2 bowls) Ready Brek (60g, 40g) or 3 Weetabix (2½, 2)
Niacin	8 mg	11 mg	12 mg	80g chicken breast (70g, 50g) or 300g lentil soup (200g, 150g)
B6	0.7 mg	0.9 mg	1 mg	120g salmon fillet (110g, 90g)
B12	0.5µg	0.8µg	1µg	2 boiled eggs (1½, 1)
Folate	70µg	100µg	150µg	75g (3 tbsp) broccoli (50g, 35g)
Vit C	30 mg	30 mg	30 mg	40g (5) strawberries or 1 kiwi
Vit A	400µg	400µg	500µg	60g (2 tbsp) carrots (50g)
Vit D	7µg	–	–	1 pilchard
Calcium	350 mg	450 mg	550 mg	65g Cheddar cheese (50g, 35g) or 460ml milk (375ml, 290ml)
Magnesium	85 mg	120 mg	200 mg	300g hummus (160g, 140g)
Sodium	500 mg	700 mg	1200 mg	200g baked beans (125g, 90g)
Potassium	800 mg	1100 mg	2000 mg	300g (1 large) baked potato (175g, 125g)
Iron	6.9 mg	6.1 mg	8.7 mg	240g beef (170g, 190g) or 175g couscous (120g, 140g)
Zinc	5 mg	6.5 mg	7 mg	120g Quorn (100g, 90g)
Selenium	15µg	20µg	30µg	40g tuna (25g, 20g)

I hope I haven't bewildered you completely. Although it's important to understand how various foods should fit into your child's schedule, at the end of the day all parents should feel free to go with the flow. There will be times when your child will only want to eat a specific type of food, meal after meal, for a few days, and this is fine in the grand scheme of things. Remember that the less anxious you are about what and how they're eating, the more likely they are to want to eat the foods you think they should be tucking into – it's reverse psychology a lot of the time to some extent, and the more anxious and pushy you are, the more likely they are to just close their mouth and refuse to play ball. If it's pasta a few days running, I bet they'll soon switch on to something else.

Don't panic! All parents should feel free to go with the flow.

CHAPTER TWO

Your Child's Eating Day

Kids are like cars – they need regular refuelling, but the amount of fuel they need largely depends on how active they are. Is your child more sedate, not seeming to burn up food quickly, or more like my daughter, Maya, who seems to use up whatever she eats within a couple of hours? Like adults, some kids tend to be more hungry at lunchtime, so it's good to think about maybe having their main cooked meal then; others just want a lighter sandwich-style/egg on toast, soup, etc. lunch, preferring to eat a more substantial tea later on. Nowadays, more than ever before, what children eat during the day will also depend on whether they're at home (what sort of cooking skills/confidence and time does the parent or carer/nanny have?), or at school (how conscious of healthy food are the headteacher and staff?). The appearance of ready-made meals for kids on supermarket shelves has also meant that some kids are just having bling-bling meals, as they're known – i.e. something that's quickly popped into the microwave.

As you'll have read in Chapter 1, every mealtime is nutritionally best when it contains proteins and carbohydrates alongside a little fat. So my yummy recipes on pages 212–259 are all rich in these essential nutrients. It's a good idea to get into a sort of routine, with a set lunchtime (roughly anyway), and to decide whether this is going to be the main cooked meal or not. This way your child will know pretty well what to expect, and you can also see the way in which what you feed them affects how they get through the day. For example, if you're used to always giving them their main meal at lunchtime, you might find you need them to have a more active morning so that they can build up an appetite. After a larger lunch they might well feel a little more sedentary in the afternoon, their body preferring to take things a little easy while it diverts some of the oxygen to the stomach where it's needed to help digest the food (this is why kids can feel sleepy after a big meal, especially when the meal is rich in the pasta, rice, potatoes, couscous, polenta-type starches, which tend to make them feel more calm). If they're lighter-lunch kids, though they may only have a smaller appetite you do need to make sure the lunch still contains some protein as well as carbohydrate. You might be fine yourself with just a little, but they most definitely need more than a salad and fruit. Chicken, meat, fish, eggs, beans, lentils, are all high-protein foods – so a hummus and salad sandwich is an idea, as are my wraps (see page 230).

RISE AND SHINE

Starting the day with a little breakfast is important, because what children eat first thing can have a big impact on how they feel, on how they concentrate, on their ability to complete tasks, memorize things, solve problems, be creative at school or playgroup. Putting just a little something inside their stomachs can help prevent them getting tummy-ache at lunchtime, feeling weak and grumpy, stop them wanting everything in sight if you make an early morning trip to the supermarket, usually the sweet and fatty things heavily marketed to kids. After all, they've gone through the night without eating anything, so their blood sugar level will be lowish in the morning, and if you don't top it up they can develop headaches and feel exhausted.

I also find it's good to start the day sitting together for a few minutes, to have time to communicate before the day goes mad. OK, you might have to go out early to work, but try to have breakfast together at weekends, or if you're lucky enough to have a lie in

(memories!), have brunch – but more about that later.

WHAT IS A GOOD BREAKFAST?

Ideally we want to them to have something that includes carbohydrate, protein and fat, with a little fruity vitamin C thrown in. Proteins and fat take longer to digest than carbohydrates, and therefore tend to keep your child energized and feeling stong and satisfied for longer – but carbs on the other hand give almost instant energy to the brain. You've probably heard of the glycaemic index (GI) and glycaemic load of carbohydrate-rich foods – the lower GI the food, the longer it is likely to keep them energized and satisfied, so I prefer low and medium GI breakfasts to the quick-burst high GI foods.

You don't need to panic about what a high or low GI breakfast consists of, as I've listed them in the box opposite. I would avoid as much as possible the cereals and bars that are heavily marketed for kids, as they are more often than not packed full of sugar and salt. So what if they contain prebiotic fibre and calcium – your child is better off getting their nutrients from less processed foods. I know it's hard to avoid them altogether, but if they don't have them, they won't miss them – if you find that friends introduce them you could limit them to weekends. I'd be wary of many of the cereal bars that suggest they make a healthy breakfast for your child – they're usually full of sugar, fat and salt at unacceptably high levels.

* **Low GI breakfast**
  Apples, peaches, cherries, grapefruits, plums, oranges, dried apricots, nuts, milk, yoghurt (plain, that is – see page 87).
* **Medium GI breakfast**
  Porridge (see my recipes, page 218), unsweetened muesli, dark rye bread, pitta bread, slightly underripe bananas, grapes, dates, figs, kiwi fruit.
* **High GI breakfast**
  Sugar, honey, pineapple, raisins, lemons, ripe bananas, wholemeal and white bread, cornflakes and cereals such as Rice Crispies. But this doesn't mean that white bread is bad for kids, nor wholemeal – they're both fine (see fibre, page 14).

Porridge is a winner – it can be made with milk or water, as well as soya, oat or rice milk. You need some sort of sweetness, so use a little honey, brown sugar, fresh or dried fruits. Although in pure nutritional terms there is no difference between honey, brown sugar and common or garden white sugar, I prefer to use honey or brown sugar because they give a delicious caramel sweetness and you don't need to use as much in order to get the desired wonderful sweet hit. In the summer you can top it with berries and in the winter with apple purée (see page 218). I also like to add some seeds such as linseeds and sesame seeds sometimes – you can either pop them in whole, or grind them up and stir them in – the latter is better for younger kids, as whole seeds can be a little tough to digest and are also a choking hazard.

Toast is fine too – wholemeal, brown, best of both or white, with a little butter and a pure fruit spread. A topping of sliced banana and a nut butter like peanut butter is good, as are poached egg, boiled egg, eggy bread and stewed fruits, or a little low-salt yeast extract. Muffins, bagels, crispbreads, such as Swedish-style rye crackers, work well too. There's nothing wrong with croissants and pain au chocolat either – depending on what your child eats during the rest of the day, it might be an idea to keep the speciality croissants as a wonderful weekend treat – going out and getting the papers, the fresh croissants, is a favourite Saturday morning routine for Maya and me.

Some breakfast cereals are OK – Weetabix, Shredded Wheat, Cheerios are some of the best. You could top it with sliced banana, a little honey, or sugar – I prefer the unrefined cane sugar. Some of the simple puffed rice cereals are good, or an unsweetened (and no added salt either) luxury muesli.

American style pancakes with nut butter or some fresh fruits and yoghurt…yum. Whole milk yoghurt or fromage frais with fresh fruit, either on its own or with a little muesli added. Fresh fruit smoothies made with seasonal fruit, or a vegetable juice if they'll drink it – Maya spits veggie juice out!

Porridge is a winner –it's pretty much the ideal breakfast food. But toast is good too, and there's nothing wrong with a croissant, for a treat.

PACKED LUNCHES

Being the parent of a child who's at an age to be influenced by colours, cartoons, TV advertising, friends, isn't easy. Every month more products aimed at kids and parents find their way on to the supermarket shelves – promising all sorts of things from calcium to so-called natural fruit sugars. When time is short and inspiration low, when you're rushed off your feet as you try to pack them off to school or nursery, with something healthy in their Tupperware box, it can be hard to know what's good, bad or indifferent in kids' products. They may be pretty similar if you look at the bare nutritional facts – calcium in one product versus calcium in another – but the best thing to do if you can is look at the overall nutrition package, the ONP as I've named it, which also includes the quality of ingredients, and the whole habit and sensory aspect of eating. Some products may contain the same amount of calcium as milk, but it's much better for kids to get used to drinking a glass of milk than eating a heavily processed cheesy something. If we can get them to eat smaller portions of good simple adult foods we can breed a healthy nation. Packed lunches present a golden opportunity for parents to lay down healthy habits kids can keep for life.

I'm very anti ready-mixed drinks, as they're frequently very high in sugars and additives. OK, they might be fortified with vitamin C, but I'd much rather Maya had plain water and got her vitamin C from fresh fruit. If there's no choice, dilute them as much as possible. Ribena Ready-to-Drink contains 14g sugar per 250ml carton – unacceptably high. Fruit-flavoured waters can contain more sugar than cola. Plain water is healthiest – start your children drinking it when they're young and you'll establish a healthy habit for life. To make water a little funkier, try using a plastic fun bottle and refill it each day.

Fruit yoghurt, for example Muller Strawberry Fruit Corner . . . where do I start? A 150g pot gives a pretty big sugar hit (although the presence of yoghurt acids and proteins does slow the sugar absorbtion down a bit) – the label doesn't state how much sugar, just 25.6g carbohydrate per 150g pot, but I suspect, using average sugar content quoted in nutritional reference tables, that a good 10g of this is sugar. A better option would be to give your child a small pot of plain yoghurt or, if they find this too sour, a small pot of plain fromage frais, with a little tub of freshly chopped fruits or raisins or unsulphured dried apricots to stir in at school. (See yoghurt, page 87.)

Fruit winders: they may be 70% puréed fruits, but what about the glucose syrup and other ingredients that make up the remaining 30%? A better sweet option would be some of the 100% fruit bars with no added sugar – even though they'll still contain quite a lot of fruit sugar which could give them a little sugar high, it's less likely to make them as wired. You could always use just half a bar, wrapping it well before putting it in the packed lunch – this is more economical as well. This said, I would much prefer Maya to have fresh fruit or some plain, organic, unsulphured dried fruits such as mango, apricots, figs, dates, etc. The only fruit bars I keep in Maya's travel bag are Peter Rabbit Organics, as I think they're one of the best on the market.

Crisps: again, without sounding like a Peter

Rabbit fiend, I like their crisps because they don't have added salt or flavourings but taste good and vegetable-y. Alternatively, try the unsalted crisps that come with the salt separate and encourage your child not to use too much of it: remember, desire for salt can be set in place early on, and if kids don't have the taste when they're young, they won't miss it when they're older. The less salt kids eat the better. Check that crisps don't contain hydrogenated vegetable oils, fats or trans-fats, which are damaging to the heart – low-fat crisps are a slightly healthier option. One friend gives her two-year-old daughter organic cornflakes to eat like crisps, and she seems really happy eating them – but my friend's very aware that the time will soon come when Minnie notices they're not the same thing!

Many schools don't allow peanuts or any other nuts now because of fear of triggering life-threatening anaphylactic reactions in other pupils (see page 185) – they also worry about the choking aspect (you shouldn't really give whole nuts to kids under five). But if you're packing lunch for your family only, a small bag of unsalted nuts can be a good, healthy, monounsaturated-fat, high-protein addition. Choose them from a store whose turnover of nuts is high, as sometimes they're really fusty and not very nice, and from a nutritional perspective the fats in the nuts may well have turned a little rancid, which gives them a slightly bitter taste and is not good news for the body. Nut butters make good toppings for rice cakes, etc.

Chocolate fingers: something like a Twix finger contains 51.6g sugar per 100g, which means that a two finger pack weighing 56g will contain roughly 29g of sugar – pretty shocking. Instead I'd choose a plain rich-tea-style biscuit, which is much lower in sucrose, or a homemade biscuit if you have time to make them. If you want your child to have chocolate, choose a good-quality organic one like Green & Black's. Or you can get really good little chocolate mousse pots, as an occasional treat. If they need a dessert, fresh or dried fruits are best – if you think they'll struggle with peeling fruits such as clementines and apples, peel or slice them and pop them into a little plastic bag or a Tupperware container (you can buy such light tiny ones now).

I reserve some of my fiercest criticism for those stringy cheesy snacks and processed meat products – bright pink luncheon meat, ham bits, turkey-twizzler-style and formed-meat shaped dippery things, etc. – that I wouldn't be seen dead with in my shopping basket. The labels may say that they contain the same amount of nutrients as more normal unprocessed foods, and that they contain some meat – but I could shock you by telling you how they remove and process this so-called meat. (Believe me, you don't want to know. Just don't go near them.) Instead of the cheesy things, I'd much rather give Maya a glass of milk and then some proper cheese, in sandwiches or as cubes with grapes or oat biscuits. When it comes to meat, we always choose lean good-quality ham, either cut from the bone at the deli counter (we like Italian Parma-style lean ham) or prepacked – you can usually distinguish which ones are better by looking first at the price (usually a good guide that we're talking quality). 100% meat is what you go for – you don't want lots of fat, salt and inferior ingredients. I know it's all more expensive when you look at the key ingredients, but actually when you look at the value of so-called heavily processed kids' products you'll see that you're paying largely for heavily packaged, processed junk that does them no good whatsoever. At least when you buy quality ingredients such as ham and proper cheese, lean chicken, etc., your money is going on foods that can make your children healthy.

If budgets are tight, just have lean ham and other meats less often and grate cheese into sandwiches, as you end up using less and it tastes just as yummy. You can cut costs, by the way, if you cook a whole chicken yourself, as sometimes the supermarkets put a premium on having done it for you. All it needs is a little forward planning and the know-how, but it's a very healthy and delicious chicken sandwich if you've made it yourself. Note that chicken portions usually work out much more expensive than a whole chicken. You can make a delicious lean red meat sandwich from last night's roast, as long as you've kept the meat chilled. (See picnics too, page 45.)

When it comes to little pies and pasties, the problem with kid-size pies is that you generally have a higher ratio of fatty pastry to the lean good-quality ingredients inside, and they're not good value. There's nothing wrong with a slice of good-quality pork pie with some raw vegetables, and perhaps a wholemeal roll – but I'd buy a full-sized pie and pack a slice of it in their lunchbox, along with something else like a salad and some fruit for afterwards.

Real food is what makes a packed lunch healthy; kids don't need separate foods, heavily marketed cartoony products. You can really save yourself a lot of money and angst over their health if you make simple packed lunches with the sorts of foods you eat at home. I know there's peer pressure to fit in and for them all to eat the same fun things, but stick to your guns like you do with other important decisions about your child's health and life – since when did food become something that you have to toe the line on! Food for your kids is too important to compromise over.

Packed lunches present a golden opportunity to lay down healthy habits.

PICNICS

Picnics can be a good way to tempt kids into eating, so when the weather permits, think about eating outside. It makes eating together a fun thing, and taking everything out into the open air can ease some of the pressures. There's something good about just grazing and nibbling, reading the newspapers (oh, that was a reminiscent moment – more likely to be running after the ball that they refuse to fetch!).

Classically, picnics tend to be based around crusty breads, but you could choose a lighter option and go for pitta or wrap breads. When they're really fresh these are delicious filled with cold meats, cheese (cow's, sheep's or goat's, even buffalo mozzarella), mashed avocado with lemon juice and a lentil or bean pâté, hummus, (see the recipes on page 256). You could steam some new potatoes and dress them with a little butter or olive oil and a sprinkling of freshly crushed black pepper, to make a good filler to go with salads. Or you could go for rice cakes – I like the ones with sesame seeds, they're a little more interesting. Good rye crispbreads go well with smoked salmon and cream cheese – the trick to avoiding soggy crispbread is to put the toppings on when you get to the picnic, not beforehand.

I don't advocate dieting for kids, except in exceptional circumstances (see page 139), but by the same token there are some good, basic habits to get into that will establish healthier choices when it comes to avoiding high-fat foods. For example, I'd include salads that don't have heavy mayonnaise or any of the low-calorie mayonnaise lookalikes. Let the ingredients in salads sing for themselves with some fresh herbs, a little good olive oil and plenty of freshly squeezed lemon or lime. I don't like the low-cal versions of classic dips like hummus or tzatziki – they sometimes contain a lot of not-great-for-you ingredients like hydrogenated fats (linked to heart disease) and preservatives, and they taste disappointing – you're much better off having the real thing and making the calories go further by having plenty of raw vegetables alongside, to fill them up and satisfy them. Just don't encourage them to dip in with the spoon!

Again, there's nothing wrong with a good-quality traditional pork pie – other ideas for pies would be my little lentil rolls, spinach and feta pie, a good quality chicken pie or some delicious vegetable pastry number. You just need to make sure that you serve big salads alongside. Serve children just a small portion to begin with, they don't have to eat everything at once, and you can even stagger the picnic – have a break between savouries and sweets. Don't OD on crisps beforehand, make sure they're eaten as part of the meal; a few crisps on their plate is better than giving them a whole bag, as they'll always want to eat the whole packet whether they really need to or not.

For pudding, as always, fruit has to be the winner, but if you want to give it an indulgent twist, bring with you a mixing bowl, a large spoon, a tub of full-fat fromage frais, a pack of good-quality plain meringues and some berries such as raspberries and strawberries. Throw the fruit into the bowl with the fromage frais and crumble in the meringues – don't make them powdery, and leave some biggish chunks. Mix gently, and give everyone a spoon to serve themselves – yum.

A note on food-poisoning

Unfortunately memories of a good picnic are far too often blasted away when you find yourself or your child doubled up with stomach-ache, sickness or diarrhoea, the result of eating something that's gone off while you've been packing the car, sitting in traffic, and then had a few dirt-carrying bugs added on the picnic site. Some people think food-poisoning's something that happens to others and is almost a thing of the past, but it's not – and we see a dramatic rise in the summer, from picnics and barbecues. There are things you can do to reduce the risk: the first one is, if the weather is steaming hot and the food is going to be out of the fridge for a good few hours, to play really safe, avoid salads and sandwiches containing meat, fish and pâté, meat pies and pasties. If you have a good cooler-bag it should be OK, but keep salads chilled until the last minute, store them in the coolest part of the car, and lay the picnic out in a shaded place. Unpack them at the last possible moment before you eat. Take a pack of antiseptic wipes – parks and the countryside have a lot of animal mess, and you need to wipe kids' hands before they start touching food and putting it in their mouths. Keep food covered as much as possible to stop insects homing in. Never serve children homemade mayonnaise – it contains raw eggs, and kids, like pregnant women and the elderly, can become seriously ill if they get salmonella.

If you're having a barbecue, bear in mind that the biggest food-poisoning risk to kids' health comes from undercooked meat (*E.coli*, *Clostriudium perfringens* and *Staphylococcus* just love this), so make sure the coals are properly hot before you start cooking. They should be glowing, with a powdery grey surface (this usually takes a good half-hour after lighting, so don't leave lighting it till the last minute and think you can speed-cook, because all you'll do is burn the outside of the food and leave the inside raw). Turn the food regularly and move it around to make sure it cooks evenly – it should be cooked all the way through and piping hot. Finally, don't let my food-poisoning chat dampen your enthusiasm for picnicking – it's just a case of better safe than sorry.

SNACKS

Some kids seem to burn through food very fast and need topping up, so snacks are essential, and they can be a good way to get a few extra fresh fruits and vegetables into a child. A healthy snack can also help to fend off the enormous hunger that can hit children when they've gone so long without eating that their eyes become bigger than their stomach and they start raiding the fridge and eating everything in sight – a mid-afternoon snack, or a snack on the way home from school, can help keep the hunger pangs at bay. However, I would like to point out that we seem to have got into a situation where kids are having snacks more often than they physiologically need – on the bus, in the car, in the cinema, watching TV – everything seems to involve kids and eating. This means that if you're not careful your child can be taking in a lot of calories, usually from fat and sugar – fine in moderation, but damaging to their health in large amounts. The occasional convenient snack food is fine – a bag of crisps, or a biscuit – but occasional should be the operative word.

On a day-to-day basis it's much healthier to snack on rice cakes, oatcakes, dried fruits (without sulphur dioxide, see page 52), fresh fruits, which can be sliced up in a little bag for convenience, dried fruit and cereal bars – preferably those without any added sugar (see my oat and raisin shortbreads, page 000), fruit smoothies (although bear in mind these can contain about 200 kcals), small bags of unsalted nuts (not for the under-fives, because of the danger of choking, and not if they have a nut allergy), breadsticks, little bags of unsweetened muesli (add some extra dried fruits such as chopped figs and apricots). Other suggestions: hummus and raw vegetable sticks, a bowl of soup, crackers with a beany spread if you have some, or with a slice of cheese on top and an apple too, crackers with nut butter, a good homemade flapjack/oat-type biscuit, a slice of cake made with wholemeal flour (such as my carrot cake or fruit muffins, pages 250 and 000), fruit and yoghurt, good healthy fromage frais, a plain shop-bought wholemeal muffin or bagel with a pure fruit spread topping or sliced banana and a little honey drizzled on top, plain homemade popcorn, a small portion of baked fruit, say a baked apple or apricot.

Snacks are good – in moderation.

Dried fruits

Dried fruits are a constant in my house – they're so handy to carry around for those times when I need to give Maya something to keep her going, but can't stop what I'm doing. I also find a few Agen prunes and a dried fig or two go well with a pick-me-up cup of Earl Grey tea in the afternoon. Although dried fruits are not high in vitamin C or other water-soluble vitamins because their water has been removed, you get good fibre, calcium and zinc from them. Sugar content can look pretty high on the pack, but remember that dried fruits are really only fresh fruits with their water removed. They have the same amount of sugar per fruit, fresh or dried, but per 100g the sugar content will be higher in dried.

I'm fussy about the dried fruits I buy – not all the food I eat is organic, but when it comes to dried fruits there are reasons why I insist on it. Most importantly, organic fruits are not legally allowed to be exposed to the preservative sulphur dioxide. This is used routinely in quite large quantities to treat non-organic dried fruits, even though it's known to provoke extreme allergic reactions in some children and can cause shortness of breath and aggravate their guts. It's used not only to give the fruit longer life, but also to 'improve' its appearance. An unsulphured apricot is dark brown in colour, while an SO2-treated apricot looks smoother, paler and, OK, appetizing, but this appearance comes at a price I'm generally not prepared to pay. You can reduce SO2 levels by soaking and cooking the fruit, but if you prefer them uncooked you could be counteracting the health benefits with a hefty dose of unwanted sulphur dioxide.

Fortunately you can now buy organic dried fruits in supermarkets as well as in health-food stores. They are fantastic when it comes to flavouring cakes, biscuits and yoghurts, either whole, or soaked and puréed. But don't give your little one too many or they may get tummy-ache.

DINNERS TO WIND THEM DOWN

Children need the right nourishment to replenish the reserves they've used up, the foods that are going to help them feel full and nourished – a salad might be fine for you, but I suspect your child will need something far more stomach-satisfying. The meal at the end of the day should also enable them to wind down and feel comfortable enough to fall asleep.

Sleep stimulates growth, plays a crucial role in brain development and affects how well your child manages everyday life. How well your child sleeps also has a major impact on you as a parent – a bad night can cripple you the following day, leaving you feeling depressed, isolated, hardly able to drag yourself around, let alone cope with an energetic, demanding child. When children have broken nights, they can be crabby, listless, go off their food and the day can really go belly-up. For me, how well Maya sleeps is the defining factor in how I juggle each day, and I find myself clinging to routines of regular eating and activities so that we both get to the end of the day well fed, exercised and in the right state of mind and body for a good night's slumber. Here's a simple plan that should break the bad sleeping cycle for both of you.

DON'T FORGET RITUALS ARE GOOD

Kids really benefit from establishing a night-time, sleepy ritual – it helps them relax, get into the mood and wind down enough to sleep. You could start the bedtime routine with a relaxing bath (see my yummy oils, page 194), followed by a story, a goodnight cuddle and kiss, then lights out. Avoid games and larking around just before they go to bed, as this only winds them up – much as it's tempting to have a raucous play session when you've been out at work all day, this could just be counter-productive and you're better off having a settled read or a bath together. I've found that as far as possible it's important to put them to bed while they're still awake, so that they learn how to drop off on their own at bedtime, without being fed or cuddled to sleep – this way, if they wake in the night, they can settle themselves off to sleep again. Of course if they fall asleep in the car on the way home at night, you don't have to wake them up, but as a routine it's better to let them get used to going to sleep in their own bed. With older kids, encourage them to read at bedtime or to listen to some music or a talking book tape – watching TV and listening to loud music aren't conducive to them dropping off to sleep.

NIGHT-TIME FEASTING

As well as looking at the bedtime ritual, it's very useful to look at what children eat and drink before they go to bed. The wrong foods and drinks can make them restless, give them tummy-ache, etc., but if you feed them relaxing, filling foods their body unconsciously winds down.

* **S** Sling the sugary foods in the bin – they can make kids feel too wired and high.
* **L** Look at what they drink – watch the caffeine, go for milk or chamomile tea.
* **E** Eliminate the hot-wiring E numbers.
* **E** Encourage a proper meal ritual, not just a snack in front of the TV.
* **P** Plates of pasta, starchy foods, to help them sleep.

THE LIBRARY
NORTH WEST KENT COLLEGE
DERING WAY, GRAVESEND

S is for sling the sugary foods

I hope I've convinced you by now that sugary, refined, high GI foods are generally bad news and always play havoc with kids' energy levels – particularly bad news at bedtime! I therefore suggest keeping their blood sugar as level as possible at night-time by avoiding foods with glucose or sucrose, honey, cakes, biscuits, chocolates (sometimes, even though I think they're generally great foods, even overripe bananas can be a little on the high side). If they're hungry before bedtime (and to be honest, I have of late given Maya a night-time snack just before going to bed, as it helps her sleep straight through) and want a little snack, go for a low or medium GI food such as dates, figs, dried apricots, a little yoghurt or a glass of milk.

L is for look at what they drink

Caffeine is bad news for kids, and some of them can consume a lot more of it via fizzy drinks, chocolate bars, etc. than they ever used to. In adults there may be a case for a little caffeine to keep us alert, but for many kids, caffeine can tip them into jitters, anxiety and palpitations and keep them awake at night. Obviously, a very weak tea with lots of milk can be fine (see page 101). My parents once gave Maya and a friend's kids chocolate and coffee ice cream in Italy as their tea-time treat – they may have loved it, but since we were then forced to stay up till the wee small hours with little ones who usually slept well – from a two-year-old to a nine-year-old, I don't think this dessert will be on the menu again! In our house the general good-sleep rule is no strong tea, coffee, cola, fizzy so-called energy drinks, hot chocolate, chocolate biscuits, etc.

Instead go for milk drinks at bedtime. Not only does milk feel very comforting in the mouth, nicely sweet but not too much so, smooth and satisfying, but it can also become part of a routine, signifying that it's time to go to bed. You can now buy Night-time Milk, which has higher than normal levels of the hormone melatonin (they milk the cows much earlier in the morning, so that the melatonin levels in their milk are higher – poor cows!) – unlike most hormones parents worry about in the food chain, this is a goody in that it can encourage kids to sleep better. Melatonin is a natural substance that controls the body clock and helps us sleep. It's a natural hormone that plays a central part in regulating sleep patterns and, in the medical world, is often used as a drug to help people with chronic sleep problems. Melatonin is the brain's way of telling the body that it's night-time. It helps reduce the body temperature, which is necessary for a good night's sleep. A bedtime drink that provides the brain and body with additional melatonin has a theoretical reason for aiding sleep. The milk is designed to be drunk warm as part of the bedtime routine but can also be enjoyed during the day without causing drowsiness. This is due to the fact that human levels of melatonin are naturally very low during daylight hours, so it shouldn't tip your child over the melatonin-induced sleep edge!

If your child can't tolerate cow's milk, try sheep's, goat's, rice or soya milk (go for the unsweetened ones, ideally organic too, as this means GM-free) for a similar comforting, filling-the-stomach, getting-in-the-mood-for-sleep effect. I wouldn't recommend adding anything to the milk, as sweet things can energize kids and also increase the rate of tooth decay overnight (always

clean their teeth about half an hour after they've drunk the milk and before they go to bed, otherwise the teeth will be left with a coating of milk sugar, and since mouth acid levels are higher at night too, this can lead to tooth decay).

Another idea is to follow in Peter Rabbit's shoes and make a cup of chamomile tea. Chamomile roman is a traditional herbal tea that's used to wind us down, or get kids back off the ceiling if they've been to a party and come back loaded with sugar energy; a cup made with either a teabag or, better still, the flowers (which you can buy from good health-food stores), which I find have a much kinder taste and are more effective, can literally have a little one nodding off in minutes. (Don't let the chamomile steep in the water for more than three minutes, though, otherwise it can become a stimulant.)

If your child has a tummy-ache and can't settle, try some fresh mint or fennel tea, as this can settle wind and colic.

Mild chamomile tea is a winner.

Sleep-inducing oils

FROM 2–5 YEARS
Mandarin, palmarosa, chamomile roman or lavender.

In the bath, 1 drop per year to a max of 3.

OVER 5
The above, plus geranium, clary sage and nutmeg.

In the bath, 3 drops until 7 years old, 4 drops between 7 and 10.

E is for eliminate E numbers
I don't have a problem with some E numbers – vitamin C has an E number, for instance, and so does vitamin E – but there is a lot of evidence to show that some additives can exacerbate problems such as Attention Deficit Disorder (ADD), asthma, behavioural problems, allergies. I find in my practice that kids who have problems getting off to sleep can literally crack their bad sleep pattern in a few days as soon as they get away from a highly processed food diet, full of (the most common behaviour-aggravating) additives, and start eating a simple, additive-free diet. (See page 72 for a list of what I think are the really nasty E numbers.)

E is for encourage a proper meal ritual
Sometimes an aching or just an uncomfortable tummy can keep kids awake. See the section on what to do for a tummy-ache (page 128), but first

check that you're not giving them overly fatty or rich food in the evenings. Creamy sauces, fried fish, chips, pasties, olive-oil-doused dishes such as spaghetti bolognaise, crisps, nuts, creamy desserts such as gateaux, ice cream and even some frozen yoghurts (which can shockingly contain more fat – and sugar – than ice creams) may be just a little too heavy for their gut to tolerate. Keep food satisfying at night, but not too heavy. Dessert could be a simple yoghurt with a banana, or a slice of oaty flapjack (one that doesn't contain too much sugar).

P is for plates of pasta
Pasta (traditionally made with wheat, but you can now buy chickpea, spelt and rice pasta too), rice, polenta, potatoes, quinoa, couscous (again, wheat is traditional, but you can buy barley couscous in some health-food stores), breads of all sorts, gnocchi, are the perfect foods to give your child last thing in the day. Along with many of my friends and patients, I find these starchy carbohydrate foods help encourage the body to release sleepy hormones. So think about a simple bowl of pasta with tomato sauce, or a risotto, cheap and quick (don't OD on the oil – remember that rich, fatty, oily foods late in the day can trigger a tummy-ache). I also find that something starchy, even a jacket potato, is a good way to get an over-excited (or sugar-high) child to wind down.

TIMING IS IMPORTANT
Try not to give children their meal too late in the day. Tea just before bed can mean they feel uncomfortable – ideally they need to wait an hour or two before they lie down. If you're late getting home in the evening and don't have the energy, or

they're nibbling at your ankles for food, you could either go for some toast with a little butter and a good-quality, not-too-high-in-sugar, lots-of-fruit-in-it jam, or a bowl of cereal (not one full of sugar) or porridge. There is an advantage in having oats in the evening – they're filling, starchy and smooth, so there's a good comforting warm mouth-feel, as well as a slow release of sugar into the blood (of course this isn't the case if you pile on the sugar; just a little to sweeten, or a drizzle of honey, is all that's needed). Kids shouldn't have salty porridge, by the way, as too much salt has been linked to high blood pressure and also doesn't help them build strong bones. Brown sugar, although it has just as many calories in as white, has such a wonderful caramel taste that I think you need less in porridge than if you used white.

Although the above has been written with your child in mind, it's also a useful checklist to use for yourself so that you get the maximum benefit from your night's sleep.

CHAPTER THREE

Key Concerns

Since I've had Maya I've been pretty shocked to realize how much more aware of environmental and societal issues being responsible for a child's total wellbeing has made me, and how vulnerable I sometimes feel for both of us. From talking to other parents I know I'm not alone. So I've devoted this chapter to what I think are the main goodies (good bacteria, omega oils, organic foods, etc.) and what I call the baddies (salt, sugar, fast-food marketing and the dirty tricks they play, GM foods, canned fizzy drinks, etc.) – all the things I think you'd expect to see in this book. But I've also included more surprising issues, such as how being ultra clean in the home doesn't always work in your child's favour, and something not much talked about but true: the premium costs of healthy eating. I'll show you how to minimize the rise in your shopping bill and how to maximize the quantity and absorption of nutrients from the foods you buy. This isn't a plan to make you feel even more anxious about parenting, more of a resource to tap into if you want to find out my take on important issues.

MY KEY ISSUES

Advertising and other influences

However young your child is, you've probably realized by now that it's not just the foods you give them at home or pack in their lunchboxes that influence how well they eat – the pressure of advertising, the views of friends and relatives, and the places your child goes to can also have a big impact.

KIDS AS CONSUMERS: THE PRESSURE OF ADVERTISING

I'm very aware that because more and more parents and campaigning health bodies have cottoned on to the strong effect that food marketing has on our kids, some manufacturers have really stepped up their tactics as they try to influence and cajole kids into wanting to eat their products and plaguing theirparents for them, known in the marketing world as Pester Power! If they were trying to entice our kids to eat healthy products, I'd support them, but this is seldom the case – nine times out of ten it's about persuading kids to eat junk food that they know their parents wouldn't ordinarily want them to eat. I'm busy trying to get the TV and other media providers to ban TV advertising for kids' junk foods, to get them out of kids' magazines, to get them off the low shelves in supermarkets that are just at the perfect height for kids to pick these brightly coloured, cartooned packets up and demand them. Meanwhile, the Food Commission has recently found that makers of soft drinks, sweets and sugary cereals are designing websites to catch the attention of children barely six or seven years old. Cheaper than TV advertising, and completely outside the control of the Advertising Standards Authority, commercial websites are enticing youngsters with games and prizes, and encouraging them to send in their names and addresses. Children may also be asked for email addresses for themselves and their friends. In return for this direct marketing information, the children receive points that get them small gifts, games, software or mobile phone ring-tones.

Some websites require food products to be purchased beforehand, so that children can log on to the website with codes from the product wrappers, giving the children access to exclusive parts of the company's website. The companies pushing their products use these subtle and cleverly designed websites to promote brands such as Nesquik, Frosties, Panda Pops, Chewits, Skittles and Kinder Surprise, for foods such as sweets, lollies, sugared fizzy drinks, burgers and chips. How appalling is this? Keep a watchful eye on your children and monitor the websites they look at.

YOUR CHILD'S SCHOOL

When it comes to schools and nurseries, I would definitely lobby for them to serve healthy food. Despite all their protestations over the years about budgets and how they're only feeding the kids what they want, etc., it's possible, as many of you will have seen in Jamie Oliver's Feed Me Better campaign (www.feedmebetter.com), which I was lucky enough to be involved with, with the right momentum and resources behind the kitchen

staff and parents, to feed our kids much more healthily.

Since our FMB campaign, education minister Ruth Kelly has announced that from September 2006 foods high in fat, salt or sugar are to be banned from meals and vending machines in English schools – so no more fizzy drinks, no more chocolate and crisps. With nurseries, meals are more likely to be cooked in small kitchens and therefore there's not usually as much bureaucracy to cut through. Just try to work with the people who organize the food in your child's school or nursery, and if necessary get like-minded parents together – if you can present a united front they'll realize that there are a lot of you concerned parents around.

FRIENDS AND FAMILY: PRESSURE FROM NEAREST AND DEAREST

Apart from having (or trying to have) reasonable discussions about how you would like your child to eat as opposed, for example, to what your parents believe they should eat, there is little you can do with well-meaning friends and relatives. I also think it's important not to be too precious about what your child eats, over and above trying to stick to your basics – having the occasional meal at their grandparents' that you'd rather they didn't eat is not going to harm them, and having a row could.

Your kids will most likely be influenced by the foods that their peers and role models eat, and it's really hard as parents to always be on their case about not eating junk. Maya enjoys her healthy food, mealtimes are generally not a battleground and her friends tend to be like-minded, so I hope I won't have too many battles over junk food.

Genetically modified (GM) food

Just don't go there! I know some experts say genetic modification can potentially produce higher-nutrient-value products, reverse worldwide starvation, but I'm not at all convinced that this is what would really happen if we let our shops sell GM foods. No one really knows what the long-term effects of consuming genetically altered foods or ingredients might be. The food scientists and multinational companies who produce the food, and currently, to a lesser extent, the UK government seem to believe that the arguments against GM foods are based on morals, ethics, ignorance and fear rather than on actual scientific evidence that they can be harmful to our health or to our environment. I feel we have a right not to buy foods that contain genetically modified organisms (GMOs), but currently, legislation sort of helps us avoid them: the EU has set a legal tolerance level for GMOs in foods of 1%, which in practical terms means that if a food on the shelf contains less than 1% GM ingredients, it can be labelled as GM-free, or not labelled as containing GM ingredients.

GMOs are hugely unpopular in many countries, thank goodness. The UK government and industry planned early in 2004 to launch a major campaign to wear down public opposition, but with a clear lack of demand (hooray!) supermarkets have bowed to public opinion that we don't want GMOs in our foods; not only are supermarkets stating that they won't sell anything containing GMOs, but they've also invested thousands of pounds in keeping supply streams separate. Of course, our kids don't just consume foods and drinks made from ingredients brought in supermarkets – they're exposed to catering companies who source their ingredients from a huge variety of suppliers, foods stocked in corner shops aren't going to be necessarily flagged up as being GM-free, and like most aspects of our child's eating we can only do so much to protect them being exposed to the things we'd rather they didn't eat. But the following box shows you how I try to stay away from GM foods both in and out of the supermarket.

How to avoid GM foods

1. The easiest way to avoid GM foods is to buy organic, as genetic modification is **not allowed** in foods produced to the UK Soil Association organic standard.
2. Read labels carefully. When a GM content meets the legal requirements I've mentioned previously, the manufacturer has to say so on the label. Much tomato purée contains genetically modified tomatoes, unless the label states that it's GM-free or organic, of course.
3. Stay away from foods containing soya as an ingredient (unless it's organic) – approximately half the world's soya crop is now genetically modified. GM beans tend to be mixed with non-GM beans before they're distributed. If it's organic soya that's fine. The same applies to products containing corn (maize) – the majority of the world's corn is now genetically modified, so avoid processed foods containing corn, unless the label states that it's GM-free or organic.

No one really knows anything about the long-term effects of eating GM foods.

Organic food

I try to buy organic food where possible, though not exclusively. As a broad statement, although studies haven't categorically been able to show this yet, from the evidence I've seen I'm sure that organic food (in most cases – I'll come to the details later) has to be better for our kids – not least because if certified by the UK Soil Association it cannot contain GM ingredients (see above). Organic farmers tend to be more in tune with the land and strive to make the food as tasty as possible; I like the fact that they frequently look after wildlife and strive to keep rural economies alive, which I definitely think is the way ahead for our society. The organic regulations that control the use of pesticides, hormones and other things that can't be good for our kids are important enough to make me pay the extra premium that organic food, especially in the supermarkets, frequently demands. Our kids' immune systems, guts, precious growing bodies, are surely better off not being bombarded with the heavy toxins, pesticides, waxes, hormones so often found in non-organic produce.

But I think it's also important, as much as is practically possible, to buy organic produce that's **locally grown**, which means it'll be seasonal. This way we support small farmers and help our kids develop a sense of appreciation for seasonal food – it makes raspberries special in the summer and dark roasted parsnips appealing in winter if you haven't been eating them all year round. Sometimes local farms, although they aren't certified organic, can be just as passionate about the quality of their food, trying to keep pesticides low, etc., but just don't have the high organic

standards necessary for certification. Some may be under review, while for others there may be circumstances beyond their control: their land may border non-organic land, for example, and there may be worries over soil leaching, etc. All of this doesn't mean that their produce is bad and unhealthy – **I certainly would buy local non-organic food**.

FRUIT AND VEGETABLES

A down-side of organic fruits and vegetables is that frequently they don't look as attractive as non-organic; the lack of waxes can make them look dull. There are many schemes for having boxes of organic produce delivered to your door, but with some of them you can find far too little variety – too many potatoes, for example. Of course box scheme suppliers vary, so if you're thinking about having an organic box delivered, shop around. Sometimes you can't choose what gets delivered, which means you need to be creative (although this is largely a thing of the past, as many suppliers have realized we want some degree of choice). I always bung what we can't use into a big soup, especially if the vegetables are looking a little tired.

The supermarkets are in a difficult position – as consumers we demand produce throughout the year, we've fallen out of the habit of eating seasonally, and our reluctance to pay more for our food means that they have to go elsewhere for approximately 80% of the organic produce sold today – it's imported. I know the supermarkets aren't holier than thou, and I hate the environmental effect of shipping and driving organic produce, like any other fresh food, hundreds of thousands of miles. So it would help if parents brought their kids up to be OK with knobbly, muddy-looking carrots, OK with only having certain foods at different times of the year – I'm not talking about being completely saint-like, but it would help turn the supermarket tide. Support the organic box schemes with direct links to farmers and local farmers' markets as much as you can – these schemes usually give the farmers a much better price for their produce than the big supermarkets. For details of box schemes, see www.farmersmarkets.net.

MEAT AND DAIRY

I try to give Maya only organic meat, milk, eggs and poultry. I don't like the idea of animals being kept in appalling conditions (which is far more likely in non-organic farming), given antibiotics sometimes at the drop of a hat, and although the Food Standards Agency assures us that the levels of hormones fed to cattle, etc. are safe, I just don't like giving my child's young, sensitive, growing body hormones she doesn't need. I'd much rather buy good meat from a reputable butcher, even though it's usually more expensive, than from a supermarket. I keep costs down by eating meat less often. It has to be said, though, that there are some fantastic farmers producing really good meat without organic certification – perhaps their local organically certified abattoir has closed down, or they may have trouble getting hold of organically certified feed. I'm happy to buy grass-fed meat that comes from a farmer my butcher knows, even if it is extensively reared beef or lamb. For a directory of organic butchers, see www.organicbutchers.co.uk.

If I can't get organic eggs, I'd choose free-range. But like everything else, Maya will have non-organic food at friends' homes and at school, and I don't make a massive issue of it – I just try to ensure she has as much organic fresh produce as possible.

FISH

With fish, the issue's not easy. Not only is it very hard and pretty expensive to get hold of organic fish, but of course it's only possible to get organic farmed fish, which I have an issue with. Although it has to be said that the British fish farming industry has recently tried to clean up its act, environmentally fish farming has caused some degradation. This means that I only very occasionally buy organic farmed fish. Furthermore, many species of fish are under threat of extinction, because of over-fishing. The Marine Conservation society has produced a list of the twenty species of fish to avoid and the twenty-five species you can eat with a clearer conscience. See www.fishonline.org for their *Good Fish Guide*.

WHEN ORGANIC DOESN'T AUTOMATICALLY MEAN BETTER

However, the area where I'm not always swayed by the organicness of a product is the processed food area – just because a crisp is made from organic potatoes, or a packet of sweets is made with organic fruit, doesn't mean they're healthy and good for our kids. The crisps can still be fried in hydrogenated fats and be full of salt, the sweets can be full of sugar. OK, the sweets won't contain as many additives and preservatives, as organic certification (usually by the Soil Association) doesn't allow this, but they're still sweets, and bad for kids' teeth, and can mount up the calories – organic cola is a nonsense to me. So I treat any organic processed food with as much suspicion and caution as any non-organic processed food. It depends on the make of foods too – use the web and books to find out as much as you can about the companies you're supporting by buying their organic produce – support as many as you can of the good ethical ones (see www.fairtrade.org.uk). I know this takes time, but it's worth it, because as soon as you make a few good choices you can rest assured that you're giving your child a great, nutritious, organic start in life.

Finally, organic doesn't come cheap – especially meat, fish and chicken. I just eat it less often and get into the habit of cooking with cheaper organic ingredients such as pulses and lentils. If you really can't afford much organic at all, just try to get as much fresh, local produce as possible. Support a good local butcher who knows where the meat is from and ask them lots of questions – choose as much grass-fed, extensively reared beef and good local poultry and lamb as you can. With fresh produce, wash it well to remove pesticides and waxes and you're doing the best you can do. Remember, eating a healthy non-organic diet, full of fresh fruits and vegetables, is still better for you than an unhealthy diet.

Organic is great, but so is locally-grown.

Additives

When we talk about additives, most people rightly think of E numbers, but although I would generally say you should avoid these as much as you can, not all E numbers are bad! Some of them are even natural ingredients such as vitamin C and vitamin E – so it's a question of knowing the goodies and the baddies.

Some additives do us a big favour by enhancing the flavour, texture and appearance of food. We're not talking about wanting our food to look luminescent and over-processed, but often even simple preparation and food safety techniques can take the edge off the colour and texture and make it less appealing to our fussy society, so that without additives we would just not pick the food up. Other additives help stop food from becoming rancid, going off, being prone to bacterial growth.

Some E numbers have been heavily criticized, quite rightly, for what many people feel is their negative effect on kids. Some seem to make kids go wild, others have been reported to have the opposite effect of almost drugging the body, others again can give them headaches. And research still can't tell us the long-term effects of eating a diet high in additives – kids are drinking copious amounts of cola and fizzy drinks, which are just glowing with the things, as well as the junk food they're eating on the bus and at school.

The following additives have caused the most reported problems with kids:

* Tartrazine (it's in colas, cakes, processed foods, and is frequently labelled as E102)
* Sunset yellow (E110)
* Carmoisine (E122)
* Ponceau 4R (E124)
* Sodium benzoate (E211)
* Other benzoates (E210–219)
* Sulphides (E220–228)
* Nitrates and nitrites (E249–252)
* Monosodium glutamate and other glutamates (E621–623)
* Antioxidants E310–312, E320, E321

You should avoid all of these as much as possible, which is actually a lot easier than you might think because they're usually found only in processed foods – especially those targeted at children, which seems astounding, but unfortunately kids tend to go for brightly coloured things, so the additives find a way of getting into the food. Also, because fewer and fewer parents, let alone schools and snack bars, fast-food joints that give kids a one-stop junk-food hit, are cooking from fresh ingredients, in an average week a child can be exposed to an enormous amount of additives and preservatives, which worries me.

Note that organic regulations are much stricter when it comes to not allowing certain bad additives, so this is a slightly better bet. But as you'll read in the organic section (page 69), just because a food is organic doesn't mean it's healthy – it could contain lots of sugar, fat and salt.

HOW TO AVOID ADDITIVES

I have a simple five-point plan for trying to keep your child's intake of additives, particularly the bad E numbers, down.

1. Try to do as much cooking as you can with fresh simple ingredients – I hope this book will reassure you that's not too difficult, it just takes some getting used to.

2. Steer clear of brightly coloured kids' drinks, snacks, processed cakes and biscuits as much as possible. If your kids really want them, why not have one evening a week when they can choose something junky? I find that if children are allowed to have a junky food night every now and then (that's if they ask for one, of course!), you're far less likely to discover they've been secretly eating additive-ridden snacks when you're emptying their school coat pockets out and find the wrappers.

3. It sounds strange, but when you're buying processed foods you might be better off buying frozen as opposed to *some* fresh produce. The freezing process means manufacturers can preserve foods better than fresh, when they might have to add additives to keep them looking and tasting attractive. Obviously it depends on the brand you choose, but generally the shorter the shelf life of processed chilled foods, and the better quality (again, I know that generally means the more expensive), the less likely they are to have as many bad additives in them. You just know that foods that can last for ages have to have been pumped full of not-great additives, so steer clear of these as much as possible.

4. Read your labels – if the list of ingredients is long and very chemical-sounding, the likelihood is that it's not the food to go for. Be wary, though: food manufacturers have cottoned on to the fact that putting the actual E number on the list may put you off, so sometimes they make a bigger splash of using the actual name of the additive, just to, how shall I say it, 'confuse' you!

5. If you suspect that specific food additives aggravate your child, it's worth keeping a note of what they eat for a couple of weeks (see food diary, page 122) with how they're feeling/behaving written alongside. This way you should be able to detect any patterns.

It really is worth avoiding additives, especially the bad E numbers.

Fats

Many people think animal fat equals bad, vegetable fat equals good, and that we should at all costs avoid saturated animal fats and only consume foods made with vegetable fats. If you listen to the 'we'd be healthier if we ate more polyunsaturated vegetable fats' campaign, you'd think it was almost sinful to put butter on bread (as I do). Again, you may think that as long as ready-made meals such as filled pastas, cereals, cakes and biscuits are made with vegetable fat, your child's heart and overall health are safe. But unfortunately if you're not careful you could be exposing their body to lesser-known damaging fats called hydrogenated oils and trans fats.

Before you throw up your hands in confusion, I'm not saying foods high in saturated animal fats are necessarily good – they can be high in calories, and saturated fats produce LDL, the 'bad' cholesterol which can cause heart disease and other problems when they're older – but just because it's vegetable doesn't always mean it's healthy. Olive and vegetable oils such as sunflower oil in their raw state – drizzled on bread, etc. – are fine (though they're still high in calories – oil contains as many calories as butter), but as soon as we demand that vegetable oils be used in our spreads and cakes it's likely that the food-manufacturing process will turn these good fats into bad, in the process increasing our risk of heart disease.

SO, WHAT MAKES A FAT BAD?

Without being too technical, hydrogenation is a process that turns oil into solid fat by bubbling hydrogen through it. It's used in making margarine and other products from spreads and biscuits to crisps, to extend shelf-life and give us the low prices we want. It's during hydrogenation that a type of 'trans fat' or 'trans-fatty acid' is formed. Some trans fat is naturally produced in the gut of cattle, so there is a little present in meat and full fat dairy produce, but the limited research to date suggests this isn't as harmful as artificially created trans fats. According to the Food Standards Agency, trans fats raise the cholesterol in the blood, more than saturated fats, which increases the risk of coronary heart disease; some experts, myself included, believe they may be worse for you than saturated fats. Government guidelines recommend a daily intake of trans fats of about 4–5g, considerably less than the 20–30g recommended for saturated fats, which are linked to high cholesterol and heart disease – to me this indicates how damaging they can be.

In this country food that contains hydrogenated or partially hydrogenated oils or fats must declare it on the label, but the level of trans fats need not be mentioned. In America, years of campaigning and a threatened lawsuit against Kraft Foods over the trans-fat content of Oreo cookies has resulted in the Food and Drug Administration demanding that trans fats be identified on food labels by January 2006. As far as campaigners are concerned, though, labelling is only a partial solution. They want these fats gone for good.

Some food manufacturers are worried that they

won't be able to make foods with the desired shelf-life, lightness, crumb texture, crispiness, at competitive prices if they remove the hydrogenated and trans fats, but surely there has to be a healthier compromise. Even if we ended up having to spend more and settle for shorter shelf-life, I'm sure we wouldn't mind if we understood the reasons.

GOOD FATS TO GO FOR

On a practical level you can either, like me, stick to using a little butter on your child's bread (take it out of the fridge for a while before you use it so it spreads easily and you won't need so much) or drizzle it with a little olive oil like they do in Mediterranean countries. Check out avocado, pumpkin and other vegetable oils such as hemp, walnut and linseed oils, as these can be good in cakes, on salads and in cooked dishes – such as my carrot cake and homemade buscuits such as flapjacks. Walnut oil is yummy in salads containing cheese and spinach and there's nothing easier and more delicious than pouring a little hemp oil (Good Oil is a great brand) on grilled vegetables or pasta. Pumpkin oil is good in curries, avocado drizzled in a salad wrap.

If you want a vegetable spread, choose one of the margarines that specifically state they are not hydrogenated; these often contain high-quality oils, such as cold-pressed sunflower oil and olive oil. An 'olive oil' spread may actually be made mainly with vegetable oil and contain very little olive oil, but it's what's been done to the fats in the processing that counts. The same applies to 'spreadable' butter – it's the method they use that's important. Look out for 'hydrogenated', 'partially hydrogenated' and 'trans fats' on the labels, and avoid those products.

Check organic products too – they're not necessarily trans-fat-free, but most are.

Not all fats are bad – get familiar with the good ones.

Probiotics

Take note – this is exciting! It's worth sitting down with a cup of tea and working your way through a little of the science, because I strongly believe that the whole probiotic area is really important and very easy to incorporate in your child's life.

The word probiotic means 'for life', although most of us are more familiar with the name 'friendly bacteria', the phrase coined by the media. Everyone has these bacteria living in their gut, some more than others, and their main purpose seems to be to maintain a healthy digestive system. Most probiotics consist of lactic-acid – lacto and bifido – bacteria, which you may have noticed on the labels of live yoghurt (I'll come on to this in a minute). These good bacteria aid digestion by breaking down tough fibres, enzymes and other proteins found in food. Probiotic bacteria are the bacteria that can survive the stomach's acid attack and hence reach the intenstine where they work their 'magic'. Probiotics produce important nutrients such as vitamin K and ferment organic acids, which are absorbed into the bloodstream for energy. They also play an important role in fending off more harmful disease-causing organisms known as pathogens.

WHY DO WE NEED FRIENDLY BACTERIA?

The human gut is home to around 400 different species of live bacteria – adults have an astonishing 1kg of these in their gut! As well as beneficial probiotics, the gut houses harmful bacteria such as *E.coli* and salmonella. Whenever we eat we introduce harmful bacteria into the intestine – not nice but true, and incredibly important, because being 'introduced' to these bugs on a day-to-day basis enables us to develop a strong immune system. By including some probiotic bacteria such as *Lactobacilli* and *Bifidobacteria* in your child's diet, though, you allow the so-called stomach-friendly bacteria to crowd out these damaging bugs. They do this by sticking to the gut wall, acting as a barrier to infection.

Many things can upset the balance of bacteria, including stress, poor diet, alcohol, age, ill-health and even antibiotics, which can kill off good bacteria as well as the bad they have been prescribed for.

Probiotic supplements, ranging from tablets to yoghurt drinks, are said to work alongside the body's natural friendly bacteria – or gut flora – to aid digestion and rebalance temporary upsets in intestinal micro-flora. Although before you head off and buy them, hear me out a little more, as some are better than others.

HOW CAN THEY HELP US?

Research has found that probiotics can help treat diarrhoea – particularly in children – caused by antibiotics and tummy bugs.

They may also prevent food poisoning by stopping bad bacteria such as *Clostridium* taking hold, improve symptoms of lactose intolerance, reduce susceptibility to dermatitis and help control irritable bowel symptoms. Trials also suggest that probiotics can strengthen the immune system, reduce cholesterol levels and even regress tumours – though evidence for this is not conclusive. A study in Finland found that giving a daily dose of the probiotic *Lactobacillus*

rhamnosus bacteria to pregnant women and their babies during the first six months of life reduced the incidence of eczema.

Probiotics may also provide some hope for children with autism. A study carried out by the Food Microbiology Sciences Unit at the University of Reading looked at more than 200 autistic children in the US and UK. They found that children with autism had high levels of harmful *Clostridium* bacteria compared to their non-autistic siblings. It is hoped that special probiotic supplements could replace some of that bad bacteria with the good variety, so easing the symptoms of autism. There is also some evidence that probiotic bacteria have a role in the prevention of bowel cancer. So the whole area of probiotic bacteria needs our attention.

The down-side is that in order to be sure of maintaining a healthy dose of good bacteria in the gut your child really needs to take probiotics indefinitely, which can be a hassle and expensive. However, if you don't manage to keep them going long-term, it's not going to damage your child. I do, though, recommend taking probiotics for getting over short-term problems like a tummy bug or if they're taking antibiotics for a chest infection. For longer-term benefits regular daily intake is required, but in Maya's case rather than buying a supplement I tend to give her a small bowl of live bio yoghurt containing probiotic bacteria most days, which is no hardship because she loves it with fruit or honey. I don't get hung up on days when she doesn't want it, as she soon will, and anyway she's not going to come to any harm from not having her dose of friendly bacteria. Although the live yoghurt probably won't have as many live bacteria as a supplement, I still think it's a good

idea to give her this live-bacteria-rich yoghurt, as a preventative measure (and it's a yummy dessert rich in calcium and a good way to get other nutrients such as magnesium into her body). I find Maya's gut has really settled down since she started having the yoghurt – it used to be a bit all over the place, which I'd put down to the change from her Indian diet to a western one, and the trauma involved in the adoption. But I'm also sure the live yoghurt has helped.

If Maya needs to take antibiotics or is getting over a bout of diarrhoea or a sickness bug, I do tend to give her a daily capsule of probiotic bacteria (containing at least a billion bacteria per dose and needing to be kept in the fridge to keep them alive) for a couple of weeks. I have seen some kids' guts recover very quickly from being very runny or painfully constipated after taking probiotics.

ARE PROBIOTIC SUPPLEMENTS ANY USE?

It has to be said that experts are divided on how beneficial probiotic supplements can be to a healthy child, and indeed to adults and I certainly feel that the adverts implying they'll give you a spring in your step are misleading. I also think the presence of large amounts of sugar in some of the drinks negates any overall health benefit that the probiotic may provide – sugar causing dental caries and obesity is far more worrying in my mind. To maximize the chances of the supplement actually working, take it with food, and make sure the ones you buy have been refrigerated in the shop, as many of the bacteria will die if they're kept too warm. You need to check the labels to make sure they contain one or all of the names below – you can buy single strains, or a mix of the different bacteria, and both are great.

Although you see many probiotic drinks on the market, I prefer the capsules or tablets because they don't contain sugar, additives, etc. and they're a much cheaper option for kids who can't or won't eat yoghurt. **Note that if your child is lactose-intolerant you need to check the label, as some supplements contain lactose.** I simply break the capsule open and either sprinkle it over Maya's cereal or put it into a glass of milk or diluted fruit juice. With older, more willing kids you can of course just give them the capsule or tablet to take.

WHAT ABOUT THOSE QUICK-SHOT PROBIOTIC DRINKS?

Demand for probiotics has resulted in untested products flooding the market. And as probiotic drinks are not regulated, because they are classed as foods, it is up to the manufacturers to ensure that any health claims they make are truthful. In one study, researchers in Belgium found that only 20% of the fifty-five probiotic products they looked at contained all the helpful organisms listed on their labels. Nine products failed to contain even one!

To establish if a probiotic yoghurt drink (or any probiotic supplement) can benefit your health you need to know the particular strain of bacteria it contains. I suggest looking out for the following names:

* Lactobacillus acidophilus
* Lactobacillus casei
* Lactobacillus delbrueckii
* Bifidobacterium adolescentis
* Bifidobacterium longum
* Bifidobacterium infantis

These bacteria are resilient enough to withstand the acid conditions of the stomach, but all the same some of them will not survive. The dose the product contains is important, so that enough of them are still alive when they reach the intestine – **a supplement needs to contain at least a billion bacteria per capsule to be effective**. Once the product contains sufficient quantities of bacteria there is little difference between the drinks beyond the level of fat and sugar they contain.

Prebiotics

Prebiotics are carbohydrates that feed the friendly bacteria. These foods aren't digestible by the body's own enzymes, so they go through the stomach unaffected, and once they reach the colon they help build up a high-density population of friendly bacteria. The two main prebiotics are insulin and oligofructose. Foods richest in prebiotics are asparagus, bananas, barley, chicory, garlic, Jerusalem artichokes, leeks, milk, onions, tomatoes, wheat and yoghurt.

Current thinking is that to have a positve impact on our gut bacteria we should give our bodies roughly 5g of prebiotic sugars a day. It is estimated that in Europe we eat anything from 3–11g a day. A bowl of French Onion soup contains 6–18g of insulin. Vegetables stored for a long time are low in prebiotics – as usual fresh is best. It is difficult to get enough prebiotic inside our kids from a normal diet so I suggest that you top up with a prebiotic supplement.

Recently, food manufacturers have started to add prebiotics such as insulin to more readily available foods such as breakfast cereals like Muddles. As usual the manufacturers shout about the plus side of their product but they would apparently prefer us not to notice the fact that although they contain good prebiotic they also contain high levels of sugar. There are however some good natural juices and yoghurts coming onto the market that contain some prebiotics, which I hope won't fall into the 'too high in sugar trap'. Watch this space.

Note that you may find that your child becomes a little windy when they start boosting their intake of prebiotic foods, but if you persevere, the gassines with subide!

Probiotics and prebiotics are exciting developments in the field of nutrition. They're not a quick fix but they can contribute to a healthy digestive system.

Sugar

This is an area of Maya's diet that I am passionate about, so I hope you'll forgive a little rant. So many parents are unaware of how much sugar their children are eating and the damage it could be doing. If you can start children off on a healthy and naturally low-sugar diet, though, they won't miss the extreme sweetness of so many refined sweet foods.

Sugar provides calories – 4 per gram – but they are empty calories, since sugar doesn't contain any other nutrients. Of course we need some carbohydrate (and that's what sugar is) because it is an essential energy source – but refined, processed sugar just isn't necessary in our diet. For thousands of years of human evolution we didn't have any sugar and physiologically we haven't changed from the cave men and women so we shouldn't need it now!

But the fact is we like eating refined sugars – sweets, gateaux, drinks – and we're big-time consumers, not least because the food manufacturers, lobbyists and advertisers throw billions of pounds at the message that sugar is fine and indeed great for us to eat. But that just isn't the case. Too much sugar isn't good for us, either adults or kids (it causes dental caries, may be a factor in the development of heart disease, it's also linked to certain cancers and is suspected of having a bearing on low IQ). Many parents, myself included, find their kids turn into wild 'little monsters' who are difficult to control after consuming quickly-absorbed sweet foods – fizzy drinks, for example. While the sugar industry fiercely – and I mean fiercely – denies these claims, it's strange that a well-known sugar manufacturer spends literally millions of pounds creating a product that mimics sugar but is not 'nutritionally bad' for you.

HOW MUCH SUGAR ARE WE EATING?

The issue of how much sugar we're eating is especially hard to fathom because there are so many names bandied about – sucrose, glucose, fructose, starch, carbohydrate, corn syrup and so on – that it's not easy to make an informed choice as to whether a product has too much or an OK amount of sugar. It's this confusion that the sugar industry is currently thriving on, while we consumers trip up when we try to make positive health choices and end up eating sugars in astronomical proportions (the average British person eats approximately 30 kilos of sugar per year, and one in ten adults eats over 60 kilos – over 9 stone).

We find sugar in unexpected places: in cough mixtures, savoury dishes such as ready-made meals, soups, sandwich spreads – and low-fat foods allow manufacturers to add sugar to alleged slimming products. The weight-loss drink Slim-Fast has been found by the Food Standards Agency to contain 61.9% sugar. According to the latest National Diet and Nutrition Survey (NDNS), over a quarter of the sugar consumed by 4 to 18-year-olds comes from soft drinks … aaagh! A 500ml bottle of cola has 53.5g of sugar – that's the equivalent of five lollipops. 'Healthier' juices for children can contain the same sugar as two lollipops. And so-called 'healthy' yoghurt drinks can have the same sugar content as four lollipops.

It's best not to have too much refined,

processed sweet food in a child's diet, not only because I think kids are better off without it, their teeth are healthier, behaviour tends to be more consistently good, weight tends to be better, etc., but also because these foods tend to be high also in fats, additives and preservatives. A diet high in sugar can be a factor in promoting insulin (the hormone that regulates blood sugar levels) resistance. This can mean that over time, the effect that insulin has on the body is weakened, so that more and more insulin is needed to clear the body of unwanted sugars. Eventually this can lead to diabetes (see page 171), and is one of the five factors in the increasingly common adult condition called Syndrome X.

Of course, kids love sugary things, but as you'll see from my yummy cakes and desserts section (page 247), you can make so many delicious treat foods for kids without having to resort to highly processed chocolate and biscuits. Many of my recipes include ingredients that can hit the tastebuds in a sweet and luxurious way but aren't derived from traditional cane sugar. Coconut shavings, almond milk, amaranth, star anise, carrots, banana, puréed fruits, soaked and dried fruits – the list of ways you can make your child's diet sweet and healthy is endless. I know it takes time to make cakes, puddings and biscuits, but it is so worthwhile. They last a good time if stored in airtight tins, and some can be frozen, so you could do a big bake at the weekends to last you all through the week.

However, most kids want to have the occasional processed treat so that they feel normal and like everyone else. As a rough guide, if you look at the label and find there is more than 10g of sugar through, this is a lot and you would do better to find an alternative treat. However, if you ban 'naughty foods' completely, you may find them bingeing on sweet junk in secret, which is to my mind much worse. Better they feel they can eat in front of you and that you can control how much they have, than to start getting into the deception game.

THE GLYCAEMIC INDEX

The glycaemic index (GI) is a ranking of foods from 0 to 100 according to how quickly each food (when eaten in isolation in the fasting state, i.e. on an empty stomach) will raise blood sugar levels. You will probably know from seeing tables of foods listed according to their glycaemic index that there is a huge variety of foods that contain sugar; but other factors such as fibre, fat and protein content also influence how quickly they are absorbed into the body.

As a general rule, I think kids are better off sticking to the lower and medium GI foods that are also natural and unprocessed. It's fine on occasions to have the high GI foods but they're best eaten as part of a meal, say a wholemeal oat apple crumble after a healthy main course, as the body deals best with sugar when there is fibre, fat, and protein from other foods around.

High GI foods

Honey; sugar of all sorts; chocolate; sweet still and fizzy drinks, bananas, watermelons, figs, dried dates and raisins; mashed potatoes, cooked carrots, squashes, parsnips and swedes; white and wholemeal bread; rye-based crispbreads; couscous, rice cakes and wholegrain cereals (including bran flakes); popcorn.

Medium GI foods

Grapes, oranges, fresh dates, mangoes and kiwi fruits; raw carrots, sweetcorn, peas and potatoes (apart from mashed); white and wholegrain pasta; porridge and oatmeal; wholegrain rye bread (including pumpernickel); brown and white rice.

Low GI foods

Apples, pears, peaches, grapefruits, plums, cherries and dried apricots; avocados; green, leafy vegetables and most other vegetables (but see above); lentils and beans; soya products.

DECIPHERING THE LABEL

Some food companies have become sneaky in their food-labelling antics, which although currently lawful are very hard to understand. They can get round packing our everyday foods with sugar, not wanting us to know how much there is in the product, by leaving out a figure that relates to the total sugar content.

When it comes to reading food labels, however, it would be useful to know not just about fructose, glucose, etc. but about any added sugars and, crucially, to know a total sugar figure. For example, and as a benchmark, the latest World Health Organization/Food and Agriculture Organization report recommends that our sugar intake should account for a maximum of 10% of our energy intake. However, I think that 10% calories from sugar is a lot and you should aim for 5%. In a day this works out to roughly a maximum as follows:

* 1–3 years old, a maximum of 31g for boys and 29g for girls.
* 4–6 years, a maximum of 43g boys and 39g for girls.
* 7–10 years, 55g for boys and 46g for girls.

If you look at refined sugar snacks like chocolate bars, a 50g bar of milk chocolate can contain nearly 29g of sugar, the whole day's allowance for a girl of three! And a cola can contain 55g sugar just in 500ml.

On food labels there is a nutrition panel, where you can see how much sugar the food contains. As a rough guide, if the product contains more than one-fifth of your child's suggested maximum intake per day, it's too high in sugar. And the higher up the list of ingredients sugar, and all the previously mentioned other names for sugar, come, the more sugar it will contain.

If your child already takes in quite a lot of sugar, try to wean them off it slowly, say over the course of a month, as you'll probably find they'll rebel big-time if you suddenly call a halt. You could dilute juices with water, and reduce processed sweet foods by limiting them to every other day, or just weekends. Whatever works for you all, but do try to get them off the sweet stuff as much as possible. I promise you'll notice so many positive changes in their general wellbeing.

I WANT SOME SWEETS!

Kids are big consumers of sweets and confectionery, especially now that some schools have abolished set school meals. They're either given packed lunches, which frequently include a sweet thing or two, or money to spend in the school tuckshop, and as a result kids' weight is rocketing, their teeth are decaying and their behaviour is deteriorating. But I guess you know this.

It's hard as a health-conscious parent to know whether it's better to give your child a little shop-bought, high-sugar, high-fat and most likely additive-riddled sweet every now and then or ban them altogether (in which case your child may start to eat them in secret). It's better that you know what they eat and are able to control it rather than force them into keeping things from you because they know you'll flip your lid – well, this is the tack I take. I also don't want Maya to feel too different from every other child around – it's not fair to her. If you're pretty laid back about your kids eating the occasional sweet now and then, you're less likely to find them wanting to pig out on the junk when they go to other friends' houses/parties as a rebellion thing.

This said, I don't want Maya to eat sweets every day; when she gets a bit older I plan to operate a once-a-week treat system when she'll have the choice of buying a little something from the shop if she wants it and eating it after she has had a healthy meal. But I'll try to steer her away from poor-quality sweet things containing additives such as tartrazine (see page 72) and coax her into choosing something from a good health-food store or supermarket, something with a little bit of something good in it, such as oats, good cocoa butter, or dried fruits.

I'd rather kids had a small organic good-quality chocolate bar than a bag of iridescent sweets. While your child is young, see if you can be quick and subtle enough to break the chocolate or other treat bar in half – you could rewrap the halves in little pink and white bags, alongside some chopped dried fruits, unsalted nuts, seeds, small rice cakes, dried cranberries and raspberries, a sort of goody bag. Cut dried fruit bars such as Peter Rabbit bars into small pieces and wrap them in shiny paper or foil, to look like a sweet.

You can make your own sweets too, a great idea for kids' parties. Melt some good-quality highish-cocoa-bean chocolate – if your child will go for a 70% one, great, but it can be a bit bitter and strong (though this means they tend not to want more than a couple of squares, which can be a good thing) – alternatively use an organic milk chocolate. Dip slices of banana, cherries, dried fruits like apricots, dates, figs, into the chocolate and lay them on bakewell paper to set.

I think a big part of dealing with the issue of sweet rewards is balance – on the one hand not making a huge fuss about the occasional naughty treat and on the other thinking about how you sell them the healthier foods. If you make a treat bag of healthy foods, be positive – if you are, they're just as likely to see nectarines and chopped figs as sweet treat foods as they are sweet things in the shop. And lead by example at your child's birthday party – I can guarantee that when the other parents see how yummy the food is and how well the kids behave during and after the party they'll all soon be copying you!

Watch the wording

Watch out for words like organic, no added sugar, sugar-free, natural, pure, fresh, etc. Just because sweets are labelled organic doesn't mean they contain any less sugar, and organic sugar might be fairer traded (which to me is a tick in its box) but it can still cause tooth decay and weight gain, etc. It's about quality and what the whole sweet is like. If it's organic it generally contains fewer or no additives, such as tartrazine. No-added-sugar sweets can still contain some sugar – and could be high in fat and anything else. 'Natural' is one of the most abused words in food labelling, like 'pure' and 'fresh' – so don't just buy something because it has these words on the label.

WHAT ABOUT HONEY?

First, honey mustn't be given to children under the age of one because it can occasionally cause infant botulism. But because it has very useful antiseptic properties and because it has a higher water content than sugar, which means it has fewer calories and is less sweet than sugar, I think it's good to include it in moderation in your child's diet after the first year. Watch that you don't OD on it thinking that just because it's natural it's much better than sugar – it can still cause tooth decay, aggravate sugar-sensitive kids and lead to obesity. Biscuits with honey in them aren't necessarily healthy, as the health-food stores frequently mislead us into thinking. Also, common or garden bog-standard honey doesn't have any of the antibacterial properties that good-quality honey has – it can help heal wounds and mouth ulcers and it can definitely soothe a sore throat, but if colds and sore throats are due to a viral infection, which they frequently are, the honey won't do anything to combat the infection, over and above the soothing effect.

Ideally choose an organic honey from bees that frequent only one flower, or the New Zealand Manuka honey (which is dark and strong, so it might not suit all kids' tastebuds, but it's a great medicine-cabinet must-have). Look for pure honeycomb too – this is more likely to have the healing X factor that seems to help annihilate bad bugs.

Kids' yoghurt and fromage frais

What a nightmare! You only have to wander down the supermarket aisles to see how many different styles, types, colours, consistencies of yoghurt and fromage frais there are. Some are great for your child – they can be a valuable source of calcium and zinc for kids – but so often there is so much other crap in them, astronomical levels of sugar for instance, that for me this takes them into the to-be-avoided-at-all-costs zone. I hate the way many of the yoghurts aimed at kids have crunchy, sweet chocolate chips added, and so many additives and preservatives that we just shouldn't be putting into our kids' bodies. Just because a yoghurt has beautiful fresh-looking fruits on the pack doesn't mean that it actually contains any real fruit.

I've made a really clear choice when it comes to yoghurt – I go for a natural full-fat yoghurt or fromage frais and add a little drizzle of honey, a dollop of apple purée or some chopped dried fruits; I stir some muesli into it if we want a little crunch, an easy way to get a little oat fibre and good seeds inside Maya. I don't go for low-fat yoghurts because first, they contain a lot of added sugar, and second, I don't think there's a reason for going for low-fat anything – I'd much rather have a creamy-tasting, good, unadulterated full-cream yoghurt that satisfies Maya after one bowlful than give her low-fat yoghurt that's weak in comparison. Kids need their fats. Whole-milk natural yoghurt contains only 3g of fat per 100g, and a natural full-fat fromage frais (8% fat) contains, as the label implies, 8g of fat per 100g, with the lower-fat natural yoghurts containing 0.7g of fat and a 0% fromage frais having, as it says, no fat in it worth measuring. You would have to

consume an awful lot of yoghurt to make it contribute such a significant difference in fat grams. Friends of mine who go for low-fat yoghurt only find that their kids are still hungry afterwards. Fromage frais or Greek yoghurt with a drizzle of honey and a chopped banana is a family favourite.

As you will see in the section on probiotics (page 77), probiotic live or bio yoghurt helps keep our kids' guts full of friendly bacteria, which can reduce the chances of food poisoning, constipation and diarrhoea. Remember always to give your child live yoghurt during and after a course of antibiotics, as the antibiotics tend to zap the good bacteria as well as the ones they're meant to be getting rid of. Yoghurt helps replenish the gut.

Note that yoghurt may even be tolerated by children who are intolerant of raw cow's milk, as the fermentation processes involved in the yoghurt can make it more digestible. However, seek your doctor's advice if you're worried about trying this and this only applies to intolerance, not allergy. Greek yoghurt tends to be made from ewe's (i.e. sheep's) milk, which can be good for kids who can't tolerate cow's milk proteins. Soya yoghurt is of course fine for vegan kids, but do check that you choose a calcium-enriched one – normal soya yoghurts usually contain only in the region of 15mg/100g of calcium, compared to the classic cow's milk yoghurt which hits the 160mg/100g mark – this can make a big calcium difference to a young child. See my section on how to bring your child up as vegetarian or vegan (pages 112–119).

I did a supermarket sweep to check out the other types of kids' yoghurt and found that almost

all the child-oriented brands I looked at contained more than 10g per sugar per 100g – which counts in my book as a lot. Nestlé's Disney fromage frais contains 18.9g of sugar per 100g! Although I'm generally a big fan of organic yoghurts, you go from natural yoghurt, which has very little or no sugar added, to 12g of sugar per 100g in a Yeo Valley raspberry yoghurt – which is shocking. OK, it's still organic, but you're best sticking to plain yoghurt and adding a little fresh or puréed fruit of your own if you want to add a little sweetness. (Remember, if you start your child with no added sugar in things like yoghurt, they won't miss it. The problems arise when you've been giving them really sweet kids' yoghurt and suddenly expect them to go all natural – it will taste sour. Of course you could wean them off the sweet taste gradually by 'diluting' the sweeter yoghurt with some natural yoghurt.)

Five ways to sweeten natural yoghurt

By putting fresh, dried and puréed fruits and honey into your yoghurt you are adding sugar, but you are still probably adding less than there is in processed yoghurts; anyway, you are also adding other nutrients such as vitamin C from the berries, antibacterial properties from the honey, fibre from the banana – it's a much healthier nutrient package altogether. However, watch you don't OD on the sweetness by adding too much honey or fruits – great as they are, they can give your child a sweet hit which could send their moods all over the place.

* Mashed or sliced banana
* Chopped-up dried fruits such as Medjool dates, figs or apricots (try to choose organic, as non-organic dates may have been preserved with sulphur dioxide, which I don't like, see page 52)
* Grated apple
* Tangerine or clementine segments
* Big juicy raisins and thick slices of pear

You can also freeze yoghurts with fresh fruit inside (see my recipes on page 254). The main reason I prefer to make my own is that because legislation isn't tight over the use of the word 'yoghurt', so many of the commercial ones can still contain cream and loads of sugar, so the fat and sugar levels can be very high. Ice cream and yoghurt machines vary a lot in price, but the cheaper ones work well and can be a good investment if your child loves frozen puddings in the summer as much as our crowd does.

Salt

I have to admit that although I am a bit of a salt addict – a bar of chocolate can sit in my fridge for weeks, but give me salty crisps, olives, strong cheeses, sprinklings of sea salt on salads and I'm gone – with Maya I go to great lengths in order that she doesn't consume too much salt. I never use salt if I'm cooking just for her, try to use the minimum if I'm cooking for both of us, and try to keep her away from very salty snacks such as crisps and processed foods. **Too much salt is bad for our kids.**

Salt consists of 40% sodium and 60% chloride, two minerals which are present in small amounts in virtually all basic foods, from fruits and vegetables to tap water. While we do need some sodium in our diet because it helps balance our body fluids and is necessary to help our muscles and nerves function properly, none of us needs the levels of salt we come across in our everyday life – we live in a very salty society. Even if you're not adding salt to anything fresh, you can easily stumble across it in bread, breakfast cereals, even foods your tongue wouldn't detect as salty. Experts now think that we consume a vast percentage, as high as 75%, of all the salt we consume from processed foods, while only 9% is added in cooking at home and 6% added at the table. A recent survey by the Food Commission, an organization that campaigns for 'safer, healthier food in the UK', has found that some manufacturers are putting just as much salt in puddings as they are in crisps and bacon!

WHY WORRY? AND HOW MUCH IS TOO MUCH?

Too much salt causes high blood pressure, which increases our risk of developing heart disease and stroke. Diets high in salt have also been linked to asthma, stomach cancer, brittle bones and fluid retention – it's bad news. Although I'm not a huge fan of tables and limits, when it comes to salt, as with sugar, I think it's good to know what sort of figures we should be aiming towards with our kids. It's pretty shocking how much salt you can stack up in a day, especially if you're relying heavily on processed foods.

Remember salt is 40% sodium, so to work out how much salt something contains you need to multiply the sodium level by 2.5 – you'll soon get used to it! So 1g (100mg) of sodium equals 2.5g of salt (2,500mg). The Food Standards Agency states that a high salt product is one with 0.5g or more of sodium per 100g product and a low salt product is one with 0.1g of sodium per 100g product, with a medium salt somewhere in between, as anything containing 0.1–0.5g of sodium per 100g product.

Here are the maximum recommended daily amounts of salt in the diet for children:

* 1–3 years old, 2g of salt (equivalent to 800mg of sodium)
* 4–6 years, 3g of salt (equivalent to 1.2g of sodium)
* 7–10 years, 5g of salt (equivalent to 2g of sodium)

The World Health Organization has set targets at 5g of salt per day for adults.

HOW TO SPOT HIGH-SALT FOODS

Although in many foods your tastebuds can be a good judge of salt, unfortunately the mouth doesn't often pick up on sodium in processed foods because very often it's disguised by lots of sugar. Breakfast cereals, for instance, don't usually taste salty, but they are in fact a big source of sodium in the diet (although some manufacturers are quite rightly reducing the salt content of cereals – about time!). Bread and tinned foods like baked beans and soups can also be very high in salt. Basically, the thing to do is get into the habit of scrutinizing labels, always remembering not to confuse salt and sodium. On the nutritional label you'll find out how much sodium each food contains, although you also need to be aware that sometimes the value isn't given per portion size – it may be given per 100g, so if you eat 200g of the product in a normal portion, this means you'll be consuming twice as much.

Sometimes manufacturers don't have to declare how much salt is in the food (don't ask me why, it's too complicated!), but you can get a very rough idea of how much sodium there is in it by seeing how far up the list of ingredients sodium appears – if it's near the top, this means that there's quite a lot of sodium in it. A personal cut-off point for me is if there is 500mg of sodium per 100g foods, which is an awful lot.

HOW TO AVOID SALT WITHOUT SACRIFICING FLAVOUR

One of the reasons why it's really important not to add salt to your child's food early on is so that you won't give them a craving for it – like sugar, if you keep the levels low, they won't miss what they don't eat, but if you add lots of salt when they're young and then expect them to eat much lower levels of salt when they're older you will probably get complaints that the food tastes bland. If you've already been in the habit of adding salt, and maybe a few very high-salt foods have been standard in your family's diet, try over the next few weeks gradually to reduce the amount of salt you add to food – don't do it all at once, otherwise they will notice big-time.

Use flavourings such as lemon juice, pepper, fresh herbs, or a little tamari or soy sauce – although these sauces do contain quite a bit of salt in themselves, they also offer other flavourings such as chilli and spices, which to my mind makes them a little better than pure salt. Just try from when your kids are at as early an age as possible not to add salt to vegetables and cooking, or to have it on the table for them to sprinkle over their food – it's just habit that we add it to food at this stage, even before we've tasted it. Remember that kids aren't the best ones to judge when something needs some extra salt – you need to step in here, and remember they'll copy you too. If you gradually reduce the amount of salt in their diet, within weeks their tastebuds will re-set their oh-this-tastes-salty thermostat so that they will start to recognize when something is far too salty, even rejecting foods you've previously given them!

With processed foods, choose chilled ready-made meals and soups rather than the longer-life or tinned varieties, as salt is generally used for long-term preservation. If you buy beans and lentils in tins, already soaked (which I do), rinse them in plenty of fresh cold water before you use them, to get rid of as much of the brine, and hence the salt, as possible.

Fast food

I've really tried to shift my prejudice against takeaway foods, but the furthest I can go is to say that once in a while is OK. I know many large fast-food companies and restaurants are making positive changes to their menus (fat levels are coming down, so are salt and sugar content), but the poor quality of the food and the disastrous nutritional package, stuffed with additives, fat, sugar and salt, means that fast food is simply not a healthy option.

If you're in the habit of going out for a takeaway because you're not sure how to make quick meals, have a look through my recipes. I'm sure there'll be something to take your fancy – even homemade versions of burgers with lean meat, or little chicken kebabs or falafel, can be just as novel for kids. (OK, I know the big fast-food giants can offer all sorts of enticements for kids as well as the food, but I try to ignore these!) But if you do want to have takeaway foods and know occasions will crop up when there is little choice in the matter, the following tips can help you choose what I think are the best options.

Incidentally, please join me in voicing your opinion of so-called kids' menus, which are usually nothing more than fish or chicken goujons and chips, cheesy macaroni style pasta, beef burgers, you know the score. Why should our kids be given the same menu in nearly every restaurant? If we all moan enough, restaurants will have to change to something more imaginative and nutritious.

BURGER BARS
Some of the salads in the large burger joints have more fat and calories in them than the burgers.

The fat the food is fried in can be reused and heated to such high temperatures that the fats start breaking down into trans fats, and if they overcook chips it increases the amount of acryl amide, a chemical thought to be potentially cancer-causing (the dark brown edges of chips in particular are particularly risky). However, I have to admit the big burger companies do seem to be doing better on their cooking techniques, so there are less trans fats than there used to be.

The problem with burger bar chips is that they're cut so thinly that when they're cooked they're much higher in fat than homemade ones – the best chips, if you're going to make them yourself as I sometimes do, are thick straight-cut chips, fried in oil, not lard. Watch out for microwave chips, as they're thinly cut, so like burger bar chips there is a greater surface area for the fat to cling to, hence higher fat and calorie content. Both microwave and oven chips, which can be lower in fat and calories, can be high in additives and preservatives.

Try to choose some salad, with dressing on the side, for them to eat (if you can persuade them!) along with the burger. There are chicken and fish options, as well as veggie burgers, but these can have just as much fat and calories as beef burgers. Chicken burgers are a particular worry – people perceive chicken as a healthy option, but unfortunately, due to more intensive farming methods, the chicken has a higher fat level these days than it used to, which can mean that a chicken burger is higher in calories thn a lean red meat burger. The mayonnaise in chicken burgers really whacks the fat levels up too – so keep the

quantity down as much as possible. Lean pieces of chicken are better than breaded, deep-fried ones.

Drinking water is much better for teeth than very sweet fizzy drinks, and fresh fruit afterwards would of course be the ideal.

'CHISH AND FIPS' (AS WE ALWAYS CALLED THEM)

I can still remember as a child sitting on the sea wall in North Wales eating fish and chips out of newspaper – this was our once-a-holiday 'chish and fips' treat! There is nothing wrong with good fish lightly battered, freshly cooked alongside some thick chips, with mushy peas for a little fibre – served with mint sauce in Nottingham, where I grew up! But sadly the freshly cooked piece of fish scenario doesn't happen much these days, as most fish and chip shops seem to like the double-frying method for quicker turnaround business – good old fish and chips is more likely to be astronomically high in fat, and may well be hefty in trans fats. It really is crucial to choose a good fish and chip shop where you see the fish go in unfried, and which serves just small portions of the traditional thick chips, preferably fried in oil rather than in the northern favourite, lard, which is astronomically high in saturated animal fats. (If you make fish and chips at home, try the Peter Rabbit brand of tomato ketchup, which has no added sugar, salt or additives – it's fantastic.)

PIZZA

I can find a few more positive things to say about pizzas. OK, I'm biased, because I love Italian food! But if the pizzas are freshly made, with a high-quality fresh tomato sauce and a simple topping like a Margarita, they can be perfectly fine. What I have a problem with are the toppings that have six cheeses, inferior meat, and are just dripping in fat, salt and calories. Choose a good-quality pizza place, try to persuade the kids to eat some salad with just a little dressing (remember to order it on the side, as these dressings can be really salty and fatty in themselves and kids tend to pile loads on), and stick to simpler toppings if you can. Although thicker-based pizzas do have a higher ratio of bread dough to potentially fattier topping, which makes them, theoretically, a healthier choice for kids, I don't think they're as yummy, and neither does Maya – we prefer to have a simple thin-crust pizza with just tomatoes and mozzarella on top. Watch out for the microwaveable pizzas and some of the oven-ready ones, as they can be high in fat, sugar, additives and preservatives. As with all takeaways, try not to get swept down the fizzy drink and dessert route – less is more.

EASTERN

I've always loved good Indian food, and now, since Maya's from India, I love it even more, though I have to admit we haven't yet had takeaway Indian, or any other cuisine such as Chinese, or Thai. Unless you're really careful about where they're made, like all other takeaways they can be very high in fat, salt and sugar. Chinese food can be hefty on the monosodium glutamate (MSG) front too. Some nutritionists suggest that you stick to the vegetable dishes, but unless it's a good takeaway, they too can be astronomically heavy on everything. So just choose the best takeaway you can find. With Indian, go for the lighter grilled meats and fish dishes, or vegetables, which are not drowned in sauces rich in cream – there are so many delicious spiced dry dishes which when served with plain boiled rice and a simple vegetable dish can be pretty healthy. The same applies with Chinese and Thai – watch out for coconutty and creamy sauces and keep the accompaniments, rice, noodles, etc. simple. Try not to over-order, as this only encourages people to eat too much.

Noodle bars and dim sum restaurants have also become popular, and as long as you're careful not to order too many salty pickles and dips, they can be good options – Maya and I frequent noodle bars, as she likes sucking up the long messy noodles!

With kebabs and other Eastern grilled meat cuisines, if you're sure about the quality of the produce, a wrap or kebab with some lean protein like fish, chicken, seafood with salad and a little dressing is a good option. Avoid the rotating meats and the fried-ten-times falafel that are dowsed with so much fat and sit heavily in the gut afterwards – oh, student memories!

JAPANESE

Japanese food is, to me, the exception among the fast-food options – I love sushi and sashimi and many of the cooked dishes. I've not yet got Maya on to raw fish, as I think she'll just spit it out, but I know friends who take their slightly older kids and it works well – choose the leaner good-quality ingredients. As with all takeaway options, the quality of the establishment is crucial. And remember to be careful with rice that's been cooked a long time before you eat it: unless it's properly chilled, it can, and frequently does, cause food poisoning! Japanese food also tends to be pretty expensive.

Some fast-foods are definitely better than others. Be wary of take-aways, though.

Kids' drinks

Children need plenty of fluid to help their gut digest food well, hydrate their skin, help them regulate their body temperature and feel energized and healthy. When kids are well hydrated, which means they have enough water in their body, they're more likely to be able to concentrate well at school, play sports with consistent energy levels, and are less likely to suffer headaches and digestive problems such as constipation. School-age children need between six and eight glasses of water a day, younger children about half to three-quarters of this amount, but it all depends on how active they are – the more they run around, the hotter they get and the more water they lose through their sweat and breathing, so you need to give them more fluid to compensate for these losses.

But although water is the simplest, most easily available, nutritionally pure drink you could give your child, it just isn't that fashionable nowadays, as the drinks industry seems to have persuaded many kids and their parents that there are much nicer, more fun, even so-called healthy drinks containing calcium and vitamin C that can take its place. So what to give your child to drink can become one more decision to have to make.

FRUIT JUICE, FIZZY DRINKS ...

There are so many options – juices, cordials, canned fizzy drinks, so-called fruit juices containing natural sugars, yoghurt drinks that imply they're healthy by including the word 'yoghurt' when they contain more sugar than a can of cola. I could list many more. Understanding what goes into these drinks doesn't make happy reading. Carbonated drinks contain carbonated water, with sugar or artificial sweeteners, colourings, additives, preservatives and some form of acid. A 330ml can of typical carbonated fruit drink contains approx 95 kcals and 5 teaspoons of sugar – you wouldn't give your child this sugar on a spoon, so why from a can? They offer no positive nutritional benefits – I don't buy into the argument that manufacturers put forward saying kids need the sugar to give them energy. This is rubbish – it's more likely to cause tooth decay and obesity in our young ones. You might think the odd can of drink is OK, and yes, as a treat, I would agree, but some kids are literally drinking the equivalent of 500g of sugar per day in canned drinks. Frightening but true: studies have shown that some children drink seven or so cans a day – at 85g of sugar a pop!

The diet drinks aren't any better because they, like the normal versions, contain acids that have been linked to drawing the calcium from our bones (and some think the phosphorus content of canned drinks also contributes) – kids need to hold on to their calcium, not lose it. The combination of sugar and acids in many canned drinks means our kid's teeth are in for a heavy hit. Preservatives such as tartrazine can aggravate behaviour, especially if your child suffers from ADD (see page 153).

WATER IS STILL THE BEST OPTION

I've had a clear rule with Maya from the beginning – she only drinks milk or water. She likes water (good girl!), asks for it when she's thirsty and usually refuses any sweet drinks that friends offer her. I've even had to stop my mum offering her sweet drinks – it might only be a little fruit squash mixed in, but she has enough natural sugar in her diet, and she likes water, so why add something she doesn't need? Frequently these squashes and high juices have so much sugar, preservatives and acids in them that they're really no better than a can of pop. If you want your child to have fruit juice, buy (or make) unsweetened pure fruit juice, dilute it well – at least two parts water to one of juice – and offer it just once a day, as an integral part of a planned snack. This way, fruit juice can be a treat food, providing useful vitamin C. If you get into the habit of always offering fruit juice, you will be damaging your kids' teeth, and the highly processed, sweetened, coloured and preserved ready-made juices (even the ones with berries, cartoon characters, so-called juice drinks – which incidentally can contain just 5% juice, so how the manufacturers can imply they are healthy drinks or full of fruit I don't know!) will give your child the very clear message that water on its own is boring. Note that although some flavoured waters offer the occasional palatable change from plain water, many contain additives and a lot of sugar. And just because they have a strawberry on the label doesn't mean the water's been near a real one!

Bottled or tap?

The bottled water industry is one of the fastest growing in the UK. But in terms of benefits to health, it is worth bearing in mind that the bacterial and chemical composition of tap water is generally subject to much tighter regulation, making it a surer bet and thousands of times cheaper than many bottled waters. You could install a water purification system at home, or simply use a water filter jug, which might make your water taste better or put your mind more at ease (and it's definitely a cheaper alternative to bottled water), but make sure you follow the instructions and change the filter regularly. If you prefer bottled water, opt for one labelled 'natural mineral water' because this type is subject to the strictest regulations. And make sure you drink it within twenty-four hours of opening to prevent the proliferation of bacteria.

Sparkling water

Although sparkling water should be fine for children, you may find that if they drink it quickly it can give them a little problem with gas, or tummy-ache. If they like the bubbles, choose a brand that's less fizzy. Check the labels on both sparkling and still bottled water to make sure they're not too high in sodium (salt). Ideally bottled water should have 20mg of sodium per litre or less, and a moderate sodium level would be somewhere between 20 and 200mg, but you should definitely avoid those with levels above this – they're far too salty for young bodies.

Five ways to make a glass of water appealing

* Add a straw.
* Serve the water in a funny cartooned or coloured glass or a little water bottle that they don't mind carrying around with them.
* Chilled water can sometimes taste better, and you can even add ice cubes, perhaps with pieces of fruit frozen inside.
* Add some pieces of fresh fruit or lemon slices.
* Let them see you drinking it as well.

FRUIT AND VEGETABLE JUICES – REAL ONES!

I'm a fan of fruit smoothies and juices for kids, as it's a great, fun, easy way to get them some vitamins and minerals and fruit sugars, especially if they're not big breakfast fans. But there are some down-sides. First, the juicing process – which is when you put the whole fruit into a machine and the pulp gets removed and a clear juice comes out into a glass – removes the majority of the fibre from the juice. This means the sugars in the juice can be quickly absorbed, which can, depending on the fruit or vegetable they contain and whether your child drinks more than say one glass at a time, give them a sugar high and then a sugar crash. Smoothies that are made from putting the whole fruit, say bananas or soft fruits, into a blender and mixing hang on to more of the fibre,

but because they've been liquidized they're downed more quickly and the body can get more of a 'sugar hit' than when your child eats the individual fruits, which takes longer.

The acids in fruit juices and smoothies can also be very troublesome for our kids' teeth, but don't clean their teeth straight afterwards. The acid and sugar levels in the mouth are at their highest then, so damage to the teeth if you brush them is inevitable. The best thing is to give some plain water afterwards, and if you can get them to eat a little piece of cheese this rebalances the acid levels and you can clean their teeth later. For this reason, you shouldn't give kids fresh fruit juice before bedtime. Drinking through a straw helps reduce the contact the juice has with their teeth.

You can add vegetables to the juice, such as carrots and celery to apple juice if you're making your own, but this doesn't seem to be that popular with kids – you're lucky if they drink it. And if you make your own juices, they should be drunk as soon as possible to get the maximum levels of vitamins, as some disappear with time. I generally say that kids shouldn't have more than one 200ml glass of fresh juice per day and that they should make up the rest of their fluid intake from water. Too much fresh juice can give kids indigestion, a bloated tummy, diarrhoea or constipation, and can make them put on too much weight, as it can contain a fair few calories.

A lower-cost option is to go for Tetrapack UHT juices. These, surprisingly, can contain just as many vitamins, minerals and phytonutrients as the freshly squeezed ones you buy in the supermarket – and they are so much cheaper. But again, just one glass a day. Try to pick one that doesn't contain the preservatives listed on page 72 – and organic is preferable, as these will contain fewer pesticide and herbicide residues.

TEA, COFFEE, HOT CHOCOLATE

I don't have a problem with kids having the occasional cup of tea as it's a comforting antioxidant-packed drink and also enables them to have some milk – much better than canned fizzy drinks. But I'd keep it weak so that they don't get the caffeine hit. Try chai, which has lots of milk and spices in it so can be a good way to get kids to take milk, if they don't like drinking it straight. It is lovely and weak, and can give a delicious spicy, warming moment to a hectic day. Boil a 1 inch stick of cinnamon, 8 cardamon pods and 8 whole cloves in 2 cups of water. Once boiling, turn the heat down and simmer for 10 minutes. Add 3 cups of milk and sugar to taste and bring to a simmer again. Add 3 teaspoons of loose black tea, cover and turn off the heat. Allow to sit for 2 minutes before straining and serving.

Coffee, however, is a different matter: it contains slightly more caffeine, which can aggravate behaviour in hyperactive kids, make some children feel jittery, nervous, anxious, disrupt their sleep, affect concentration at school. So although the British Coffee Association, who represent the coffee industry, say studies show that kids can consume between 50 and 100mg of caffeine without suffering any problems, I would say avoid it. Incidentally, colas can contain between 30 and 55mg of caffeine per 330ml can. If you compare that to a single espresso, containing roughly 100mg (and you'd never normally consider giving your child this), you'll see just how worrying the fact that kids drink so much cola is!

Hot chocolate drinks can contain quite a lot of a caffeine-like substance called Theobromine and sugar, which could just have the opposite effect on your child from the one you want at bedtime. If they're going to drink hot chocolate, give it to them earlier in the day to allow more time for the caffeine from the cocoa beans to work out of their system and not keep them awake. Try to use good-quality organic chocolate like Green & Black's. It's easy to make: just melt one square of chocolate in a small pan of warmed milk (which could be cow's, sheep's, goat's, rice or soya milk).

Finally, be wary of malted milk drinks, even the low-fat ones, as they can be full of sugar. Hot milk on its own is a good settling drink for getting kids to sleep well – and check out night-time milk, which contains higher levels of melatonin, the hormone that helps you sleep. But clean their teeth afterwards as it contains sugar, albeit natural.

UHT juices are just as good as freshly-squeezed ones, and much cheaper.

Costs

I know many people in my profession will try to convince you that eating healthily is no more expensive than your usual diet, but the fact is that feeding your child good nutritious food doesn't come cheap. Organic produce can cost more, so do so-called premium healthy food lines, and food wastage can be high because some days they just won't eat what you prepare for them. But there are lots of ways you can reduce the costs without compromising on the key healthy nutrients, things you can do to shop economically, and to reduce the amount of food you throw out.

* Ready-made meals and prepared products like pastry, chopped vegetables, fruits, peeled this and that, are more expensive than doing it yourself. So if you have the time, try to pull back some pennies by buying the vegetables unwashed, and preparing them yourself.
* Try to become a more confident cook, as you can really save a lot of money making simple meals for your child, instead of having to rely on ready-made things. And they'll usually be much healthier, as you can control the amount of ingredients such as salt, sugar, fat, etc., that you put in, and you won't need to add preservatives. If you work during the week, try to cook big batches at weekends and freeze them in small portions. A classic mistake is to freeze a whole serves-six lasagne when only two of you will want to eat it – if you portioned it out you wouldn't end up throwing so many leftovers away. Wrap foods well so that you don't lose any to freezer spoilage. This also applies to wrapping foods in the fridge, so that they don't dry out or

spoil before they should. Not closing lids or rewrapping cheese, etc. can mean you have to throw a lot of food out.
* Frozen vegetables and fruits can be very economical – they're generally cheaper, and because they're frozen you tend not to lose as many nutrients to food spoilage. I particularly like frozen berries, which you can throw into a smoothie or crumble in the winter, when fresh berries would be very expensive. Don't ever feel bad about not giving your child blueberries and mangoes regularly – the common or garden apple, pear and banana are just as nutritious and much cheaper.
* Buy seasonally, as foods are cheaper when they're plentiful.
* If you tend to do one large shop a week, watch you don't over-buy food – make a meal plan for the week, or check your cupboards and freezer before you go out, as it's so easy to buy things you already have when you're tired and have a child screaming to go home.
* Buy direct from farmers and suppliers - look at the following websites:
  www.soilassociation.org
  www.foodloversbritain.com
  www.fairtradeonline.com
* Club together with other parents locally to share delivery costs.
* To find a cooperative near you, which can keep costs lower, look at www.sustainweb.org, which lists 300 organizations on its database.
* Put things into the freezer that you don't plan on eating straight away, such as whole chickens or meat products, even milk, so you don't find

yourself hurrying to use up foods before they go off, or just missing the sell-by dates.

* Shopping more often and for specific meals, rather than just buying what you think you might use, can save money and reduce the amount you throw away – but I know it takes more time. As an online food shopper, I've just recently changed to having two deliveries per week instead of one big one, as although it costs me another delivery charge, say £5, I'm throwing away much less and not feeling as if I'm racing against time before salads, fruits, vegetables and fresh produce go off.

* Even if vegetables are looking limp, don't throw them away – often they'll still be fine for casseroles and soups. Try to get into the habit of using recipes like bubble and squeak or fricassee for leftovers.

* Freezing meals means you can be more responsive when your child wants to eat something specific. You can just grab it from the freezer, rather than having to go out and buy the ingredients (by which time they might have changed their mind – we've all been there!), perhaps having to pay higher prices from a small corner shop if you can't get to your supermarket. It also means you won't have to go through the process of cooking something that they'll refuse and having to throw it away. Defrosting and reheating meals in a microwave is perfectly healthy, as long as you follow the manufacturer's instructions.

* Economy lines, although they seem better value, can often actually be more expensive if you look at the amount of good ingredients they contain.

For instance, cheaper sausages can contain less meat than premium lines, as can chicken nuggets, fish pies – you're paying more money for fillers and cheaper ingredients like poor-quality fat. I know it costs more to buy better sausages, beef burgers, pasta, biscuits, etc., but you can make them go a lot further by adding other cheaper, but still great ingredients. For example, make a sausage casserole using premium sausages and add chickpeas or lentils or some brown rice to make it feed more people.

* Try to avoid products aimed specially for kids. They are usually not only poor-quality, but they can also be expensive – you end up paying a premium for the cartoon or hip character on the packaging.

* Choose one supermarket or shop for your premium ingredients, the ones I think are worth spending the money on, say fresh vegetables, fruits, meat, chicken, etc. Then with branded products like baked beans, loo rolls, dry goods, where supermarkets can really compete well on price, go for the cheapest and best value.

* Tap water is much, much cheaper than bottled (see page 98).

* If you're a confident cook, buy the more economical, unfashionable cuts of meat or cheaper fish – cuts of meat like brisket of beef can be just as healthy and nutritious. The cheaper cuts of meat often take longer to cook, though, and you need to know how to cook them so they don't dry out. Trendy foods like sea bass can be expensive, so instead go for a simple white fish like grouper.

* Watch the big supermarkets' pricing antics, as although they may say they've reduced the price on 200 or so foods, they are sometimes economical with the truth, shall I say. Be on your guard, and do some price comparisons before you commit.

Dirt is good!

You might think I've veered a little off track here, but there is some method in my madness. We live in an obsessive society when it comes to cleaning, and our dislike of dirt and over-use of detergents and antiseptics means that not only are our kids being exposed to more chemicals in the home than they ever used to be, but there is also quite a lot of evidence to show that it's not helping them develop an appropriate level of immunity. Although the evidence isn't conclusive, it does seem that if children are not exposed to a minimum level of dirt and bugs, their immune system can't develop an acceptable way to react to things in the environment – they can become over-reactive and develop conditions such as asthma, other types of allergies and diseases such as diabetes. In short, kids need to be allowed to be dirty – it's part of growing up and an important part of their development.

HOW TO AVOID CHEMICALS

So when it comes to what you use to clean your children and their immediate environment, try not to use chemicals all the time – good old warm water and a little soap or lemon can often do the trick. Here are my top ten tips to help you avoid ODing on the chemicals:

1. Don't get seduced by the persuasive product marketing for kids – just buy the essentials for their skin and hygiene care. They seldom need more than a few basics, and I'm sure some skin irritations and rashes are triggered by over-use of soaps and creams.
2. Avoid baby and kids' wipes, which can contain parabens and propylene glycol – a common ingredient in antifreeze. A damp flannel will usually do the job just as well.
3. Over-washing with chemically based shampoos and conditioners strips the hair of its natural oils. If you usually shampoo your child's hair daily, leave it for a day or two and see if it makes any difference.
4. Cut down on bubble baths, which can contain skin-irritating detergents. I'm not saying we should say goodbye to building bubble-bath castles, but really all your child needs to get clean is a bath full of warm water. If you want to use an essential oil, for example to help them calm down, look for organic oils (they can be the best quality) and see my yummy oils (page 194).
5. Much as I definitely approve of protecting our kids from sun damage, use sunscreens appropriately and cover their skin or keep them out of the sun completely as other measures too. Avoid unnecessary use of products with a high sun-protection factor – at night they don't need these, so take more than sun cream on holiday.
6. Become label-savvy. I hope by now I have persuaded you how crucial it is to read food labels – get into the habit of doing the same with toiletries. The label won't tell you everything, but it will help you see how

chemical-riddled some products are – I tend to opt for organic brands as they generally contain fewer baddies.

7. If you want to be sure a product is organic, look out for Soil Association certification. Do bear in mind, though, that as with food, you shouldn't blindly trust the concept of 'organic'. Words like 'natural' and 'hypoallergenic' generally mean little in the beauty industry. I like organic baby products (www.organicbabies.com, www.spiexiaorganics.com) but again, I use the minimal amount on Maya.

8. Follow the instructions. It's easy to use far more than you need to. Less is more.

9. If you're taking your kids swimming, ozone pools have fewer chemicals. When visiting chlorine pools, make sure they shower first. If everyone washed before getting in, there'd be less need for so many chemicals in the water.

10. Look at great websites such as www.Greenpeace.co.uk for lists of products to avoid, as well as companies with good track records such as Green People, www.greenpeople.co.uk and the following:
www.organic babies.com.
www.absolute – aromas.com
www.Aubrey-organics.com
www.theorganicpharmacy.com
www.drhauschka.co.uk
www.livingnature.com
www.nealsyardremedies.com
www.weleda.com

MESS IS GOOD TOO!

Try not to be an overly fussy parent when it comes to kids making a bit of mess while they're eating. They need not to have to worry about the mess aspect if they're to enjoy their food. In one extreme case, I've seen a parent who cleaned away every splat of food from their child's mouth and hands the minute it landed there, resulting in the child wanting to eat only a very limited and nutritionally restricted dry-food diet. So don't wipe up every drip as soon as they've made it – let food be fun; otherwise they might start using 'getting messy' as a controlling game, if they see that it really winds you up. Extreme messiness isn't the answer either, but as in most things there should be a balance between seeing that they are clean and possess acceptable table manners, and being relaxed enough to let kids be kids and therefore do a little experimenting with foods and texture.

Food should be fun!

THE LIBRARY
NORTH WEST KENT COLLEGE
DERING WAY, GRAVESEND

Maximizing nutrients

If kids eat a well-balanced diet and are generally well, they don't need to take any vitamin and mineral supplements. Supplements can be expensive, some can be full of E numbers and sugar, and some parents can be lulled into thinking that because their child takes a multivitamin and mineral they don't need to keep on at them to eat more fresh fruits and vegetables. This isn't the case: the body is more likely to absorb nutrients from food than from any tablet. Foods offer a nutrient package, like fibre, alongside what is usually two or three vitamins or minerals in each food, and some of the vitamins and minerals help each other to be absorbed. Furthermore, kids need to learn to eat well, and there aren't any short cuts. The food we get in the supermarkets hasn't lost all its nutrients by the time we eat it –it will have lost some, but not enough to mean that it's nutritionally worthless.

Having said all that, if you want to give your child a multivitamin and mineral supplement that's designed for kids and that doesn't exceed the dietary recommended values (DRVs), there isn't anything wrong with this. But don't start self-prescribing more than one supplement, or giving them one of yours, as you could give your child the wrong dose and cause some damage, for example liver damage from too much vitamin A, or mouth ulcers from too much vitamin C. A general good-quality multivitamin and mineral is enough, unless prescribed by your doctor or dietician. Choose a sugar-free and additive-free one if possible – like medicines, supplements can be full of sugar.

Finally, giving kids a supplement can be a way to break a vicious cycle of angst over food. If meals have got very fraught, and your child has stopped eating, a tablet could help you feel confident that at least they're getting some basics. You can have a breathing space and return with renewed vigour a few days later to try and emotively cajole them into eating something better.

HOW TO GET THE MOST NUTRITIONAL VALUE

Here are ten ways to maximize the nutrients in your child's food (plus a healthy cooking-fat tip).

1. Steaming and microwaving vegetables (yes, microwaves are fine if used correctly) ensures you don't lose soluble nutrients into the water – if you have green-coloured water in the bottom of the steamer after cooking broccoli, the vegetable will still contain more vitamins than if you'd boiled it.

2. If you do boil vegetables, keep the cooking time to a minimum. The longer you cook the veg for, the fewer nutrients will be left – they're sensitive (especially Vitamin C and Folate) both to heat and to length of cooking. Try to use the cooking water in soups or gravies, to recycle some of the nutrients. Even though soups are cooked for a long time, you keep all the nutrients in and don't drain them off so it's a worthwhile and healthy thing to make. Did you know that the body actually absorbs more beta-carotene from carrot soup than it does from raw carrots? So it's definitely worth including soups in your kids' diet.

3. Try to prepare your vegetables and fruits at the last minute – the longer they're left with cut

and peeled surfaces exposed to the air, the more nutrients like vitamin C will oxidize and disappear. I'm generally a fan of preparing your own vegetables and fruits, but the ready-prepped vegetables you can buy in specially sealed and stored bags are more nutritious than produce that's been sitting in the fruit bowl or the fridge for days. Yes, in an ideal world we would all have time to go to the local market three times a week for fresh produce that's been picked in its prime and is seasonal and nutritious, but that isn't reality for most of us – we need to rely on freshly prepared easy-to-cook convenience foods.

4. We should use frozen vegetables more – they can contain more vitamins and minerals than fresh, because they are frozen so soon after picking. I also think they're a great standby to have in the freezer for when time's gone against you and you need something quick. Their texture can be disappointing, but peas, beans, spinach and corn work well, especially cooked from frozen – throw them into soups to lift nutrient levels.

5. If you make fresh juice, drink it straight away – the longer you leave it the fewer nutrients you'll glean, and the textures and tastes can alter pretty quickly too. If you buy supermarket fresh juice, use it within the recommended time – and because these can contain quite a lot of sugar, which isn't that great for us, I'd recommend diluting them with water. (This is especially important with little ones, because sugary, acidic juices can damage their teeth.)

6. If deep-frying, make sure your fat is at the correct temperature. If it's too hot, the fat breaks down and can form damaging trans fats; too cool, and the food will soak up too much fat and have too high a calorie content. Having the right temperature for oils and pans is essential when frying – think about using a kitchen thermometer or a special heat-spot pan. A good test is to drop in a cube of bread – it should sizzle gently straight away, and the fat shouldn't smoke (discard it if it does).

7. If you're making chips, cut them thick rather than crinkly – the surface area of crinkly vegetables is larger, therefore more nutrients will be lost in cooking, and if you fry them the fat content will be higher.

8. Choose organic fresh produce whenever possible. I think it tastes better, and nutrient values can be higher.

9. Think about scrubbing vegetables and fruits rather than peeling – you lose valuable nutrients in the peel. I know stories about pesticides and residues can be scary, but in the UK we have some of the lowest levels in the world. And of course, if you buy as much organic as possible, that will reduce your exposure to these chemicals too.

10. Even if you don't buy organic (I know it's expensive), try to support local weekend markets – you'll probably find great freshly picked produce that's high on the nutrient scale.

Essential fatty acids

Yes, yes, yes! There's so much fantastic research around to show that it's well worth including these essential fatty acids in your children's diet. We're talking super-great fats here – especially ones called omega-3 fatty acids.

The parents who are most likely to have heard of omega-3 fatty acids are those who have children with attention deficit disorder (ADD). Kids with ADD have been shown to be deficient in omega-3 fatty acids, so boosting their intake of omega-3-rich foods can have a real impact on their behaviour (see page 153). But there are plenty of reasons for every parent to boost their child's intake of omega-3 fatty acids, as they've been shown to be effective at keeping our hearts healthy, helping with conditions such as eczema, asthma, dyslexia, helping to keep our immune systems strong and encouraging a good level of concentration and memory. Omega-3 and omega-6 fatty acids seem to be the most important, but most kids get enough omega-6 fatty acid naturally and it's the omega-3 that's important to focus on.

Omega-3 fatty acids are found mainly in oily fish, such as kippers, herring, mackerel, salmon (ideally I'd choose organic salmon, wild if possible, not farmed), sardines, fresh tuna (tinned tuna doesn't count, although tinned versions of the other fish do), and mackerel. But you've also probably heard about the worries over toxins such as PCBs in oily fish, which may well have put many of you off eating salmon, etc. Too much oily fish could potentially affect unborn babies, so girls and women of childbearing age should stick to just two portions of oily fish per week. Boys, like men and women past childbearing age, can eat up to four portions (the Food Standards Agency calls a portion 140g fish), although, with the recent concerns over the mercury levels in tuna, I would suggest boys don't eat more than two portions of tuna a week.

HOW TO INCREASE THEIR INTAKE

In my experience, it can be tricky to get kids to eat oily fish twice a week. You might pop salmon into a pie once a week, or eat a smoked salmon bagel, sardines on toast, smoked mackerel pâté in a pitta bread with a natural yoghurt and mint dressing, but it's not that easy to be consistent with two portions a week for a child. So I tend to look to the vegetarian sources of omega oils, which are hemp oil, flaxseed/linseed oil, walnuts and walnut oil. Hemp and flaxseed or linseed oils can be used as salad dressings – I don't use pure hemp oil in mine because I think it's a little strong, but I mix it half and half with olive oil, a little mustard and seasoning and it's absolutely fine.

Another idea is to mix the whole seeds into cereals. You can buy roasted seeds, which are good as a snack mixed with dried fruits such as sultanas, or tossed into salads, especially ones with avocado in them. Or you can grind the hemp and the linseeds up (which actually means your child's body will glean more of the fatty acids) and stir them into muesli or porridge, or milk pudding. You could also use them in cakes and biscuits (see my carrot cake on page 250). With flaxseeds the essential fatty acids need to be kept as fresh as possible, so keep them in your freezer and only grind small amounts of them down at a time. A good health-food store will keep their stock of flaxseeds in the fridge.

If you can't get your child to take omega oils in any of these forms, you could give them a supplement such as morEPA – the usual dose is between 500 and 1,000mg per day for children of school age – but I would only recommend taking a supplement if you have noticed that your child is lacking in concentration or suffers from dyslexia, dyspraxia, autism, ADD, or an allergic condition such as eczema or asthma. One great new supplement to try is called MorDHA-mini, which is an essential fatty acid supplement for children from the age of 6 months to five years. The DHA, which stands for Docosahexaenoic acid, one of the omega-3 fatty acids that is critical for growth, function and brain development, is sourced from fish oils, but the capsules come in stawberry flavour, which is one of the easiest ways to ensure kids get enough omega-3 in their diets, if they're not fish eaters. For kids over the age of five, the more critical fatty acid is EPA, Eicosapentaenoic acid, so the better supplement is the grown-up version MorEPA. Kids take just one capsule daily. You can buy both from www.healthyandessential.co.uk

There are plenty of reasons for every parent to boost their child's intake of omega-3 fatty acids.

The vegetarian child

There are always some parents who prefer not to give their kids meat and fish, usually for moral reasons, but I've also noticed that since the food scares involving BSE and *E.coli*, and Jamie Oliver's Channel 4 programme *School Dinners*, exposing the awful meat products our kids are being fed at school, more parents, and some children old enough to make such choices, are turning their backs on animal products.

IS IT EVER A BAD IDEA TO LET YOUR CHILD GO VEGETARIAN?

If you are not yourself vegetarian, it can be a bit worrying if your child is insisting on it. Obviously this tends to happen only with older children, not very little ones, and while vegetarianism can be a healthy choice, there are some concerns. Some kids won't eat meat and fish because they don't like the texture of it – I remember my sister sitting for what seemed like hours trying to chew meat, until eventually she would spit it out. She's now vegetarian and has brought her children up to be too – she was just put off the texture. (I'm not trying to stop you bringing your children up as vegetarians, but if you think this may be the only reason why they're avoiding meat and other animal produce, you could try mincing it so that it's not such a big deal for them to chew it.)

Most vegetarian children will eat eggs and dairy, so I'll cover that first and then move on to vegan kids, who are strictly animal-produce-free. When it comes to being vegetarian the first thing to remember is to try not to make an enormous song and dance about it, as this could either set you up for rebelliousness (especially with the older

children), or they could get picked on at school – with all styles of eating, keep it as relaxed as possible. If you show that that you're really riled by them choosing to be vegetarian, you might just get a backlash.

If you're worried that your child (especially a girl) has decided to become vegetarian because of undue worries and concerns about weight and is trying to find a way to cut food intake down drastically, reducing it to simple meals like green salad, you need to look at the bigger picture and seek advice about eating disorders. I'm not saying all girls who decide to become vegetarian have a body image problem, but it can happen (and it can happen to boys too).

BEING VEGETARIAN CAN BE A HEALTHY CHOICE

Having acknowledged that there are sometimes legitimate concerns, especially for non-vegetarian parents, it has to be said, as I'm sure the vegetarians among you already know, that there are also numerous benefits. Studies have shown that children brought up on a vegetarian diet consume more fresh fruits and vegetables and are less likely to suffer from diseases such as obesity, bowel cancer and heart disease as an adults.

GO BIG ON VARIETY

For non-vegetarian parents looking after a lone vegetarian child, there is some basic advice I would always give: you need to ensure that your children get plenty of variety in their vegetarian diet. Don't just give them the vegetables you have with your main meal or expect them to live off

pasta and tomato sauce – things need to be a little more sophisticated than that. Children need variety to ensure they get a spectrum of all the essential nutrients.

NOT TOO MUCH FIBRE

As you will have read in Chapter 1, fibre needs to be finely balanced in your child's diet. If they have too little they could become constipated, while too much can leave them lacking in energy and anaemic. Because a vegetarian diet tends naturally to focus on vegetables, you need to watch that your child doesn't have too much fibre, especially under the age of five. Signs you should watch out for include their weight not increasing as it should do, or the fact that they might be always complaining of feeling tired and you notice they're being more grumpy than usual. I generally say you shouldn't really give a child under five more than a third of their bread, rice and cereals as wholemeal but you can give over-fives two-thirds wholemeal to white. This just a rough guide, but it could ensure that your child gets enough energy and also the goodness of wholemeal and fibre.

In addition to the fibre issue, you need to ensure that the protein, energy, vitamin and mineral intake is sufficient to meet the child's growing needs.

PROTEIN

Kids need protein because the amino acids the protein foods contain have a huge role to play in their digestive, muscular, hormonal and immune systems. With all children we need to include a variety of proteins in their diet to ensure that they have the essential amino acids. The reason why protein becomes more of an issue with a vegetarian diet is that with animal produce the proteins are what we call complete, that is they contain sufficient amounts of all of the eight essential amino acids the body requires. But vegetable proteins, with the exception of soya and seaweed, which in my world aren't consumed much in a child's diet, are incomplete, and to get round this you need to have a variety of different vegetable proteins to ensure that your child gets enough of all of the amino acids needed to thrive.

It used to be thought that for vegetarians to metabolize the amino acids, a vegetable protein such as beans needed to be accompanied by a cereal, say toast, at each meal, but we now know that this isn't necessary. It's just a good idea to ensure that kids have as many of the different proteins from the following chart, with some cereal thrown in, throughout the week.

Make sure vegetarian kids eat a wide variety of foods.

Sources of protein in a vegetarian diet

Legumes

Chickpeas

Butter beans

Black-eyed beans

Kidney beans

Borlotti beans

Haricot beans (used for baked beans)

Pulses

Lentils

Split peas

Green peas

Soya products

Miso (fermented soya-bean paste

Tofu (soya-bean curd)

Tempeh (soya meat alternative)

Tamari (wheat-free soy sauce)

Nuts and seeds

Almonds

Brazils

Hazelnuts

Pine nuts

Walnuts

Cashews

Peanuts

Sesame seeds

Sunflower seeds

Pumpkin seeds

Linseeds – also known as flaxseeds (they're a bit hard to digest for little ones, so I tend to whiz them to a fine powder in a blender with some sunflower seeds and pumpkin seeds and stir them into muesli or porridge.

With children under the age of five you should avoid whole nuts and stick to nut butters (assuming they don't have a nut allergy). Other great grains containing a little protein include quinoa and spelt.

VITAMINS AND MINERALS

You need to check that your vegetarian child has a plentiful supply of five key minerals – calcium, magnesium, iron, zinc and selenium – as these are required to build and maintain their bones, heart and immune system and also to help ensure that their body remains healthy. It is much easier to ensure that they take in enough minerals generally if they eat dairy produce, even if that means using milk, yoghurt or cheese in cooking because they won't drink a glass of milk, but the chart on page 29 will also give you some a few of the non-animal sources of these essential minerals.

ENERGY

As I mentioned before, vegetarian children need to have some good healthy sources of energy in their diet, which can most usefully come from fats and carbohydrates. As you will have read in Chapter 1, there are two main types of fat: those that come from animal foods such as butter, cream, cheese, yoghurt, milk, and those that come from vegetables, seeds, nuts, olives, avocados, hemp and nut oils, as well as the many other vegetable oils such sunflower and safflower oils we can readily find in the supermarkets and health-food stores. Loads of my recipes are made without animal products, not because I'm vegetarian but because I think they're delicious made with milks like almond milk, or oils such as hemp oil, nut butters, seeds and other energy-rich ingredients, and also because I think it can be useful to give you some inspiring ideas about how yummy vegetarian foods can be.

Animal fats

I do think vegetarian children can benefit greatly from including dairy foods – butter, cream, cheese, and yoghurt etc. – in their diet. These animal fats contain 9 kcals per gram, which means they're great for energy. Dairy foods can also give them a good source of calcium and vitamin D – although butter and cream aren't all that rich in calcium. However, you need to watch that they don't consume too much dairy, otherwise they might either put on too much weight or start having problems with the amount of saturated fat in their diet, which can lead to heart disease and some types of cancer.

Vegetable fats

The other source of fat available to vegetarians comes from vegetable fats in avocados, nuts, seeds (hemp, pumpkin, sunflower, linseeds, sesame), coconut (milk, flesh, oil), olives, olive oil, hemp oil, avocado oil, nut oils and nut butters (for example, almond, hazelnut or peanut butter). All these vegetable oils contain just as many calories per gram, but with the exception of coconut (which has a high saturated fat content) the fat tends to be mainly unsaturated fat, which is better for our hearts. They can still in excess put too much weight on children, but as long as they don't eat too much of them, the fat can be good fat (especially the seeds and their oils, as they're rich in the beneficial omega-3 fatty acids – see page 110).

I still use coconut in cooking sometimes because a little won't do any harm and it does have a delicious flavour, but I wouldn't rely on coconut oil as a child's source of fat. Although soya and soya products contain plenty of protein, they tend to be very low in fat, so they're good for kids' hearts but not great for energy-boosting – you therefore need to ensure you add some other vegetable source of energy to their diet.

Watch the fast veggie foods

You need to watch that ready-made vegetarian foods don't contain hydrogenated or trans fats – check the labels. Ready-made veggie meals can also be very high in calories, as the manufacturers sometimes pile in a lot of oil and cheese, which can be a problem for kids who have an excess weight issue. Fast-food outlets like burger bars can produce very fatty, high-calorie veggie burgers with not many vegetables in them, so if your child is too heavy or has problems with digestion, you should be wary of these.

Carbohydtrates

The other source of energy you can use in your vegetarian child's diet is of course carbohydrates, because it provides 4 kcals per gram. But as with all children, you need to ensure the carbs are the healthiest and least bulky, so fruit purées and compotes, such as the fruit compote on page 220, are great things to have in your fridge.

THE VEGAN DIET

It's a lot easier to follow a vegan diet these days, now that the supermarkets have cottoned on to meat substitutes such as soya and tofu, fortified soya milks and soya yoghurts. But as I've mentioned above, the problem with quite a few ready-made veggie foods is that they can be high in hydrogenated fats, which have been linked to heart disease. This doesn't mean you can't grab a tofu burger every now and then, but try as much as you can to make up your child's foods from fresh ingredients. You'll see from the lists below that there are lots of yummy vegan recipes in this book, which everyone will love, whether vegan or not. (Read pages 142–46 for advice about energy intakes.)

My favourite vegan foods to think about using in your child's diet are:

* **Seed pastes** like tahini, which can be stirred into bean salads and of course is the basis of hummus (a staple in our house) – good for breakfast if Maya isn't in a sweet mood, or with pasta, on top of jacket potatoes, etc.
* **Nut butters** such as peanut butter (though this is best avoided until they're three if there is a history of asthma, allergies, eczema, etc. in your family), cashew butter, hazelnut and almond butter – yummy on bread and rice cakes and good in vegetable casseroles and bakes. Whole nuts, once they're over the age of five.
* **Oils such as olive or hemp oil** (see page 110 on how to sneak this fantastically healthy omega-rich oil into their diet). Don't skimp on the oil in a vegan diet, as kids really need the calories – drizzle it over vegetables, dip breads such as fluffy white ciabatta in oil at the table. Try to buy speciality breads made with olive oil such as focaccia, as they're energy-rich. Watch that when you're cooking with oils such as olive oil, you don't over-heat them – if the oil's smoking it's too hot. Don't use iron cookware with oils and don't re-use the oil, as re-used and over-hot oil will have partially broken down into more damaging fats.
* **Avocados** are wonderfully creamy and rich in fat – good on jacket potatoes, in salads, sandwiches, on rice cakes spread with peanut butter – yummy!

Pay special attention to the B vitamins

You need to watch that your vegan child gets enough vitamin B12, as this is a nutrient that is often low in this diet. You can buy fortified soya drinks, spirulina (a form of algae), low-salt yeast spreads (the full-blown ones are far too high in salt for kids) to pop on slices of hot toast, fortified cereals such as breakfast cereals – but I'm not a big fan of these, as they're frequently screaming with sugar and salt, and hence not the best food for a vegan child.

These are just a few of the important things to concentrate on in a vegan child's diet; however, I would recommend that you also see a dietician if you're bringing up your child as a vegan, as it may be that you need some help juggling all the different nutrients and foods. A vegan child is also highly likely to need a supplement containing vitamin B12 (see the box), as well as possibly needing a supplement containing other key nutrients. We're not even sure whether vegetable sources of B12 are actually absorbed and useful for children, so since B12 deficiency causes anaemia and needs to be treated carefully – the symptoms are similar to iron deficiency anaemia i.e. tiredness etc. – you need to get specialist help.

It's getting easier to follow a vegan diet but it's still worth seeing a dietician for advice if you're contemplating it.

CHAPTER FOUR

Curing Everyday Problems with Food

KEEPING A FOOD DIARY

Keeping a food diary can be one of the best ways not only to check how your child's diet is going, but also to see the effect specific foods are having. It's a really good idea to keep a diary before you seek professional advice about a specific concern – if you suspect they have a food intolerance, for example – as this should help your doctor or dietician sort out a programme of advice for you. The exception is if your child is ill, or suffers a severe allergic reaction, in which case you should seek professional advice immediately.

Try to record things as your child eats and drinks them – or ask what they've eaten at the end of the school day and also ask any parents or teachers, etc. You could keep the diary in secret if you feel it's more appropriate. Here's an example of what to record.

Date and time	Food and drink consumed	Quantity	Symptoms
	Try to give as much detail as possible about ingredients too. Your child could collect and stick on the labels of anything they buy, such as confectionery, to make them feel part of the process.	(household measures, e.g. teaspoon, slice)	e.g. are they hyper, constipated, nauseous? Do they have tummy-ache? This can be both before and after they've eaten the food if you notice something like a rash appearing.

GENERAL CONCERNS

Boosting concentration

All of us as parents want to know how we can get our children to concentrate more and maximize their chances of doing as well as they can at school. The answer lies in providing the brain with the power foods it needs to perform its miraculous tasks. There are five main points to look at for brain power: brilliant breakfasts, sustaining sugars, intelligent fats, wonderful water and cutting out the brain-cloggers, as I call them.

First, what children eat in the morning plays a key part in getting them off on the right foot. Several studies have shown a strong link between good nutrition early in the day and a child's brain power. Eating breakfast has been shown to positively influence ability to solve problems, and can significantly boost concentration and memory – wow! Other studies have shown that kids who eat breakfast tend to be far more creative, have more good energy and can keep going much longer, their batteries remaining charged and alive. I also think that if they start the day off well and eat something healthy and nutritious before they leave the house in the morning, children are far less likely to want to nibble or snack on the sugary and fatty foods and snacks poor in vitamins and minerals that tend to be everywhere outside the home, saying eat me now!

As you'll see from Chapter 1, it's good to go for the complex carbohydrates, which have fibre in. The fibre slows down the absorption of the carbohydrate, which not only makes kids feel satisfied for longer, but also means that because the breakdown of the sugars is slower, they should

find their energy levels, moods, concentration, everything that is to do with their brain and how they're feeling, much steadier. Those cereals that have a lot of refined sugars in them tend to give the child a kick to start off with, but it can easily mean they feel shaky, frazzled, cloggy-brained, unable to sit still afterwards. Instead opt for a no-added-sugar muesli, porridge (see my porridge, page 218), Weetabix or what I call grown-up Shredded Wheat (Shreddies are much higher in sugar, so I wouldn't go for those), any of my cereal-based start-the-day recipes (page 215–22), a sandwich made with wholemeal bread, or a toasted wholemeal bagel with a little butter and pure fruit spread with no added sugar in it.

If your kids really don't want to sit down and chomp through any of the above, think about making them a fresh fruit smoothie, which would give them a great fruit boost.

SUSTAINING SUGARS

There is an enormous amount of evidence to show that our kids' academic work level improves when they receive regular nutritious meals. Kids who skip meals, or don't have a good breakfast, are much more likely to wane, feel grumpy, be disruptive because their blood sugar levels are lower than their body would like them to be. I see this with lots of kids that I treat in my clinic: if we manage to give them a good breakfast, lunch and supper, with healthy snacks in between, they feel much stronger both mentally and physically and this has an amazing impact on their school performance.

It's best to have plenty of whole grains, fresh

fruits and vegetables, lean proteins, throughout the day, in other words to follow the basic healthy eating advice in Chapter 1, which includes foods with a low glycaemic index (GI) value – i.e. food that won't send the sugar levels rocketing in your child's body. The rapid surges and crashes in blood sugar which go hand in hand with eating a very rapidly absorbed, high GI food trigger the body to release loads of blood-sugar-lowering insulin so that blood sugar levels come quickly down. These rapid sugar swings do seem to affect kids' concentration and moods, so try to stay away from high GI foods (see page 38). This means trying to persuade the school/playgroup/nursery not to serve sweet drinks and sweet biscuits – water and fruit would be much, much healthier. And tell them they'll notice a positive difference in kids' behaviour and moods as a result.

Try giving your child a healthy snack late in the afternoon, or in the car on the way home, as typically kids need a little boost just to keep them going with their homework (see my ideas for snacks on page 49).

INTELLIGENT FATS

Research has shown that a diet rich in omega-3 fatty acids appears to boost brain power. You should definitely try to get your child to eat omega-rich fish, such as sardines, fresh tuna, mackerel, herrings, according to Food Standards Agency recommendations: girls two 140g portions a week, boys four (see page 110).

I have seen great results, too, with kids who have learning difficulties, once they start eating oily fish and having a healthy diet as well, or alternatively taking an omega oil supplement such as morEPA or EyeQ or a supplement containing

500mg of omega-3 fatty acids. You can also get useful omega-3 fats from sunflower and hemp seeds and other nuts and seeds (see page 110). Take a look at www.healthspan.co.uk for vegetarian omega oil supplements.

WONDERFUL WATER

Water is one of the cheapest and best brain power foods. I find that kids who drink enough water, and I mean just water, not juices or fizzy drinks, are much better able to concentrate and carry out the basic good-behaviour tasks – from playing well and tactically in school sports to sharing toys in the playground. Lack of water induces tiredness, grumpiness and lack of concentration, so try to encourage your child to drink plenty in the course of the day. Children who are active should drink 6–8 small glasses of water every day. Older kids, once they get into the water thing, can drink more like 6 large glasses a day and feel and perform well at school. Getting your child to feel this well hydrated can be amazing, especially if they've been drinking the fizzy, additive-riddled carbonated drinks which are one of the classic brain-cloggers.

BRAIN-CLOGGERS

There is some evidence linking too much caffeine and certain E numbers such as tartrazine with poor concentration – so I would suggest that you try as much as possible to keep both caffeine and the E numbers listed on page 72 out of your child's diet. The evidence surrounding caffeine tends to be more to do with it preventing kids from resting and sleeping well at night, with the result that they're more likely to be sleepy and less able to concentrate during the day, but anecdotally, I also

see some kids who have difficulty concentrating finding it much harder to do so if they've drunk cola or any other caffeine-rich drink, even chocolate, which is full of another caffine-like substance. Once they get off the caffeine high-roller-coasters, their ability to concentrate improves.

Too much fatty food can sit heavily in the gut, which can mean the body would much rather sleep than concentrate on the tasks in hand – so just check your kids don't OD on fat-laden fast food (which can also be riddled with E numbers and sugar). If you suspect that their lack of concentration may be down to Attention Deficit Disorder (ADD), read pages 152–156 and seek professional help. Once kids have the right treatment, including diet, and support, the results can be pretty astounding.

PROBLEMS AFFECTING CONCENTRATION
Not eating

Not eating much will aggravate concentration levels, so if this is the case with your child, try to get to the bottom of why they're off their food. It might be that they're being bullied at school and that not eating is their way of expressing their fear. This is especially common with kids who carry a little more weight than others and are being teased about it – it can be very tempting for them to just stop eating and hope the problems go away, which of course they never do because the bullies will just find another thing to tease or bully them about.

So keep an open mind over whether your child not concentrating or eating is something to do with other kids, or with worries about their school work or about their home or friend situation. And of course if your child is losing weight, or not putting on weight, or seems overly worried about their body image, and you suspect that they might be heading down the anorexia nervosa route, seek professional help.

Not enough variety

Restricted and unbalanced eating could mean your child missing out on essential brain nutrients such as iron and the B vitamins. This can frequently happen when kids decide they want to be vegetarian, which can be at a very young age nowadays, and if they're fussy eaters when it comes to the non-animal foods this could mean their body becoming deficient in essential nutrients. B vitamins are found in red meat, chicken, eggs, whole-grain cereals, brown rice, green leafy vegetables, cheese, yoghurt and milk. If your child is vegetarian and you want to check that they're getting the right balance of nutrients, see pages 112–115, and bear in mind that lack of iron (which can be a bit harder to boost in a vegetarian diet) in particular could be accounting for their tiredness and lack of concentration. It may be that your child needs a vitamin and mineral supplement, but over and above taking a general multivitamin and mineral which lists and meets the dietary reference values (DRVs) listed on page 29, you should discuss this with your doctor.

Feeling sick in the morning

This sometimes happens to children when they've had a disturbed night's sleep and their tummy feels all over the place, or if they're being bullied at school (as a child who was bullied I remember feeling generally anxious about leaving home and facing lessons, and having a knot in my stomach). Even though they don't feel like eating, you're better off trying to get them to nibble on something small and easy that'll sit in the tummy – sometimes it feels as if you need something to soak up the stomach acids, although physiologically this isn't the case.

Having nothing in the stomach will only exacerbate both a low-blood-sugar, low-energy, low-mood, nauseous stomach feeling, so get them to nibble some dry cereal, ideally not a sugar-loaded one but something simple like Rice Crispies or cornflakes. They can have milk, or some 'gentle' fruit juice like apple juice, poured over the top, but more often than not something drier seems to suit an upset/nervy stomach better. Try a slice of white toast with just the thinnest scraping of butter and a pure fruit spread, plain biscuits (perhaps water biscuits or rice cakes), or, if you think they might go for a little something warmer, porridge made with water or skimmed milk and plain, natural yoghurt mixed with a little honey. Although fruits are usually great in the morning, skip the citrus and berries and go instead for bananas, which can have a binding, settling effect, and papayas, maybe chopped and mixed with a little natural yoghurt.

The advantage of consuming live yoghurt containing cultures such as lactobacillus, bifidus and acidophilus is that these probiotic bacteria help restore a healthy bacterial balance within the gut, which tends to be thrown out of synch by an infection. Try to get your child to eat a small pot of live, natural yoghurt every day for a month after they've been under the weather.

REMEDIES FOR NAUSEA

If you think they may just have eaten too much the night before, or you find them feeling nauseous later on in the day, there are two great remedies you could try. The first was given to me by Caroline Peppercorn, a very dear friend who has to be one of the best mums I know, and consists of cutting a lemon in quarters, placing it in a pan with a cup of water, bringing it up to the boil for about 8–10 minutes, then pouring the lemon water into a mug and adding a good teaspoon of honey. The combination of the tartness of the lemon and the sweetness of the honey seems to soothe the stomach and helps get rid of the sickly feeling kids can also get with a stomach bug or if their eyes have been bigger than their stomach and they've eaten too much.

The second recipe is a traditional Indian remedy for an upset stomach. I was initially sceptical about whether Maya would eat it, but she does occasionally, and I also wondered about the curative powers of a dish that contained so much yoghurt (an overload of milky foods can aggravate an upset digestive system), but when chilled, the combination of rice (I use basmati), stomach-settling ginger and calming yoghurt makes a soothing paste which does seem to work! If you think your child will go for it, do try it.

Curd rice

250g rice

500g yoghurt

1 tablespoon vegetable oil

1 tablespoon mustard seeds

1 sprig of curry leaves

½ tablespoon green chillies, chopped

1 tablespoon fresh root ginger, chopped

Freshly ground black pepper

First steam the rice. When it's cooked, add the yoghurt, mix well and set aside.

Heat the vegetable oil in a pan and add the mustard seeds. When they start spluttering, add the curry leaves. Now add the chopped green chillies and ginger, stir well and remove from the heat.

Sprinkle a little freshly ground black pepper over the rice and yoghurt mixture. Pour the chilli seasoning over the top and combine thoroughly. Chill before serving.

Try to get your child to eat a small pot of live, natural yoghurt every day for a month after they've been under the weather.

Food as a power game: kids, food and psychology

FUSSY AND LAZY EATERS

Until I became a mum, I hadn't realized how emotionally wearing mealtimes could be. So often we start with the best intentions, preparing something we're convinced our child will like, proud of ourselves for being so imaginative, or for managing to find time in a busy day to prepare something fresh instead of relying on jars or frozen ready-made kids' meals, but within seconds a refusal to eat can become the straw that breaks the camel's back, and from there it all goes rapidly downhill, with frustration on everyone's part.

It can be incredibly wearing to have a fussy eating child, even if lasts for only a few meals, especially if you throw in a few spoonfuls of worry that they aren't getting enough nutrients – something I'd like to put your mind at ease about. It's very rare to find a child who doesn't catch up on a few days of apparently not eating well – toddlers will eat when they're hungry, and they'll grow out of their fussiness, usually when they're around other children who eat well, because they want to be the same and not feel different. Older kids can go from one extreme to the other, not wanting to eat anything during the whole day and then you find them later on, burying their heads in the fridge!

So many different influences can have a positive effect on your child's eating – from a new friend, peer pressure, not wanting to be different from everyone else, to reading a book about Popeye who likes spinach. My daughter started wanting to eat raw carrots and spinach leaves because Pickles, my friend's rabbit, liked eating the ones she'd sneak into the cage. How many parents have seen their kids wolf something down at a friend's house and then had the 'but I don't like it' protests when it's put in front of them at home!

Older siblings, friends and cousins can have an enormous effect on whether kids like something or not too. They can change like the weather. My friends' older kids suddenly snap into eating more at the weirdest moments; it's almost as if their brains are too busy dealing with other stuff to eat, but then all of a sudden their stomach feels too empty to take it any more – sometimes it's just before they go to bed and they suddenly want to eat two large bowls of cereal – which I don't see anything wrong with, as long as it doesn't become a habit that means they don't eat proper meals.

The more positive you stay about the whole eating experience, the less you make a big song and dance about it and the cooler you are about them eating or not eating, the less likely your child is to use food as a controlling power game. The more they see that they can get you wound up, can get your attention big-time if they misbehave and throw a strop, the more problems you lay down for the future.

How to take the strain off

Even though every child is different, the following tricks and tips can help.

* Don't worry that sometimes you need to give them something less than perfectly healthy – we all have to resort to this occasionally. I just try to make the thing they'll eat as healthy as possible – it could be a slice of homemade cake, a yoghurt, a rice cake and peanut butter – just

make sure you've got some of these staples in the house. As long as you try to get them to eat a more substantial meal as soon as possible and keep trying new foods, the odd occasion when you give them a not-ideal meal food because they just need to eat something is OK.

* Sit down to eat with your child as much as possible; children need to see you eating the same type of food as them. Eating round a table is a crucial part of development – it develops communication as well as eating skills. If work schedules make this difficult, just try for weekends – the more you eat together the more likely it is that your child will want to take part in eating. Remember always that children will eat when they're hungry, so stay cool and with time you'll see them eating well – and even if they're teenagers before they're eating broccoli, it'll be worth the wait.

* Though I'm not a fan of eating in front of the TV, it can take the pressure away from the table environment if you think this has got a little bit out of hand. If children are glued to their favourite DVD they're not so aware of what they're doing, and will happily put food in their mouths that you've been nagging them about for ages – and then decide to eat it. Once they've started to relax and will eat while watching TV, try to shorten the amount of time the TV's on, say by five minutes each day, so that eventually they'll be eating without it and without making a fuss.

* Even if they're eating on their own, resist the temptation to watch and fuss over them or react to them not eating – keep a watchful eye from a distance, while doing something else.

* With young ones, tap into any stories or characters involving food – such as Maisy or Bob the Builder. Talk about how they like the food – sometimes Maya's rabbit joins us at the table and we pretend to feed him first and make appreciative noises, so that she wants to join in the game too.

* Use food and non-food things such as a trip to the cinema as rewards. As soon as children are old enough to understand the concept of rewards, make a chart where they get stars or something if they achieve the (small, achievable) goals you set. It's important to have non-food rewards, so that, for example, sweets aren't the only thing they see as a reward for good behaviour. Of course the occasional treat is fine – having sweets one regular day of the week after tea is a good way for children to enjoy some, but not too many. It stops them secretly eating sweets as a big rebellion, which can happen with mums who are very strict about sugar – the child will eat them in secret, which is tougher to tackle.

* Check that the reason they're not hungry at mealtimes isn't because they've been eating too many snacks or filling up with fizzy drinks. Kids should have structure to their days and because food is everywhere now – corner shops, petrol stations, cinemas – it's almost as if our society has become feeding-food-to-children mad. They don't need snacks all the time, especially as this might well put them off wanting to eat a nutritious meal.

* If getting your child to be less fussy is the big problem, I suggest trying each new food 8–10 times, leaving days in between, before you give up on it – persistence usually works, especially if you also become imaginative about how you

cook and incorporate the new food. I'm not talking making vegetables into faces here, more like occasionally sneaking foods into sauces, roasting vegetables or sneaking vegetables such as cauliflower into macaroni cheese. I've weaned Maya slowly on to cooked tomatoes this way, by just putting small amounts in her scrambled eggs. Blending and puréeing foods to disguise them in soups and pasta sauces, or putting carrots in with the mashed potatoes, etc. usually works well. Even making little filo parcels, for example with cheese and leeks, can be a good way to get more vegetables inside them. But I wouldn't recommend always being deceptive about foods (and it's usually very demanding timewise to be constantly thinking laterally), otherwise you'll never get them to eat a string bean or a normal-looking undisguised vegetable – I'd try a combination of persisting with some simple foods cooked on their own, while at the same time putting some undisclosed foods in sauces to give you the peace of mind that they're getting enough nutrients.

* Try fruit smoothies, and let your child be involved in choosing the fruits that go into the blender – serve with a curly straw and in a fun glass/beaker.

* Get them involved in the choices sometimes. Making their own muesli in the morning, by just putting out jars of the different grains, or using a base muesli and getting them to add the dried fruits, seeds, etc. can give them more of an appetite than just plonking a bowl of the same cereal down in front of them. You can sneak ground nutritious seeds into the muesli, so that even if it's just a bowl of cereal for tea, you know they're getting a pretty nutritious meal.

* Try to take your child shopping at a time when it's not a mad dash. That way you can spend a few minutes talking about the foods you're putting in your trolley – so they learn the names, see foods as fun. Let them help unpack the shopping and put things away in the right place. It takes time, I know, but involving children in shopping and cooking wherever possible is one of the most effective ways for food to become part of their life in a fun and positive way. Expecting them to eat foods that just land on the plate with no story seldom works with fussy eaters.

* Try to cook together. Whatever their age, they're never too young to help out, even if this does make a huge mess and means the meal takes ten times as long to get ready. Try not to be too concerned – it can really make a difference to how included they feel with food – and get them to taste things as you're going along. I still remember the taste of uncooked cake mixture, as my mum used to give us the spoon to lick. Let them peel the vegetables with a safe peeler or, if they're not old enough to use real kitchen implements, one of their kids' knives and just let them play with food. Let them see that to make an apple pie, you roll pastry out and slice apples into it. If your weekdays don't allow you time to cook together – if it's all you can do to keep the train of being a parent on the tracks – think about cooking together at weekends.

See the picnic section on page 45 – taking food outside can make kids' appetite increase, take the pressure off you and bring some fun into sharing food.

HUNGRY ALL THE TIME

All kids go through stages of complaining they're hungry all the time, having probably been not fussed about eating much for a few days. Hunger is a natural mechanism that ensures they get something to eat when their body needs it – usually when they've been running around a lot outside or playing a lot of sport. What distinguishes what you do about it depends on why you think they're asking for something to eat. It sounds obvious, but a simple checklist can help you fathom out whether it's a physical hunger or they're feeling hungry because of wanting comfort and don't need any extra energy, i.e. food.

Try to work out whether they've been growing more than usual recently. If so, their body probably needs extra fuel to meet the increased demand – in which case they should be eating bigger, healthy meals and also substantial snacks to meet this hunger. Have they just been through a famine stage of not being bothered about food? If so, help them catch up by serving bigger portions and good snacks. It's important, though, to stick to a rough meal-planning and timing structure and not just let them graze all day, as they could start thinking they can have food whenever they like and this could pose other issues and problems in the future.

Have they been eating good meals and snacks, but it seems to be boredom or comfort eating? If so, try to find out what's behind the hunger. Are they feeling insecure about something? Remember that kids sometimes have problems expressing their emotions, and asking for more food can be a call for more attention.

Do they see you nibbling all the time and think this is the norm? Have you got into the habit of having food for every occasion, from travelling in the car to sitting in the doctor's waiting-room, so that asking for food and eating is no longer solely related to being physically hungry and in need of sustenance? Are they drinking enough water? Sometimes kids ask for food when physiologically they're thirsty, so try giving them water before anything else.

Are they bored and just wanting to pick at something while watching TV? Try not to encourage this habit, as so often adults I see report back that they got into the habit of eating for boredom while young and they wish they hadn't. If they want a snack, get them to sit at the table and concentrate so that they're satisfied after eating it and know when it's time to stop – there's a beginning and an end. The contrary situation is nibbling on food while watching TV or playing a computer game, when the brain doesn't recognize how much they've eaten, so they end up over-eating and wanting even more afterwards.

Are they rushing their food? Try to get them to eat slowly, as this gives more time for the body to recognize when they've had enough. Last but not least, just make sure their meals have a good balance of carbohydrates, proteins and some good fats, as meals that are too light, like a salad full of raw foods, will leave them complaining later on. Equally something that's very sweet, fatty and low in fibre and protein, usually fast-food junk, will satiate them only for a short time, which is why people get addicted to fast food – it doesn't satisfy them for long and they also crave the fatty and salty hit.

Too much energy, or too little

TIRED ALL THE TIME

You'll notice that just as we parents go through peaks and troughs with our energy levels, our children will do the same – Maya will have a few days when all she really wants is quiet time, sleeps and cuddles, and then quickly snap into being forever on the go, unstoppable. But if you've noticed your child's energy levels flagging consistently, or at nursery or school they seem to be struggling with keeping going and staying awake, it's worth looking through the following points, as there are several nutritional things you might need to address and therefore food and drink things you can try to give them more joie de vivre.

* First of all, check for dehydration, as many kids don't drink enough water and tiredness can be a key symptom. Others include dark-coloured urine (it should be very pale), thirst, headaches, and finding running around and exercising hard. It's especially easy for children to become dehydrated when the weather's hot, when they're doing lots of running around, playing sports – they lose a lot more water then and can get dehydrated far more quickly than adults, as they're smaller and don't tend to take as much notice of being thirsty. They may also need more water if they've eaten a sugary or salty snack such as a treat packet of crisps.
* Check they're eating enough, but not too much – see Chapter 1. Even if you think they're eating well, sometimes it's good just to reread the key points. Also make sure they're getting a varied diet – if they're narrow in their food choices they can be lacking in essential energy-boosting nutrients such as the B vitamins. If your child is underweight, try to boost non-wholegrain sources of B vitamins (see page 25) as these will also give them more calories and protein and you'll find they can eat more of them before getting full. If they're a little on the heavy side you can incorporate some of the wholegrains, the cereals, wholemeal bread (don't forget the white-looking, mid-range goodness breads if they won't touch anything that looks brown!). Rice is also a good source of energy and B vitamins.
* Check your child isn't anaemic. Anaemia is the lack of haemoglobin, which carries oxygen in the blood around the body so that our cells can use it to produce energy. The symptoms of anaemia focus largely on energy levels, so if your child is constantly tired, looks pale, maybe has a headache or suffers from dizziness or shortness of breath, frequent crying, poor memory, frequent colds and infection, you need to take them to your GP. He will carry out a simple blood test to see if they are indeed suffering from the most common type and cause of anaemia, too little iron in the diet, and if the result is positive, you will need to focus on boosting their intake of iron (see page 27 for good sources) and of foods rich in vitamin C, such as fresh fruits and vegetables (kiwi fruits and blueberries are two of the best vitamin C fruits, but all of the vitamin C foods help the body absorb iron). It also helps to minimize the amount of tannins they drink i.e. tea (and in case you're wondering, kids shouldn't drink

coffee). The odd cup of very weak tea can be comforting, but it shouldn't have had more than a dip of the teabag – tannins can reduce the amount of iron and other essential nutrients the body can absorb.

* Are they eating too many high GI, sweet foods? These could be sending their sugar levels and energy levels shooting up and down, leaving them dragging their feet far too early in the day. Go more for the low and middle GI foods (see page 84).
* Check they're not having too much fibre, as that would mean they might not be getting enough energy in their diet. I have a rule that kids up to the age of seven or eight should have one-third wholegrain to two-thirds more refined, such as white rice, white pasta, bread, etc., but after this they can increase to two-thirds wholemeal. It really depends on their weight. Just ask yourself whether you're maybe overdoing the high-fibre foods.
* Not having regular enough meals – is their schedule a little mad? Have they started doing new activities, or have you, so that mealtimes have become later? If they're going through a real growth spurt they may need more nutritious snacks to keep their energy levels up.
* Your GP should check whether they're diabetic if they also display some of the following signs: increased thirst, possible blurred vision, always having to do a pee and feeling or behaving excessively tired (see page 171).
* The other condition to think about when you've gone through all the above is coeliac disease. It's especially important to consider it if you have this autoimmune disease in your family or notice that your children have problems digesting

gluten and have fatty, foul-smelling stools. See page 156, and seek the advice of your GP before cutting gluten out of your child's diet.

Check they're getting enough exercise, as lack of fresh air and good old cardio activity can make them feel tired. Make sure their sleeping environment and schedule are conducive to getting a good night's sleep –make sure they're not watching too much TV or playing games too late, as it could be these are causing dreams or stopping them getting off to sleep early. Try lavender and other essential oils (see page 194) to help them sleep. Finally, if they're still very tired, it may be nothing nutritional or physical, more an emotional thing, so talk to them.

WILD THING!
We've all been there, whether they've just passed the tired phase and have gone into fifth gear, over-compensating with an excitement and energy that borders on wildness, or they've just come back from a friend's birthday party, or are fed up with staying indoors in bad weather and are almost thrashing around with frustration that they can't get out. Whatever the cause, what you next put into their mouth can either make the situation ten times worse, or calm them down. I'm not talking about kids who suffer from ADD (see page 153), but sometimes kids can almost appear as if they're high on drugs, as if they've taken speed – when this happens what we need is a natural remedy to bring them down and mellow them out.

Reach for the water
I'd reach first for a mellowing drink – ideally water, still or sparkling, at room temperature, or a glass of

cool or warm milk. But don't reach for the caffeine or for sugar-containing drinks like cola or commercially made fruit juices, as pouring sugar or caffeine on a wired child in my experience can be like pouring petrol on a fire. I also wouldn't go for any of the diet-processed sugar-free drinks, as the combination of artificial sweeteners and E numbers such as tartrazine can be just as explosive. If your child will take a warm drink you could try some chamomile tea, as this is really calming. Try if you can to sit them down with you, have a cuddle and speak in a calm voice so that gradually you take the steam out of them – yelling at them to calm down isn't going to work. Read them a story, or just talk about something easy-going. Switch the TV and music off, unless it's relaxing music – maybe even have a warm bath, perhaps together. Sometimes Maya's wired because she's just feeling a little insecure, so a soak and play together can do us both a lot of good.

Steer clear of sugary foods

Keep away from chocolates, biscuits, sweets, pastries, etc. and go for some filling but 'sedating' pasta, potatoes, rice, couscous, gnocchi, polenta – it can be amazing how quickly a filling bowl of rice or pasta can calm a child down.

Lower your healthy eating expectations

I wouldn't be too fussed on these occasions about them eating their vegetables, as you're probably not going to win with this one if they're overly sensitive. So quit while you're ahead. Another quick wind-down meal is baked beans on toast – I like Whole Earth baked beans because they're organic and we both love the taste, but just because they're sweetened with apple juice doesn't get away from the fact that they're pretty sweet (although apple juice has a low GI value, so they have less of a sugar-high effect – the only thing to be aware of is that the sugar is bad for their teeth). Serve them with wholemeal toast or scooped inside some warmed wholemeal pitta breads with a little grated cheese on top. If you have the time, and can cook ahead, try making my home-made baked beans (page 217).

Keep handy snacks around

If you're driving along with a wild thing in the back of the car, stop and give them some water and a few plain oatcakes or rice cakes to take the sting out the storm. If you notice that they tend to be wild and over-tired at a pretty similar time each day, think about having smaller meals more often, as it could be that they're hungry and are over-compensating with their behaviour. (See page 194 for some calming essential oils.)

A note on ADD

See page 153 if you want to explore the Attention Deficit Disorder (ADD) issue further. However, if you do suspect they're suffering from ADD I would urge you to seek professional advice from your doctor and a paediatric dietician.

What to do if your child is becoming overweight

This scenario is unbelievably common. Our family lives have changed significantly over the last decade, and latest statistics say that over a million kids in this country are clinically overweight. Schools seem to be doing much less sport and physical activities, TV and computers are more likely to occupy your kid in the evening than playing outside, parents are time-pressured, so nipping to the shops tends to be in the car, food preparation needs to be minimal, so processed and convenience foods, eating out, are all much commoner.

Food seems to be everywhere, and you seldom see a child sitting on a bus without something to eat or drink. Food has become the chief pacifier, and also a way that parents perhaps over-compensate for not having time to spend with their kids. The break-up of the traditional family means that separated parents can end up over-feeding and treating their kids at the weekend – especially fathers who don't have the cooking skills to make them something healthy to eat; they end up going to pizza places or getting a takeaway, and on the odd occasion of course there is no problem with that. But when it happens every weekend, and there is a lot of eating and snacking going on generally, not much burning up of calories, our kids can pile on more and more weight.

On the other hand, many parents who bring their kids to see me in the practice are understandably anxious that their child doesn't go on any sort of crash diet, doesn't feel isolated by having to follow something different from everyone else, and when it comes to girls (although boys can equally be affected this way), they're worried

that if they start putting their daughter on a diet she'll swing the other way and perhaps become anorexic. It's a fine balancing act to follow, as the last thing you want to do is make eating a battleground.

I'm not going to try to come up with all the answers – it would be impossible in one chapter – but I've come up with three areas and mini-points that I've found really work with kids who are piling on too many kilos. Don't try to take every point on board straight away, just look on the next few weeks as a time when you see what you can do to make family eating, and therefore your children's eating, as healthy as possible.

LAYING GOOD FOUNDATIONS

Before you start dashing out to the supermarket and checking labels for fat content, or serving your child salad and grilled chicken (which will probably be rejected anyway!), take a really good look at what might be the reasons behind your child putting on too many kilos. Has something changed at home, are they having difficulties at school, have they fallen out with their best friend, has their support structure changed so that perhaps they're seeing less of either parent, might they be eating for comfort reasons? Many kids start wanting more oral satisfaction when they're feeling insecure or a little wobbly, and you could find that they're asking for more biscuits and snacks than they would normally. Take some time to talk to them about what's going on and see if you can build in some non-food time and treats that will help them feel better.

Has your own weight gone up recently? Have you

been cutting corners in making meals, perhaps having more pizzas and takeaways? I'm not wanting to sound judgemental here, but sometimes when life is so manic we need to stop, step back and see what's really going on. Perhaps as a family you're not eating in reality as healthily as you think, and maybe you're nibbling at crisps and chocolates while watching TV yourself. Remember that kids often copy behaviour, so you need to watch what you're doing over the next few months too.

Are you maybe over-treating them with food? Are you packing snacks for even the smallest of journeys? Are you buying fizzy drinks and popcorn more often than you really need to at the cinema – how about taking in a bottle of water and some fresh fruit to nibble if you really think they need something to eat? On the other hand, why not just try watching a movie without eating or drinking anything?

In my practice, I seldom ask kids about their weight as such, I usually start talking about whether they'd like to have more energy, whether they'd like to do better at running, to get into the school sports team. Would they like to feel less different from other kids, who may also be picking on them for being a bit bigger around the waist? I was bullied as a child because I was a little chunkier than other girls – I remember being humiliated in the girls' toilets when they told me to try to squeeze into a blatantly too small skirt belonging to another girl. Kids can be super-cruel about weight, and if your child is being picked on, helping them to believe that they can change their body for the better by eating better, making changes to the family schedule, is one positive thing you can do to help. I like to get kids to focus on a role model, not a stick-thin pop star or model

but a sports star like David Beckham. Younger kids could choose a cartoon character like Popeye.

Do speak to your child if you think bullying may be a problem, as it can be one of the loneliest aspects of childhood and if it's serious, get in touch with Childline (www.childline.org.uk), for some advice, both for you and your child, who may like to talk to someone other than you, especially if they see that the whole bullying thing upsets you too. When I was bullied at school, by girls who picked on the fact that I was a little chunkier than they were (it was just a little puppy fat, nothing major), I used to hide how upset it made me from my parents, which with hindsight, wasn't the best way to get through it. Try to get your child to talk.

To weigh or not to weigh?

I wouldn't recommend that you start putting children on the scales. It can lead to weight obsession, and is often unrealistic anyway because of kids' growth spurts. This said, some kids respond well to measuring their waistband with a tape measure, or say once a week hopping on to the scales and at the same time checking their height – it really depends on the age of your child, and how well you think they'll respond. See below for my rough body mass index (BMI) guide as to whether a child is clinically overweight or not.

If you think they might well do well with some sort of incentive chart (maybe if they lose a kilo in a month they could go on a special outing) it's a good thing to try and can sometimes work. If you've been told by the doctor that your child is seriously overweight, weighing them can be useful, but I'd suggest focusing more on how they feel – for example, whether they can run more easily without feeling tired when the weight comes off a bit. Remember that kids grow, so one good way to look at this stage in their life is to think that they need to grow into their weight – just need to elongate. Even if their weight stays the same, for some kids as they grow taller this can be fine – it depends on how overweight they are. If you do weigh them, don't do it more than once a week and make sure the scales are in the same place, you do it at the same time of day, and they're wearing the same type of clothes each time, so that the results are comparative. Remember that weight loss is never linear – some weeks they'll lose more than others. It's your job to keep them motivated and not disappointed if some weeks their weight doesn't change.

Is your child technically overweight?

The best way to find out if your child comes into the technically overweight category is to work out their body mass index (BMI), as follows:

1. Note down their height in metres and square this figure, i.e. multiply it by itself, e.g. 1.25m times 1.25.
2. Write down your child's weight in kilograms.
3. Divide the weight in kilos by the height in metres and this will give you the BMI.

There are a few tables out there that give slightly different figures, and also it depends on how muscly or fat your child is, how they feel about their body, how many bits wobble, etc., but here's the way I work out how big the problem is. Children are overweight if their BMI is above the following figures.

Aged 2, boys over 18.4 and girls over 18
Aged 3, boys over 17.9 and girls over 17.6
Aged 4, boys over 17.6 and girls over 17.3
Aged 5, boys over 17.4 and girls over 17.1
Aged 6, boys over 17.6 and girls over 17.3
Aged 7, boys over 17.9 and girls over 17.8
Aged 8, boys over 18.4 and girls over 18.3
Aged 9, boys over 19.1 and girls over 19.1
Aged 10, boys over 19.8 and girls over 19.9

Look at your meal patterns

Every child is different – some kids are more hungry in the morning than others, for instance – but generally it's good to get them to sit down at the table and to structure the day around three meals per day, at pretty regular times. If you let the mealtimes wander, they can end up being so ravenously hungry that they'll eat far more than they really need. You'll also find that they'll be around your ankles demanding snacks such as crisps and biscuits if you've pushed their hunger too much, and then you'll find they're too full to eat a nutritious meal. So, difficult as it is, try to keep to roughly regular mealtimes and get them to sit down at the table, preferably with you, to eat. Eating in front of the TV means they not only miss out on all the socially educational aspects of eating together, learning good table manners, etc., but from a weight point of view, you'll find they're so distracted by the TV that they don't notice what they're eating. Laying good foundations so that they appreciate their food, eating as slowly as possible, giving them enough time to eat their food, is one of the best things you can do for a child.

As a working mum I can't always sit with Maya, as she sometimes eats before I get home. But I ask her nanny to sit with her, and even if I'm around and wanting to eat later, either with another adult or when it's peaceful and I can relax more, I still try to sit with her and drink a cup of tea or something so that I'm part of her eating experience. At weekends we always eat together and make a thing of buying the food, talking about what we're going to eat, so that eating and appreciating is well enclosed in her psyche.

If the meal plan has gone out of the window, think about giving kids a healthy snack to keep them going – give them some fruit in the back of the car, sit them down at the table with some hummus and raw vegetables, or in winter serve them a bowl of soup as soon as they get in, to take the edge off their hunger and give you time to make something healthy.

Serve a little less

Often we just serve the same amounts on their plates out of habit, and since many of us still have the mentality that we should finish everything on the plate, this can mean that sometimes our kids eat more than they need. So try two things. First, serve less – they can always have seconds if they really need more. Second, use a smaller plate and don't insist that they always finish everything before they leave the table. Of course they need to eat enough, so that they don't want to pick at not-so-healthy things after the meal, but you're trying to teach your child to eat less, so you need to trust them a little.

It frequently takes time between eating and swallowing food and the recognition of that to kick in, so eating slowly and pacing the meal is important. Try to allow a small gap between the main course and the dessert, and they might not need to eat as much. They'll also appreciate the dessert more.

HOW TO CUT DOWN

The food and nutritional aspects of helping your child to lose weight are pretty similar to the diet principles most adults should follow, but you need to be very careful that you don't put them on anything faddy or crash-diet-like. What does work is looking at obvious ways to minimize the amount of unnecessary fats and sugars – honing in on cutting out the surplus while not depriving them of essential nutrients. Before we move on to consider ways to do this, one of the most important aspects of feeding a child who has piled on too many kilos is to be make sure you're well stocked in foods they can eat freely – have big bowls of fresh fruit around, and try to make their eating habits part of your whole family's, even if there are just the two of you. Don't expect them to eat different diet food while you tuck into fish and chips – if you're underweight yourself, find other moments in the day to stock up on your extras. And have some treat days each week – maybe make the weekends the time when you relax the rules.

Here are some good general tips for every day.

Make food yummy!

Kids are not going to go for the salad without the dressing, the skinless chicken breast – you need to try as much as possible to make sure that the food tastes delicious. I know chicken skin adds more calories to the breast, but if it's a crispy, well-cooked skin they'll enjoy the chicken much more than a poached anaemic-looking white thing. Of course keep fats, oils, salt down, but this doesn't mean you need to ban them – some good olive oil

over new potatoes or fresh courgettes will make them more appealing. It helps also to think about how the food looks on the plate – I'm not talking sculpting vegetables but you need to sell the food to them by making it look good. Try as much as possible to make sure there are two or three different colours, tastes and textures on the plate and encourage them to rotate and switch between the different foods. The more variety and different textures and tastes a child has in one meal, the more likely their brain is to register that they've eaten enough. This sounds like a lot of effort, but it can be one of the most successful tips with kids – it truly works if you give them something more than just a simple bowl of pasta with nothing else to break down the taste and texture sensations.

Ways to get a child's weight down
* Ban fizzy drinks – kids don't need them. They shouldn't drink diet drinks either, as these are full of sweeteners and acids, which aren't good for them. Persevere with getting them on to drinking water – if they just kick up a lot, gradually wean them off sweet juices by watering them down.
* Make sure they're drinking enough water, as this not only helps keep them hydrated, but sometimes kids think they need food when really it's water their body needs. It can also help take the edge off their hunger.
* Change breakfast – five days out of seven (save the weekends for treats) – to wholemeal toast, wholemeal muffins, porridge, a higher-fibre breakfast cereal such as Weetabix, Shredded Wheat, Bran Flakes, unsweetened muesli. You can change your milk to semi-skimmed after

they're two, but I wouldn't shift to skimmed milk until they're over five.
* Ease off the obvious baddies: keep frying down to a minimum – grill, microwave or steam instead. Even though vegetable oils such as olive oil are generally regarded as good fats, they still have just as many calories as butter and other animal fats – so watch the quantity. If kids really see fried foods like chips as a lifeline, you could maybe have them as a treat one day a week. Keep away from pastries, batters, thick creamy sauces, and make cakes and biscuits a once-a-week treat too.
* Avoid low-fat and low-sugar processed foods. Not only are many of them full of preservatives, since something has to be put in as a replacement when something big like fat or sugar is taken out, but they can also be pretty high in salt and even in the end higher in calories than the standard biscuit – a low-fat digestive-style biscuit can have more calories in than the normal one. They're usually more expensive and don't taste as good, so they don't satisfy the tastebuds and the fullness part of the brain called the hypothalamus, so you might end up giving them two to hit the spot, as opposed to one delicious proper biscuit. It's much better to try to keep sweet foods other than fresh fruits as once-a-week treat foods. Like so many things with kids, it's how you sell them – if you make a yummy fresh fruit salad and go on about how delicious it is, and you eat it yourself too, you're much more likely to see it go down than if you just plonk a boring banana in front of them.
* If you make puddings, think about keeping fibre up, fats and sugars down. For instance, a fruit

crumble can just as easily be made with a topping of wholemeal flour, oats and brown sugar as with a refined white crumble mix – OK, brown sugar has just as many calories in as white, but to me it tastes far sweeter and more caramel-like, so you can add less. You can also substitute fructose in puddings, as this is sweeter for fewer calories. With yoghurt, choose plain varieties and add fresh fruits to them, instead of buying the fruity versions which can be extremely high in sugar.

* Include pasta, rice and potatoes in your child's diet, as these give them beneficial carbohydrates and other minerals, but try to use wholemeal pasta, brown rice, jacket potatoes as much as you can. Although wholemeal pasta and rice have a different texture, they are so much more satisfying than the white equivalent. If you just can't get these past their lips, just make sure you give them a smaller portion of the white kind, and serve a good vegetable dish or a salad with them. With risotto, you don't need to add lots of butter and cheese at the end – it still tastes good with just a little.

* Homemade soups are a fantastically healthy, naturally low-calorie food for kids – serve chunky, beany, vegetable ones, and if you need to disguise the ingredients, whiz the soup up in a food processor. Just a bowlful will give you enough vegetable and pulse fibre goodness to satisfy their voracious appetite. It's a good starter to a meal too.

* With pasta, go for non-creamy sauces. Keep the proteins (meat, fish, eggs, chicken, seafood, etc.) as lean as possible, and ditch pies and sausage rolls. Eggs are fantastically satisfying, nourishing and pretty low in calories – if you need a quick supper make scrambled eggs in a non-stick pan, with just a little butter, or an omelette. Serve with wholemeal toast or bagel.

* I wouldn't go down the low-fat cheese or butter route, just keep the quantity down. Cheeses like Gouda, cottage cheese, Edam are naturally lower in fat. Cutting the rind off soft cheese like Brie and Camembert reduces their fat content. Grate cheese to use in sandwiches or on jacket potatoes – the greater surface area on the cheese means that the tastebuds register more cheese flavour for less consumption. Incidentally, one of the best ways with a jacket potato is to scoop the white flesh out when it's cooked, mash it in a bowl with a fork, a little butter or olive oil (you could even use a little yoghurt or fromage frais instead of butter), cheese, a little mustard (which brings out the cheesy flavour), seasoning – place the filling back in the skin and toast under a grill till crispy and hot.

* Dried fruits usually go down well, as they're nicely sweet and moreish (see page 52). Watch that they just eat a few at a time – make them up a little mixed bag instead of expecting them to stop after only a few out of a large packet.

* Veggies are great for helping to fill kids up with very few calories – once you know they've had enough energy from the other aspects of the meal. We all know that steamed veggies are usually the best, but sometimes our kids don't like them this way, so try roasting them with a little olive oil, stuff them, make ratatouille. If they'll eat the vegetables but only with a little olive oil or butter, it's still worthwhile – the plus side of the veg outweighs the few extra calories.

* Try as much as possible to make food from fresh ingredients, instead of relying heavily on

convenience foods. Even the slightly healthier kids' ranges can be high in fats, sugars, salt and preservatives, so try to grab the culinary fear over lack of time by the horns – it doesn't really take much longer. (Find out how to make healthy burgers, fish fingers, etc. on pages 233–34.)

BURNING UP THE CALORIES

Despite there being new diet theories flying around all the time, one thing remains constant: losing weight is to do with burning calories, and kids will lose weight if they burn up more than they consume. Lack of exercise has to be one of the main reasons why today's kids are suffering from obesity and all its associated health problems, such as heart disease and diabetes. The statistics are shocking: national data suggests that apart from young kids (4–6 years old), between 40% and 69% of children in Britain are largely inactive, spending less than one hour a day participating in activities of moderate intensity. In 2004 the Chief Medical Officer, in a report called 'At least five a week: evidence on the impact of physical activity and it's relationship to health', recommended that children have a minimum of sixty minutes of at least moderate-intensity exercise every day. It also recommended that activities that increase muscle strength and flexibility and improve bone strength, such as weight-bearing exercise – gym, running, tennis, hockey, football, etc. – should be included at least twice a week.

Walk with them, take them cycling or swimming at the weekends – as a family make exercise part of an enjoyable activity. It's unrealistic to expect children to lose excess weight just by eating healthy food; they need to burn up calories too.

Exercise is good for them in so many ways – it helps them to feel confident, secure in their own body, it produces endorphins which can help keep them happy, burns off anxiety and bad moods, pushes oxygen around their body and tires them out! That's on top of the long-term health benefits of reducing their chance of developing diabetes, heart disease, certain cancers, joint problems, etc. There are now loads of great kids' fitness clubs around if you think they need a little group support, even dance classes, karate, yoga. But if at the beginning you think they're a little too body-sensitive to take their clothes off and get into the swimming-pool, just get them walking and cycling, or buy a skipping rope – a fantastic fun way to burn some calories!

What if exercising gives my child an even bigger appetite?

This can often happen. The first thing to do is to give them plenty of water to rehydrate them. Next you should try a snack such as fresh fruit or some raw veggies and hummus, if you're at home. Alternatively, offer rice cakes or dried fruits, a few unsalted nuts (not if they're under five though). What you need to watch is that you don't fall into the trap of thinking that because they've been active and exercising hard they need even bigger portions – they don't, and you'll actually be surprised how few extra calories exercise burns. I'm not saying it's not worth exercising, but if all you do is give them another couple of hundred extra calories in a bigger meal, you'll be back to square one. You just need to try to distract them from feeling so hungry. What is great about muscle-building exercise is that the more muscle a child has, the more calories they burn off and the fitter they feel – so keep on with the exercise, but don't OD on the food afterwards.

Sticking with it

If you think that sticking to a losing weight diet is hard enough for adults, magnify that a few times for kids. They need you to keep encouraging them and to work out a practical lifestyle that helps them. There is little point in watching them losing weight over a few weeks, making all these great changes, then going back to the way things were before – this will only put their weight up again and probably mean that they balloon even more. They need consistency too – if they're spending their time between parents, for example, you need to get your ex-other-half to support them too. This is especially important for kids who spend the weekends with a dad who doesn't know how to cook – buy him a cookery book, or talk about restaurants where there will be options your child can eat. I've come across parents who give confusing messages, too – one might say the child has a weight problem and needs to lose weight, only to find the other one undoing the good work by rewarding the child with sweets, saying oh, don't let the other parent see them. Food is frequently used as an emotional tool to gain approval – try not to do this. And if you're overweight yourself, lead by good example.

Of course there will be blips, they will go to parties, to friends for weekends, but just try to keep the norm as healthy as possible, so that it's easy for them to get back on track. And remember that not every overweight child becomes an overweight adult – some kids just go through different rates of growth. They change hormonally, and sometimes, like me, they lose their puppy fat

and don't have a problem in adulthood. Even if you as an adult can remember being like them, genetically they're different individuals. Try not to go off at the deep end and impose rules that are too strict, as they will only want to break them. Finally, seldom is a child overweight just because of their genes or any hormonal/gland problem. OK, family history comes into it if there is a tendency to have weight issues, but frequently there are lots of things you can do behaviour- and lifestyle-wise to override these issues. Stay positive and you will see results.

The bottom line is, kids will lose weight if they burn more calories than they consume.

SPECIFIC CONDITIONS

Asthma

Asthma is a disease of the airways that carry air into and out of the lungs. These tubes become sensitive and inflamed, and when an asthma attack occurs the airways swell, making it hard to breathe. In severe cases this can be life-threatening, as my twelve-year-old nephew recently experienced. The son of a friend has just been diagnosed with asthma, and having witnessed both my brother and my nephew experiencing serious asthma attacks, this whole area of how foods can influence the way our kids breathe is very close to my heart.

Asthma is the most common long-term disease in the west, reportedly killing 1,500 people a year in Britain and costing the NHS an annual £850 million. An alarming European Commission study has furthermore found that 13.2 per cent of British children have asthma, almost double the European Union average of 7.2 per cent – you only need to look in the playground and in school clinics to see how many kids now have to carry their inhalers around with them. As to why more of our kids are becoming asthmatic, the theories for this range from genetics (which is certainly the case in my atopic, i.e. allergy-prone family), pollution, bringing our kids up in overly clean home environments (see page 105) and low levels of vitamin E during pregnancy, to low-fat, high-salt diets.

While I can't say that nutrition can cure asthma, changing the way children eat can definitely have a positive effect on their breathing. It's worth keeping a food diary recording what your child eats and how his or her breathing has been – because sometimes an allergic reaction to a food molecule can be the cause of an asthma attack. Specific additives such as tartrazine, used in canned drinks and other processed foods, are commonly to blame, but even the most natural foods, such as oranges, can be the culprit (which, for some asthmatics, makes the half-time quarter of fresh orange the last thing they should be eating), or milk or wheat, and if this is the case, you should seek help from a paediatric dietician to ensure your child's diet is nutritionally well balanced when you remove such a big food group. Jamie Oliver in his *School Dinners* programme found that simply giving kids in Greenwich healthy food that wasn't full of preservatives, fat and general gunk at lunchtime meant that they didn't have to use their inhalers as often, and I'm convinced we'd see this effect in all our schools and kids.

I know keeping a food diary (see page 122) is laborious, but identifying any triggers can reduce the amount of inhaler your child has to use. According to the National Asthma Campaign, food and drink aren't particularly common triggers for kids with asthma; but food allergies can produce symptoms very similar to an asthma attack such as wheezing, and these can make asthma worse. The most common triggers I've found with kids with asthma are shellfish, eggs, peanuts, sesame, fish, products containing sulphites (E numbers 220–227) and wheat – those kids who react badly to tartrazine may also react to aspirin. Benzoic acid (E210), found in fruit drinks and some fruit products, can set other kids off, as can, occasionally, milk, although to slightly confuse the issue, many studies have shown that kids who drink milk every day are less likely to suffer from asthma in the first place. It therefore seems that if your child does develop asthma, milk might not be great, but this is only the case if they have an allergic reaction to it – if they don't, they should still keep it in their diet (see page 189). If you're at all worried by any aspect of food allergy, seek professional advice.

BOOST ANTIOXIDANTS

In case you need another reason for not giving in to the pester-power surrounding heavily marketed processed kids' foods and for persevering with putting fresh vegetables and fruits (raw carrots, cucumber, cherry tomatoes, radishes, etc.) into packed lunches and sneaking them into sauces, research shows that our kids are becoming asthmatic because they aren't consuming enough antioxidant-rich fresh fruits and vegetables. One particular antioxidant seems to be effective: vitamin E, found in oily fish (salmon, mackerel, sardines, fresh tuna), nuts (whole nuts only allowed after the age of five and to be avoided if they're allergic) and seeds (almonds, hazelnuts, sunflower and hemp seeds), vegetable oils such as wheat germ oil, avocados, wholegrain cereals and, strangely, sun-dried tomatoes – the ones stored in oil, rather than the dried packet tomatoes. The phytonutrients in apples can also help to improve lung function, making drinking a glass of freshly squeezed apple juice one of the healthiest ways for an asthmatic child to start the day.

THINK ABOUT OILY FISH

I'm not going to tell you again … well, OK, maybe one last time! Omega-3 really is a superfood, and is particularly good for asthmatics. (See page 110 for more details on sources and how much to eat.)

WATCH THE SALT

Since high salt intakes have been implicated in aggravating breathing, you should watch your kids' salt intake (see page 90). Try to avoid putting it into foods after weaning, as they won't miss it, and keep processed salty foods such as crisps as a treat, rather than a staple. Purists may suggest that we ban white bread because it is surprisingly high in salt, but practically I'd target the salty snacks, fast foods and breakfast cereals first – kids need starch, and white bread also gives them energy and calcium. Of course manufacturers could always lower the salt content, or if you have the time you could bake your own in one of the great bread-making machines that you can buy now, as this means you don't need to add the salt.

MINDFUL OF MAGNESIUM

Finally, unsalted nuts and seeds are rich in magnesium, a mineral that relaxes the muscles, and reduces the reactivity of the MAST cells (allergy cells) in the airways, making them a great snack. If you're worried about kids choking on nuts (or if they have an allergy to them), a useful alternative source of magnesium is soya milk (ideally non-GM, organic) – blend it with fresh fruits in the morning to make a quick, no-fuss breakfast or good energizing snack.

KEEP THEM ACTIVE

Sensible exercising not only helps keep your child's lungs and breathing healthy, but also helps keep their weight in check, an issue if they're having to take powerful steroid medication, which can have a tendency to increase their appetite and therefore their weight. You don't want your child to pile on the weight because this will make them feel less healthy and less inclined to keep active. If you can keep on top of their weight (see page 139) and also keep them fit and active you'll find their lung function improves along with their moods. Exercise encourages the body to produce endorphins, which make them feel happier and also generally sleep better if they've had a physically active day. Do check with your doctor about how much exercise your asthmatic child should be doing, and always make sure an inhaler is to hand.

Remember, of course, that the less exercise kids do, the more weight they're likely to pile on, the fewer endorphins aka happy hormones they'll produce, and the poorer their lung function generally becomes.

Diet is a key factor in controlling asthma. And exercise is great for asthmatic kids.

Attention Deficit Disorder (ADD)

Astonishingly, recent official Department of Health figures suggest that one in twenty children aged between the ages of six and sixteen in the UK have ADD, with the figures being much higher in the USA. Medication costs the NHS £10 million a year. No one really knew about ADD ten years ago, but now there are at least a few cases in most schools and I don't see the numbers waning. Interestingly, boys are four times as likely to have the condition than girls. What is important is not to self-diagnose, or accept a doctor's diagnosis and drug prescription without them seeing your child. If you suspect that your child has the symptoms of ADD, which can range from insomnia, to lack of concentration, to hyperactivity (they just won't sit still and can be like little hurricanes in the room), moodiness and frequent destructive outbursts, take them to your GP, who can then refer you all to a paediatric team of experts for assessment and advice. Children with Attention Deficit (Hyperactive) Disorder, commonly known as ADHD, ADD and HKD (Hyperkinetic disorder) can not only drive their parents to take antidepressants, but can even destroy marriages.

If this wasn't worrying enough, the conventional course of treatment for ADD has been amphetamine-type drugs like Ritalin. In the USA this is a major drug of misuse and addiction – kids are being bullied for their Ritalin, as other kids who don't have ADD like to take them for a kick. More recently, atomoxetine (Straterra) has been used for the treatment of ADHD. Atomoxetine is a non-stimulant medication that has been shown to be effective in children with ADHD, as an alternative treatment option in kids who are intolerant or unresponsive to stimulants such as Ritalin. I'm not saying that kids with ADD shouldn't be taking these drugs – I realize that in some cases they can be a lifeline for both the kids and their families – but it worries me that not many parents know that dietary adjustments and behaviour-modification therapy can be very effective alternative or complimentary therapies to the drugs, with certainly fewer negative side-effects. We don't hear much about this, because the drug companies and certain areas of the food industry move heaven and earth to stop this information getting out, and in comparison with the huge sums of money invested in drug and food research, scientists who try to find links between food and behaviour problems such as ADD can struggle for funding.

It has to be said that some of the studies into food and mood/behaviour throw up mixed results, but from my experience and those of many colleagues working in this area, changing the diet of kids with ADD can definitely make a huge difference. Since the side-effects of dietary and behavioural change, apart from being hard work and needing lots of determination, are minimal, I urge all parents of kids with ADD or other behavioural issues to look at some key aspects of their diet. I have turned kids with huge behavioural issues around, and the results can literally be life-changing.

We have four key areas to focus on. The first is the general overall healthiness of the diet: small healthy meals often, lots of water, lots of fresh fruits and vegetables is the general background theme to try to achieve first. And strip out the baddies – the sugars and additives.

SUGAR

It's my opinion that as soon as parents get rid of the very sweet high GI foods from the diet of a child with ADD they'll notice a positive difference in their behaviour. They might seem more moody or lethargic to begin with, but this is just the stage of being weaned off the rapidly absorbed sugars crisis, and they'll soon, usually within days, start to find a more consistent energy level. When it comes to what sweetish thing you can give them instead, we need to look at the low GI foods (see page 84 for good low-sugar foods).

Try to give your child small healthy meals often, and make them as full of fresh ingredients as possible. This way you will also reduce your child's exposure to additives and preservatives, which in some cases can really upset behaviour.

THE SALICYLATE ISSUE

On rare occasions, kids with ADD have been shown to be reactive to a group of naturally occurring chemicals known as salicylates, which can irritate their behaviour. This applies very much to a minority of cases, but if you want to try removing the salicylate-rich foods from your child's diet to see if behaviour improves, see the box:

Foods rich in salicylates

Oranges	Grapes
Almonds	Nectarines
Apples	Tangerines
Apricots	Peaches
Tomatoes	Plums
Cherries	Peppers
Cranberries	Prunes
Cucumbers	Raisins

As you'll see, it's a huge list of healthy foods, but if you notice your child craving and eating a lot of any food on the list, just try taking the quantity down and trying to get a more balanced amount into their overall diet. (I have to say that tomatoes are the only thing on the list that I've really experienced as a trigger).

ADDITIVES

As you'll have read on pages 000–000, we need some additives in our foods to stop them going off, to give good texture, etc. But when it comes to kids and additives, I try to keep well away from the following list, as it's my experience that kids who eat a diet free of these additives (in addition to looking at other areas of their diet and lifestyle) are much healthier, more evenly behaved and can concentrate better.

* Tartrazine E102
* Sunset yellow E110
* Carmoisine E122
* Ponceau 4R E124

* Sodium benzoate E211
* Other benzoates E210 – 219
* Sulphides E220 – 228
* Nitrate and nitrites E249 – 252
* Monosodium glutamate and other glutamates E621 – 623
* Antioxidants E310 – 312, E320, E321

I am not saying that all these additives have been linked with ADD, but if you steer clear of them, which you can if you use fresh produce as much as possible, it helps their behaviour and concentration. And since they don't need them, why put them inside their bodies?

THE GOODIES

Finally, but very importantly, one of the most exciting areas of research into the relationship between foods and behaviour focuses on getting children to eat more of the oily fish that's rich in omega-3 fatty acids, such as sardines, salmon (preferably wild), trout, herrings and mackerel. The reason why oily fish can come to the rescue is that it contains the beneficial fatty acids docosahexaenoic acid (DHA) and eicosapent-aenoic acid (EPA), which positively influence the signals that are sent back and forth between the brain and parts of the body. EPA in particular has been shown in many studies, largely those carried out by Dr Alexander Richardson, Senior Research Fellow and co-director of the charity Food and Behaviour (FAB), to have the power to stabilize mood swings and generally improve the mood, behaviour, concentration and learning abilities of children with ADD – which of course benefits everyone around them, too.

Vegetarian non-fish sources of omega-3 fatty

acids include linseeds (flaxseeds), sunflower, pumpkin and sesame seeds, walnuts, hemp seeds and their oils. However, it has to be said that it can be pretty difficult to get kids to consistently eat enough omega-3 fatty acids to stabilize their behaviour and other symptoms of ADD, so I would discuss giving them a 500mg omega-3 supplement three times a day, or else one capsule of a supplement called MorEPA, which will provide a highly concentrated source of EPA.

Sometimes kids with ADD can have food intolerances, and as soon as they avoid the not-tolerated food, most typically wheat or milk, their behaviour can improve. Ask to be referred to a paediatric dietician for some professional support. I would stress how useful it is to keep a detailed diary of what your child eats, just in rough household measure quantities, with their symptoms/behaviour alongside, for a good couple of weeks, as this can give you and any professionals from whom you seek advice a real idea of which foods could be aggravating the child's behaviour. Try to keep the diary as secret as you can, though, apart from asking them what they've eaten at friends' homes or at school, as they can quickly cotton on to playing up and performing for you, which muddies the waters!

If this sounds daunting, remember that children with a short attention span will feel positively stimulated, interested and therefore better able to concentrate and behave well if they see their parents preparing different foods and then sitting down to eat as a family – this is just one example of how eating and behaviour modification are intertwined. If there is no way that your child will eat vegetables and fruits, however, give them a daily multivitamin and mineral supplement (one which lists the DRVs or dietary reference values for the nutrients and is free of bad additives and E numbers) to ensure that their body receives some nutrients, thereby making them feel better so that in turn they start eating better.

All in all, I'd urge all parents of kids with serious behavioural problems to think about altering their diet, because the results can be astonishing. Wouldn't it be a relief to banish your household's little monster and get your loving child back?

Coeliac disease

It's alarming to be told that your child has coeliac disease, but this inflammatory condition, which is actually an autoimmune disease (an immunological disorder) that affects mainly the gut, can be very successfully managed. The gut can fully recover by sticking to a diet free from gluten. Gluten is the protein found in wheat and rye grains, and coeliacs can also have problems dealing with very similar damaging proteins found in oats and barley.

WHO GETS IT AND WHY?
Coeliac disease used to be considered rare, but not any more. More doctors and parents are aware of it, and the frequency can be as high as one in 100 people (although not everyone knows they have it). If your child with coeliac disease eats foods containing gluten, the gluten damages the lining of the small intestine, which causes symptoms such as diarrhoea, vomiting, tummy pains and a bloated tummy. Having a damaged intestine also means they will have problems absorbing essential nutrients – lack of calcium can cause your child's bones to become brittle,

especially later in life, and the poor absorption of iron can mean they become anaemic (which makes them pale, grumpy and very tired as well as stunting their growth). When gluten damages the intestine, your child will have difficulty digesting foods, so their stools can often become fatty, grey, stinky and float.

WHEN DOES IT START?
Usually the symptoms of coeliac disease start appearing when you feed children solids containing gluten, i.e. at a very young age, but sometimes the symptoms go unnoticed for years and it's only when your child doesn't seem to be thriving, complains frequently of tummy-aches and doesn't have much energy that the disease is diagnosed. Coeliac symptoms can manifest themselves at any age and, according to Coeliac UK statistics, most coeliacs are diagnosed when aged between thirty and forty-five years (which I've certainly found in my practice). If you suspect that your child has coeliac disease (maybe you have it in your family, as it is often hereditary), you need to see your doctor, who can refer you to a paediatrician for a test called a biopsy. This is when they remove a little of the intestine in a very minor operation, to see whether any of it is damaged. You need to take your child to see the doctor before taking them off gluten, as they need to be able to see what's happening in the child's body when gluten is around. If your child is diagnosed and you suspect you may have it too, get checked out.

Although all this sounds frightening, the good news is that as soon as you remove gluten from your child's diet the gut very quickly recovers. Symptoms can vanish completely, and kids with coeliac disease live very healthy lives – although coeliacs need to follow a gluten-free diet for life, it's not something they grow out of.

A PRACTICAL NOTE

The obvious sources of gluten are breads, pasta, cakes, biscuits, pastries and ready-made meals that could have flour in them – the flour might be in the sauce, for instance. To help you steer clear of gluten in manufactured products, get straight on to the Coeliac Society, who will not only reassure you that you're not alone, but will also provide you with lists of up-to-date gluten-free foods – i.e. manufactured foods that have been processed. Note that you need to keep on top of these lists and not rely on old ones, as products change all the time and something that is gluten-free now might not be when the next list is produced – this is really important.

Simple naturally gluten-free foods

Rice

Potatoes

Lentils and beans (pure unadulterated beans and lentils should be fine, but you need to check with anything processed like baked beans)

Corn- and rice-based cereals

Rice, corn (maize), buckwheat, millet, soya, gram flour

Sugar, honey, jam, some chocolates (but you need to check the labels)

Fish, chicken, eggs, lean meat, all vegetables and fruits are fine, as is milk, but you need to check yoghurts to make sure they don't contain gluten, as some use it as a stabilizer or to add a crunch)

FOODS TO AVOID

You need to avoid anything that has bread flour or gluten products in it, such as fish fingers, fish cakes, sausages. Many processed foods use bread, wheat starch as fillers, to puff them out – it's cheap, you see, so avoid all processed foods unless you know they are definitely gluten-free.

Labelling isn't everything you need it to be when you're a coeliac, as although labels will indicate the obvious presence of wheat or wheat flour where a gluten-containing flour (such as rye flour) is used as a processing aid or as a small

percentage of a compound ingredient, it does not have to be declared on a label. Regulations are getting stricter, but at the present time coeliacs are advised to use the Coeliac Society's UK food list rather than relying on information given on a label. If a product is not in the list it should be avoided. See www.coeliac.co.uk.

WHAT ABOUT OATS?

Oats have traditionally been excluded from the coeliac diet, although this is now a point of controversy, largely because some of the earlier studies which found that oats should be avoided seem to have involved very small numbers of patients, and some questionable methods. The Coeliac Society's Medical Advisory Council have published interim guidelines to help parents until we have more conclusive evidence to draw on. These guidelines say that although moderate amounts of oats can be consumed usually by adults with coeliac disease without risk of any reaction, the situation is less clear with kids. Before you give your child any oats, you need to ask your consultant for advice – your child might be highly sensitive to them. You need to be very careful of oat products as they can be contaminated with wheat at various stages of production, such as in the milling or processing – so you really need to be confident about where you source the oats from if your child is actually allowed them by your doctor.

WATCH OUT FOR WHEAT STARCH

Wheat starch is produced from wheat flour by removing the proteins, including gluten. Years ago it was believed that all the protein could be removed, but it is now recognized that it is technically impossible to remove all traces and a small amount of protein remains.

There are two types of wheat starch: commercial wheat starch, which is not sufficiently pure to be suitable for coeliacs and should be avoided, and specially manufactured wheat starch which complies with the International Gluten-free Standard. This allows it to be used in a gluten-free diet. Wheat starch of this purity is expensive and it is most commonly used in products specially manufactured for coeliacs, to provide palatable and acceptable bread and flour substitutes. These products will be labelled as gluten-free, so should be fine.

IS WHEAT-FREE OK?

No it isn't! You need to make sure you don't fall into the trap of thinking that just because something says it's wheat-free, that it's safe for coeliacs – it isn't necessarily, because often breads and cakes sold as wheat-free are made with other grains that contain gluten (or the similar damaging protein in rye, oats, etc.). Wheat-free is fine for people with wheat intolerance, but not if you have coeliac disease – only give it to your child if the label says it's gluten-free. Nowadays some people say they have an intolerance to gluten and wheat, but this is not the same as coeliac disease – although they may feel unwell after eating gluten or wheat (they may in fact show very similar symptoms, such as tummy-aches, etc.), coeliac disease needs to be treated extra carefully and it should be stressed to waiters in restaurants that you're not just a fussy parent! Sometimes I see kids who exhibit all the gut signs of having coeliac disease but the tests come back normal – in this case as long as you make sure that their diet is well-rounded it's perfectly healthy to be brought up the gluten-free way. It may be that they can manage a little bit of gluten, say flapjacks, or oatcakes containing wheat flour, every now and then and feel fine, but if they eat lots of wheat and gluten they feel lousy. They might have a problem with wheat, but feel OK after eating rye bread or casseroles containing barley. **But remember, if you're diagnosed as being coeliac, you need to avoid all gluten for the rest of your life – there are no half-measures.**

You'll see from the Coeliac Society website that you can buy many gluten-free products such as special bread and biscuits – I think the special bread is best toasted. If you're diagnosed as suffering from coeliac disease, you can get prescriptions from your GP for free gluten-free bread and other products such as cakes and biscuits – these used to be not great, but now, since coeliac disease is becoming increasingly prevalent, chefs have come to the rescue and managed to come up with many great-tasting gluten-free products. Even in the supermarkets you can find good gluten-free cereals, breads and products, which is a big relief for parents who used to have to order them from the chemist.

Remember, your child can be perfectly healthy – as long as you avoid gluten.

Inform those around you

Make sure the following people know about your child's coeliac disease and have all the information they need:

* School and nursery staff
* Relatives
* Carers
* Friends and their parents
* People who run sports and club activities

You need to be vigilant and to make sure your child knows which foods they can and can't eat – when they go to school, friends' houses, cinemas, etc. Every carer, every friend's mum, needs to know that your child isn't a faddy eater but has coeliac disease and needs to be extremely careful to avoid gluten-containing foods. It's worth getting a letter from your GP that you can photocopy to send around to playgroups, etc. I find that if you explain the situation and give people plenty of warning, don't just leave it till you're on the way round to their house for tea, most parents these days are cool about making sure their food is safe.

TAKE TIME TO EXPLAIN TO YOUR CHILD

As a parent you also need to take the time to explain the situation to your child – even if you just say something simple like 'These foods will give you tummy ache or make you poorly.' Don't just say they can't have something. Always make sure that there is an alternative for your child to eat, so that they don't have to feel too different. There are so many naturally gluten-free foods, as well as manufactured foods, that everyone in the family should be happy eating, so try as a family to cook in a gluten-free way as much as possible. Kids never want to feel different or left out – if they do, you might just find them rebelling.

WHAT TO DO IF YOU'RE NOT USED TO GLUTEN-FREE COOKING

If you're a mum, and a friend's child who has coeliac disease is coming to tea, don't panic – below is a list of naturally gluten-free recipes to get stuck into. It's best to keep it simple, as this way you'll avoid the angst.

* Jacket potatoes with cheesy topping and crispy bacon
* Scrambled eggs
* Chicken and chips
* Risotto (made with gluten-free stock cube)
* Home-made soup or casserole (as long as they are made with gluten-free stock and not thickened with flour)

Keep flour and anything containing gluten away from your cooking area and try to just have naturally gluten-free snacks for everyone – grapes or pineapple and cheese on 'safe' sticks, or dates or figs (as long as the packaging says they're gluten-free) and chunks of melon.

Make sure that everyone who might feed your child knows that he or she is not a fussy eater but has coeliac disease.

Colds and coughs

It seems as though Maya has permanently had a cold this last year, although the reality is that she hasn't, it's just that we usually don't notice the times when children are well and cold-free. Colds and coughs are par for the course for all children – most parents find that as soon as their little ones start playgroup, nursery, school, they drop like flies to the bugs that swarm around. It's an important part of their body getting its immune response mechanism right that we allow them to fight the infections as much as possible without taking drugs.

The majority of common colds and coughs are caused by a virus, which is why doctors are reluctant, and quite rightly so, to prescribe antibiotics at the drop of a hat – antibiotics are useless for getting rid of viral infections, it's only bacterial infections that are zapped by these medications. However, we can of course help ease our kids' symptoms and make them much more comfortable. We can also make their immune system stronger and much less vulnerable to coughs and colds by looking to food and a few natural remedies.

The key nutrients to focus on in the development of a good efficient immune system are zinc, selenium and vitamins A, C and E, so you need to ensure they're eating enough of the foods that contain these, especially if you've noticed they're succumbing to coughs and colds more often, or are less able to shake them off, than other children. (See the vitamins and nutrients chart on pages 25–29.)

WHEN THE COLD OR COUGH HITS ...

Make sure your child drinks plenty of fluids, especially if they're running a temperature, which is common at the beginning of the infection, as a hot body sweats more and hence loses more fluid.

Go for garlic

For older kids who don't mind strong and spicy flavours, you can do no better than trying to get some fresh garlic inside them, as it has an amazing power to combat bacterial, fungal and viral infections as well as having potential benefits for diabetes and asthma sufferers. One of the easiest, most effective ways to get rid of a sore throat is to chew a fresh garlic clove – if you can do it, great, but it doesn't go down well with young ones!

Note: You need to eat garlic as soon after peeling as possible, as its potency fades the more it is exposed to light; and fresh young garlic bulbs, which we find in summer, have maximum health benefits – much more so than a fusty old head of garlic that's been sitting in your vegetable basket for weeks. Heat negates most of garlic's healing powers – although of course the taste is great.

With older kids, and for yourself if they've generously passed their bug on to you, try this potent garlic hit. Crush 5 or 6 garlic cloves, add 6 teaspoons of apple cider vinegar, and stir. Refrigerate for 24 hours, then warm in the microwave and add a tablespoon of honey and four teaspoons of lemon juice. Leave to cool, and let 2 teaspoons trickle down your throat, with a little gargle, 3 times a day. A quicker-to-hand traditional remedy for a sore throat is a crushed garlic clove in a mug of warm milk.

If you can't stand the taste and want to go down the tablet route, be wary of useless supplements. Many experts believe the active allicin in garlic cloves is so volatile that by heating and deodorizing them so that they don't taint your breath their potency is diminished and they become virtually useless. The only really effective garlic supplements on the market are those known as real allicin products, which capture the allicin from fresh garlic and stabilize it – brands such as Allimax (recommended dose in the region of 180mg of allicin powder, usually one capsule per day) and Alliforce. Good health-food stores stock these. Garlic oil, aged garlic extract and garlic powders are inferior products with few healing properties.

Honey and lemon – a classic

First off, you mustn't give a child under one any honey because it may occasionally cause infant botulism, which is a type of food poisoning. But over one year old, honey can be one of the best and most soothing of foods to give your child when their throat is sore – it not only soothes, but because of its strong anti-bacterial and general immune-system-boosting properties, it can help them get over the cold and cough quicker. I'm not a fan of adding honey or any sugar to drinks generally, as they don't need the sweetness, but when children are feeling under the weather a little honey in a lemon drink can lift their spirits. See the section on sugars (page 86), for a reminder of which honeys are best. They are definitely not all equal!

Vitamin C

If kids are feeling up to eating something, focus on boosting their vitamin C intake – this antioxidant can help them recover more quickly and keep them from getting another bug straight afterwards, which can happen if your child's immune system is challenged by the cold virus. While I remember as a child sucking the bright orange, so nice to have, supplements, I don't use these with Maya because they're not necessary, and they're high in sugar. I make up fresh fruit smoothies and serve them with a curly straw – Maya loves them. You can also sneak lots of vitamin C into their food – chop a kiwi fruit into their yoghurt, throw blueberries or raspberries into their cereal or mash them on toast. A mid-morning snack bowl of fresh fruits, chopped up, is a good snack rich in vitamin C that will also give them some energy. Satsumas, clementines, mandarins appeal to all kids, so if they're wanting a little snack to nibble on while they watch a comfort-video, these pack some vitamin C punch too.

Non-dairy foods

Mention colds and snotty noses to many mums in the playground and they say you should avoid dairy products, as they're supposedly mucus-forming. I have never found this to be the case, and scientific research doesn't show it either – you can still eat dairy and have a clear nose and chest. However, many of you cut dairy down when your kids are snuffly. I don't have a problem with this, but since dairy produce is a major source of calcium, one of the most essential nutrients our children need to build strong bones and teeth, you should make sure they're eating plenty of other non-dairy sources.

Non-dairy calcium-containing foods

Small-boned fish such as sardines, crab, prawns, pulses like chickpeas, kidney beans (both can be made into pâtés and dips such as hummus – a favourite in my house) tofu, fortified soya milk and yoghurt, almonds, brazil nuts, peanuts, tahini (another reason for choosing hummus), white bread, white muffins, pitta bread.

Since in this country we still fortify white flour with calcium, how about white toast spread with smooth peanut butter or hummus for a comforting calcium-rich snack, or a smoothie made with banana and soya yoghurt with added calcium. Another quick comfort food Maya likes if she's feeling under the weather is pasta with hummus stirred in. You could also stir hummus into a vegetable soup to give it that creamy taste that appeals to kids.

Essential oils to ease a fever

* Eucalyptus
* Lavender
* Tea tree
* Chamomile roman
* Peppermint (in a room diffuser only)

I like to use a combination of equal measures of eucalyptus and lavender. If your child's fever is peaking, half fill a washing-up bowl with lukewarm water, add 10 drops of essential oil and mix. Make a compress with a clean handkerchief, soak in the solution and wring out. Gently bathe your child (avoiding the genitals, as they're too sensitive for oils) around the forehead, underarms, groin and lower back – rinsing and cooling the compress and repeating until the fever subsides.

To make an inhalation for under-fives, make a blend of the following oils: tea tree (8 drops), chamomile roman (7 drops), eucalyptus (10 drops). For over-fives, tea tree (8 drops), red thyme (10 drops), chamomile roman (7 drops).

Use 3 drops in a diffuser or using the water-bowl method, three times a day.

Constipation

Many of us unfortunately know how agonizingly painful constipation can be, and that's talking as adults who understand what's going on or not going on in our body, so no guesses needed as to how painful the whole issue is for a child. Technically speaking, childhood constipation is caused by an abnormal amount of waste matter building up in the lower bowel, which then becomes so hard and uncomfortable that the child is either unable, or afraid, to pass it, with the result that the waste in the bowel becomes even more compacted, thereby exacerbating the condition.

WHAT CAUSES IT?

Constipation can be caused by all sorts of factors, some of them quite complex on an emotional and psychological level. I've found with Maya that new foods either at home or at friends' houses can cause her gut to react sensitively. This is always one of the tell-tale signs that she's taking a while to adapt. Emotional distress also gets translated into digestive problems and constipation. If I've been working particularly hard and haven't been around as much, her smile and eyes might suggest that the changes haven't really bothered her, but her tummy aches and she has difficulty passing a stool. Maya's gut has always been her sensitive area, ever since I picked her up from the orphanage and brought her back to England; at that time nothing would stay in her body – food was literally passing straight through and giving her horrendous diarrhoea. Now constipation is more likely to be a reaction to emotional upset, but as with other kids, a minor illness such as a cold or chest infection may also affect her gut in the short term. Sometimes children deliberately hold in motions after a bout of diarrhoea in case they have an 'accident'. In the case of the son of a friend of mine, because after a long period of constipation one stool had ripped his anus he understandably did everything that he could to avoid the potentially painful process of going to the loo.

Sometimes medication such as a mild laxative may be necessary, but with most constipated kids checking a few things out and making tweaks to their diet can help kickstart the gut into moving. Be patient though – if you get stressed out about them not going to the loo it will only make them more anxious, which in turn might make their little bodies clamp up.

Over-enthusiastic potty training on the part of parents may be to blame, too. If you put your child under too much pressure to perform on the potty, they may deliberately choose not to do so when they're angry. Another extreme reaction is that of the child I once saw in my practice who eventually had to have her bowel emptied in hospital. Her parents, who had put her 'accidents' down to laziness, had scolded her so much that she had become frightened to go to the toilet. It's vital that you use positive feedback and do not criticize your child. If you think it will help them, and they're old enough to understand, try introducing a reward system by recording lavatorial 'successes' on a chart, rewarding them for every star, or collection of stars, that they achieve. Until they have established regular toilet habits, try to get into the habit of praising younger children and giving them a little treat each time they pass a stool. Gently encouraging your child to go to the toilet regularly will help them start to feel more confident and less scared that they'll have an 'accident'.

Constipation can also be caused by an intolerance or allergy, for example to wheat or dairy produce. If you suspect that your child becomes constipated after eating a specific type of food, keep a food diary for a couple of weeks (see page 122), also recording when the child goes to the loo and whether – and, if so, when – they have a stomach-ache, headache or other symptom. Having analysed the food diary, if you think that you can see a pattern, give your child less of the suspect food. If this strategy has positive results, ask your doctor to refer you to a paediatric dietician for advice on how best to balance your child's diet.

WHAT CAN YOU DO?

First check how much fluid they're drinking – lack of fluid, especially in the summer months or when you have the central heating blasting away, can be one of the commonest reasons why children get bunged up. Try to get them to drink plenty of plain water – if they're reluctant water-drinkers put it in fun cups, give them a straw, etc. (See page 100 for more tips on how to increase kids' water intake.) And because water is far more hydrating than sweet drinks, and therefore better able to soften a stool, serve only water with meals.

Sometimes too much milk (some kids can drink in the region of 1 litre a day, after all!) can aggravate a constipated gut, in which case try to just use the milk in cooking, on cereals, etc, rather than giving it to them to drink. This isn't always the

case, but some friends do find that milk bungs up their kids who already have a tendency to be constipated. Chamomile tea is very soothing for a constipated gut, so try them with some, either (safely) hot, or cooled.

I am a big fan of using a little good quality aloe vera juice for constipation. It is a little bitter, but it can be mixed with fresh juice or water and is great for helping to get a lazy gut moving. The usual dose is between 1 and 3 ounces per day.

When buying aloe vera juice, do check to make sure that the one you select is derived from aloe vera gel, not from aloe latex, as the latex can be too potent a laxative for kids. Also make sure the juice product contains a minimum of 98% aloe vera and that it does not have any aloin or aloe-emoin compounds, the key substances in aloe latex. You should also look for the 'IASC-certified' seal; it is allowed only on products manufatured to standards set by the International Aloe Science Council.

Be sure to drink aloe vera juice between meals to let it work it's magic.

Give kids raw vegetables to snack on, such as cucumber batons, and dried fruits such as nice plump soft prunes and figs (don't go for the hard-as-rock ones, they're more likely to get tossed aside – the semi-dried ones are far more appealing and yummily sweet).

WATCH OUT FOR THE JUNK

As Jamie Oliver found in his *School Dinners* project, kids who eat junk food are far more likely to suffer from constipation. Of course there are times when corners need to be cut, and we all

Fast-moving fruits

Certain fruits seem to have a particularly strong laxative effect, including figs, dates, apricots, papayas, prunes, rhubarb and soft fruits such as plums. A small portion of fig and apricot purée can soon get the bowel going, and a little fruit purée can be given to children as young as four months old. Having first been cooked to soften them, figs and dried fruits, for example, can be puréed and mixed with yoghurt, added to fresh fruit smoothies or served as an accompaniment to ice cream. You could also give your child a small glass of prune juice every day, either on its own or mixed with freshly squeezed orange juice.

What about a little massage?

When Maya will let me and isn't too ticklish, I massage her feet very gently with either a base massage oil (other kids have got on well with patchouli oil, which is an excellent intestinal cleansing oil) or a blend, taking 6 drops patchouli, 4 drops geranium, 15 drops mandarin diluted in 30ml vegetable base oil, then, to get things shifting, rub her tummy in a clockwise direction, starting at the lower left-hand side by the groin and rubbing right up to beneath her breasts, across and down the other side. This can help all the gut muscles to relax and move with ease, which is especially important when your child is becoming anxious and upset about not being able to go to the loo.

have to resort to the odd takeaway if we're travelling, etc., but because sweet and fatty foods tend to have a constipating effect, make sure your child isn't eating too many fast foods, crisps or chocolates. Reserve them for treats – even as rewards for regular toilet habits – and restrict your child to a couple of pieces of chocolate, for example, rather than a whole bar. (See 'I want some sweets!' on page 85.) Children who are allowed to over-indulge in convenience-type foods are also less likely to eat fruit, vegetables and whole grains, all of which are essential providers of fibre, which swells in the presence of water and stimulates the gut to move. All fruits and vegetables contain fibre, so the more of them your child eats, and the more water he drinks, the less likely he will be to become constipated. But

remember that fibre needs plenty of water to help it swell and work its magic – if you boost the fibre, and not the water, this can make constipation ten times worse.

If your child is fussy about eating chunks of vegetables, try disguising them in pasta sauces, perhaps puréeing tomato sauce with aubergines, carrots, onions and peppers. Cereals and pulses are also good sources of fibre, so try sneaking some chickpeas into home-made soups or chicken rissoles, using hummus in your child's sandwiches, or in a little bowl for him to dip cucumber or carrot batons into.

REMEDIES

You shouldn't give your child a laxative unless recommended by your doctor; however, the following supplements loosen your child's stools by adding bulk, which naturally improves the way the bowel works. One very important fact to remember with all the following remedies, though, is that they need enough water to help them work. If children don't drink enough water, these bulking agents can make their stools even harder.

Psyllium seed

This seed comes from a species of plantain called *Plantago psyllium*, and is a great source of fibre. You can buy powdered psyllium seed husks from health-food stores. I suggest you use only the seed husks and not the seeds, as the seeds can lodge in intestinal pockets and cause irritation. Dissolve the powdered husks in your child's fresh fruit juice, or in their cereal, porridge for example – but you need to get them to eat them as quickly as you can after you've mixed them as they tend to swell and can make the juice very thick and unappetizing. For kids over the age of two, the suggested dose is one flat teaspoon in water or juice – chased with another glass of water.

Flaxseed

Flaxseed is another great bulking agent, and since flax is also a very good source of the essential fatty acids and omega oils, this can be a good way to get their gut going healthily. What you need to remember with flaxseeds is that the essential fatty acids need to be kept as fresh as possible – heat and time can cause them to break down, so I suggest keeping them in your freezer and grinding small amounts of them down at a time. This is worth remembering when you shop – the best health-food stores will keep flaxseed in the fridge.

Ground flaxseeds go well in porridge (as you'll see from my recipes, pages 218–220), or a fruit smoothie, but like psyllium you can also mix them into juice or water. Like psyllium they also tend to thicken quickly, so children need to eat or drink them quickly afterwards. Dose-wise, for kids over two it's one teaspoon per cup of water, with a cup of water to drink afterwards.

Bran

Although bran is usually a little too high in fibre to merit being included in most kids' diets, if your child suffers from constipation you can add a little bran to their cereal or porridge – a teaspoon a day. The only kids who won't benefit from this are children who have an allergy or intolerance to wheat.

A word of warning

The harsher laxatives such as senna, which, rather than add bulk to your child's stool, work by irritating their bowel, are far too fierce for a child unless specifically prescribed by your doctor.

Sometimes tougher action's needed

If, having tried the above tips, your child still remains constipated, visit your doctor, who may prescribe a mild laxative. Don't abandon my nutritional advice, however, because the more you can do to help relieve your child's constipation through food, the less they will need to rely on laxative drugs. Above all, remember to be relaxed about your child's eating and toilet habits. Uptight children are likely to develop bowel problems, so the more you can do to calm them down, the fewer problems you'll all experience.

Diabetes

The most common type of diabetes, Type 1 or insulin dependent diabetes, normally develops during childhood. If you are the parent of a child with diabetes you are by no means alone, as there is evidence that it may be affecting more people than it did ten years ago. Currently approximately 1.6 million people in the UK suffer from diabetes (this includes Type 2 diabetes, which is not usually seen in children, but a few cases have been diagnosed recently). Although there is a suspicion that this increase in numbers could relate to changes in the environment, such as altered diet or different exposures to infections, Type 1 diabetes only seems to develop in people who have inherited particular genes from their parents.

WHAT CAUSES IT?

Diabetes is all to do with the hormone insulin, which enables body cells to use and store the sugar glucose. In kids who have Type 1 diabetes, the cells in the pancreas suddenly stop making insulin and the lack of this hormone causes a build-up of glucose in the blood, which disturbs the body's biochemical balance. Unused glucose is then excreted, as the body tries to rid itself of this potentially toxic substance by making large volumes of urine and giving your child an unquenchable thirst. When the blood sugar is too high kids usually feel exhausted, as the body is unable to use the sugar they take in as fuel, and they can also lose lots of weight – partly due to the fact that the body tries to glean enough energy to survive by breaking down fat and protein stores in the body. Another symptom of uncontrolled diabetes is that kids can just go off their food, which since they're frequently losing weight can get them into a horrible, worrying vicious cycle. In rarer situations the abnormally high blood sugar levels found in uncontrolled diabetes cause abdominal pain, vomiting and rapid breathing, and if not treated can cause confusion, lack of consciousness and coma. If you have any suspicion that your child might be diabetic, you **must** phone your doctor straight away, as urgent medical treatment is necessary.

Now this all sounds rather scary, but if diabetes is well managed your child's life can be completely normal and healthy – there are after all many famous people, including Gary Hall, the Olympic gold medal swimmer, Wasim Akran, the Pakistani fast bowler, and the Hollywood actress Halle Berry, who suffer from this condition. Eating and living healthily will help the body control its blood sugar levels.

As I've mentioned, there are generally two types of diabetes, Type 1 and Type 2. Type 1 is also known as insulin-dependent diabetes, and is the more common type found in children, whereas Type 2 used to be found only in overweight adults and older people. Nowadays, however, when we have such a big childhood obesity problem, we are also finding for the first time small numbers of kids with Type 2 diabetes, simply because their body fat levels have become so high that their pancreas can't produce enough insulin to look after blood sugar levels. In the majority of cases of Type 2 diabetes, kids who succeed in losing excess weight can usually manage their blood sugar well without much medical intervention – so your doctor and dietician will arrange for them to go on a healthy weight-loss diet and get plenty of exercise to help the body get back into shape.

But since Type 1 diabetes is more common in kids, I'm going to concentrate on how to manage this.

GET THE A TEAM

As a first port of call you should be referred by your doctor to a specialist paediatrician and dietician who can take you through all the fine details of juggling medication, food and lifestyle. Diabetics UK can not only offer practical advice, but runs great summer camps for kids, support groups for parents, and above all can reassure you that you're not alone and that your child being diagnosed with diabetes is not the end of the world. You may hear horror stories from elderly friends and relatives about people with diabetes losing their sight, suffering from kidney damage and even having their legs chopped off, but that isn't the case these days – we have amazingly sophisticated medication, great support, so much more information and research that enables diabetics to lead perfectly healthy lives. Listen to your diabetic team, get some good resources, read through and get to grips with the following simple points, and then close your ears to every tale that goes around.

I would also offer a word of warning about listening to so-called alternative practitioners who suggest that your child shouldn't take conventional medical treatments, such as insulin injections. This advice is extremely dangerous and you must ignore it. Kids with Type 1 diabetes need to take their insulin as prescribed – complementary treatments such as acupuncture can be used, but only as complementary, not alternative.

MANAGING DIABETES THROUGH DIET

When you're diabetic, it's all about maintaining as normal blood sugar levels as possible. Two useful terms to familiarize yourself with are **hyperglycaemia**, which means too high levels of sugar in the blood, and **hypoglycaemia**, which is the opposite, too low. Your doctor and or diabetic nurse will show you how to test the amount of glucose in your child's blood and how to record the results. The measurements obtained from the tests allow you to work out how much insulin your child needs to be given by injection.

How much insulin your child needs to take often depends on what they've eaten and how much exercise/activity they've had, but there will also be mad moments when for various reasons – they have a cold or stomach bug, are growing more than usual – it all seems to go haywire and either high blood sugar levels can start appearing, or they suffer from hypoglycaemic episodes, which we all seem to abbreviate to hypos (more about these later).

First, with your dietician and doctor, you will work out the types and amounts of food your child will eat, when they should eat them and how to tailor the insulin injections around them. Generally speaking, a diet for a child with diabetes is virtually identical to any healthy eating diet for a child, with consistent proportions of fats, protein and carbohydrates, but you need to be pretty consistent about when they eat because you rely on insulin injections to work alongside the food – there's no buffer in the body that allows for the type of flexibility non-diabetic children have.

I suggest you read Chapter 1, which takes you through what a healthy kid's diet should be, but in addition, I just want to answer some of the most commonly asked questions.

Can my diabetic child eat chocolate and other sweet foods?

Kids with diabetes can include some sweet foods in their general day-to-day diet – yes, a diabetic diet does not need to be sugar-free! As with all kids, it's best not to have too much refined, processed sweet foods in their diet.

The GI diet (see page 83) is something it's useful to be aware of as the parent of a diabetic child. However, it's not infallible – treat it as a guide. The GI index is a useful tool in managing diabetes, as it's an indicator of sugar in all sorts of foods, not just the obviously sweet ones, and it gives you crucial information on the other components of the food, which mitigate the effects of the sugars. Even for diabetic kids it's fine on occasions to have the high GI foods like chocolate and biscuits, but as always, they're best eaten as part of a meal, say a pudding after a good healthy meal, as the body deals best with the sugar they contain when there is fibre, fat, and protein from other foods around. Use my yummy cake and dessert recipes for inspiration on how to cook delicious treat foods for kids without always having to resort to highly processed chocolate and biscuits.

But as with all kids, they will most likely want to have the odd processed treat so that they feel normal and like everyone else. If you ban them completely you may find them bingeing on sweet junk in secret, which is far more damaging for their body and in the short term could send their blood sugar levels up astronomically quickly and can cause hyperglycaemic complications, which need immediate medical intervention.

Do I need to buy diabetic products?

No. I don't like them – they make kids with diabetes feel unnecessarily different when they don't need to, since eating as a diabetic is really the same as eating healthily for any child, and because the sweetness in them comes from artificial sweeteners they can cause tummy upsets and diarrhoea if you OD on them. They're expensive too.

How can I tell if their blood sugar's going too low?

The symptoms of hypoglycaemia are sweating, dizziness, confusion, tummy-ache.

What do I do if they go hypo?

You need to give them something very sweet that will be quickly absorbed – a high GI food such as a fresh fruit juice, a biscuit, honey and milk, chocolate. In extreme circumstances, if they won't eat or drink anything and you can't correct the hypo this usual way, you will have to give them an injection of glucagon, so make sure you chat through this with your diabetic team.

How do we know how well we're getting on?

Your doctor and diabetic team will check on your child's progress by doing special blood tests, but you will also probably be asked to take regular pin-prick samples of blood to check on how much insulin you need to give them.

I've heard that diabetic kids need to watch their fat intake – is this correct?

Yes, you're right. People with diabetes tend to have an increased risk of heart disease, so you need to keep their diet generally healthy: lots of fresh fruits, vegetables, lean proteins (see Chapter 1),

but pay particular attention to trying to get them to eat plenty of beans, lentils, oats and moderate amounts of fruits, as these are high in soluble fibre and have the additional benefit of keeping down cholesterol levels, which are often higher in diabetics as they get older. The fats best for kids are vegetable oils and the omega oils (oily fish, seeds, nuts, hemp oil, etc., see page 76), rather than the saturated animal fats.

Some diabetics can fall into the trap of thinking that sugar is the only thing they need to watch and that they can eat as much fat as they like. This isn't the case – sugars are part of a healthy diabetic diet, and if they OD on fat they can become overweight, which is not what you want for their whole body, including their heart. Lean mean fighting machines are what you want!

What should I do when they're ill?

Illness, however minor, even just a cold, will undoubtedly send a diabetic child's blood sugar levels up, which may mean they start showing the signs of hyperglycaemia – excessive thirst, tummy-ache, wanting to wee a lot, etc. You need to keep on top of this and treat the high levels by still giving them their insulin, as diabetic ketoacidosis, which is when the ketones go sky high, can cause a coma that can be fatal. **Don't stop giving children insulin because they're feeling unwell**. If they're not up to eating something substantial, you need to get carbohydrate and sugar inside them to balance the insulin regime by giving them milky drinks, fruit juices, yoghurt with banana or soups such as leek and potato – something easy to eat, but containing starch or sugar. Your team should be able to help you work through this scenario, but if you're at all unsure, seek medical advice straight away.

Are snacks good?

If kids are leading a full and active life, they all need a little something in between meals, as the days can be so long. See page 49 for good snack suggestions, and bear in mind that sometimes your child might need a more substantial snack such as a glass of cold milk and a healthy biscuit before bed to prevent night-time hypo or waking up hypo in the morning. Discuss this with your team once you see how their blood sugars pan out.

EXERCISE

Kids need to be active to be healthy, and this definitely includes kids with diabetes. We need to keep their hearts healthy and make sure they don't put on too much weight. But exercise 'uses up' blood sugar, so you need to take care that they eat sufficient carbohydrate before they exercise, otherwise they might suffer a hypo. Every child is different, and how vigorous the exercise is will affect what they need to eat beforehand, but this could be anything from a sandwich, banana, or a biscuit. After they've finished it's ideal if you can give them a little snack containing both carbohydrate and protein, such as a natural yoghurt and banana, or some nuts and raisins (not for under-fives), or a peanut butter or hummus sandwich. Remember, if the exercise takes their blood sugar down too low you need to get some sugar inside them quickly – it's a good idea therefore for kids to carry around some glucose tablets for those emergencies. But do encourage them to keep active, and if they get anxious and lose their confidence for fear of their blood sugar going too low, tell them about how famous sports stars have got over their fears. Note that there can be a delay between finishing the exercise and the blood sugar level dropping, so make sure they have something to eat afterwards and don't assume that because their blood sugar reading is OK it will stay like that – it could change an hour or so afterwards. If this happens a lot, get in touch with your team, as your child's insulin regime might need changing.

It's understandable that diabetc kids should want the occasional processed treat. If you're doing everything else right, it will be fine, so long as it's part of a balanced meal.

Diarrhoea

Kids can develop diarrhoea to differing degrees and for many different reasons and not all of them are physical – it could be that your child is overly anxious about something. When I picked my daughter Maya up from the orphanage in India, her way of exhibiting her distress at not knowing what was happening to her was for her gut to reject everything I put inside her. She had profuse diarrhoea for days, very worrying because she was losing vast amounts of fluid and in the heat of India that wasn't easy to compensate for. I thought it must be a bug, but tests back in England showed nothing – it was just Maya's way of responding to a big life event. As soon as she started to settle down with me at home, her gut quickly followed suit.

Sometimes your child might just be feeling anxious – emotional upsets, from being bullied at school, to being unsettled by a change in routine, to a parent maybe being away or absent from home for abnormally long periods of time, can sometimes trigger a temporary bout of diarrhoea. You may also find they get a quick bout of diarrhoea if you've been treating them for constipation (see page 166), as the gut tends to go completely the opposite way before it settles down. It's therefore best to wait a day or two before changing their diet again.

On the physical side, it could just be that their gut isn't able to digest a new food, or deal with the quantities of foods you're expecting them to cope with, or that they're having too much of one type of food, say fresh fruits or beans and lentils – just make sure their diet has variety and isn't dominated with too much of anything.

When you introduce foods children haven't had before, you may find to begin with that their stool changes consistency and most likely that it becomes somewhat runny. This is usually down to the fact that their digestion may not break down the new foods completely, so there may be undigested bits of food in the stool. If you persevere by keeping with small amounts of the new foods, their guts should soon adapt – it's just a shock being faced with something new to deal with. If the stool contains a lot of mucus, that suggests that the gut seems to be having a bit of an issue with breaking the food down, so it may be best to lay off that food for a couple of weeks or try mashing or puréeing the food, as this can make it easier to digest. Too much roughage – wholegrain cereals, wholemeal bread, fruits, vegetables, legumes, lentils – as healthy as these foods are, can be too much for them.

IS THE FOOD TOO SPICY OR RICH?

Even though I thought Maya would be used to spicy foods, like the simple daal they served at the orphanage, I've found that she takes a while to get used to new spices. There is no reason why a young gut can't tolerate spices, but sometimes, with anything new and specially with the heat of some things like chilli, you may find they have a loose stool before they become used to it.

If you start putting oil or butter in their food, or cheese in vegetable purées, you may again find that the change in fat levels may trigger a little short-term diarrhoea. The same thing may happen if you start giving them dried fruits, which although they are great foods for little ones to eat, still contain a lot of sugar; the increase in sugar levels, like the fat increase, can again unsettle their young gut.

FOOD-POISONING

If you suspect your child has food-poisoning, it's best to keep to water and simple dry foods, like rice cakes, plain dry toast, plain rice. See your doctor. The most common food-borne bugs are the following.

Salmonella

Although this is one of the most virulent food-poisoning bugs, it's thankfully not the most common. It causes severe diarrhoea, high fever, sweating and loss of fluid. Most commonly caught from undercooked eggs and chicken, but can also be caught from salads and cooked foods that have been left out of the fridge for several hours. You must seek medical attention immediately if you suspect your child has this bug.

Campylobacter

The most common food-poisoning bug, this gives our children diarrhoea, stomach cramps and tends to make them feel and be sick too. Most commonly found in chicken, shellfish and meat.

Bacillus cereus

Mums can be surprised with this one, because while you may think rice is a very safe and easy food (which if cooked and sorted properly it is), *Bacillus cereus* is found in rice that's been kept warm or improperly heated. For this reason I always make sure that Maya eats her rice straight away and put any leftovers straight into the fridge as soon as it has cooled down. I tend to use the rice again only as fried rice, as the high heat of the wok kills the unfriendly bugs. Even though this bug can give your child a very severe bout of diarrhoea and/or vomiting, it tends to pass (excuse the pun!) very quickly.

E.coli

This tends to be found in beef products that haven't been cooked properly –the raw-middle barbecued beef burger nightmare – so make sure you cook beef products all the way through. *E. coli* can spread like wildfire through schools and cause a mad rush to the loos. You can also get it from raw milk, so never give your child unpasteurised milk.

Listeria

This is the one that pregnant women fear, but unfortunately it can be dangerous for little ones too. Listeria tends to be mostly found in soft, mould-ripened cheeses (such as Brie and Camembert) and pâtés, but it can also be found in prepacked salad and hams. Because this is, however, one of the least likely causes of food-poisoning, I still give Maya soft cheese and ham and indeed salads, since we tend to be very careful with basic food hygiene in the house and she's a fit and strong little girl. There are risks with most things we do, and becoming paranoid is not the answer.

When do symptoms appear?

You will usually find that food-poisoning symptoms such as diarrhoea and vomiting start after a few hours, though sometimes it can actually take days before the bugs have reproduced enough in your child's body to make them feel ill.

Keep them at home

It's definitely best to keep your child away from schools and play groups when they have diarrhoea. However much you try to instill good hand hygiene, little ones will always put their hands where you don't want them to and these food bugs can spread incredibly easily.

Do they need antibiotics?

Many types of food-poisoning bugs are resistant to antibiotics and tend to clear up by themselves. Don't be too eager to take antibiotics, as sometimes the body needs to be allowed to fight and build up immune strength on its own. However, sometimes they are necessary, so discuss the pros and cons with your doctor.

What if they won't take anything?

While they're feeling sick or have diarrhoea, if they can't take or keep any food down, there is little point forcing them – what you need to remember is that getting **fluid** down them is essential. In order to ensure that your child's electrolyte balance stays healthy, it's best to give them some rehydration fluids. You can buy these from the pharmacy, or you could make your own if you can't leave the house – all you need is salt and sugar. Take a pinch ($1/3$ teaspoon) of salt, a pinch of lo-salt (for some potassium) and 1 teaspoon sugar to 250ml of water – literally just use the boiled water to dissolve the sugar and salt and let it cool down.

As they start to feel a little better and you want to start giving them something solid, I'd opt for a rice cake or two, some freshly cooked rice, a piece of dry toast, a mashed banana (although this is fruit, it's settling, sweet, comforting and can be usefully binding to a runny gut). Another staple for us is a little mashed potato, but I don't add any oil or butter.

WATCH THE DAIRY PRODUCE

When your child is recovering from a diarrhoea or sickness bug, their body can become temporarily intolerant of dairy. The exception is live bio yoghurt, as these contain natural bacteria such as lactobacillus and bifida which can help your child recover. Antibiotics frequently strip out all the good bacteria from your child's gut at the same time as zapping the bad ones, so taking a small pot of live probiotic yoghurt each day for a couple of weeks at least can help re-colonize their gut with healthy bacteria. Live bio yoghurt, which is the only one we have in our house, can also help prevent food-poisoning diarrhoea-causing bugs and improve your child's ability to digest food, so they are a good thing to have in your child's diet. Children sometimes like yoghurt because it's cooling and soothing to eat, so try a little bowlful with some honey drizzled over.

PECTIN

Although too many fresh fruits are hard for an unsettled gut to deal with, pectin, a form of soluble fibre found in fruits and vegetables, especially apples, carrots, rice and bananas, can help to reduce diarrhoea by absorbing water and important minerals in the bowel. So you could try your child with a raw carrot stick or some apple (still with it's skin on) if they're old enough to chew.

Grated carrot and apple is another option. Blueberries are also good, not only because they contain pectin, but also because they contain anthocyanosides, which have a mild antibiotic action that could just help fight off a gut bug or two.

What about a little massage?

Make a blend of essential oils: 5 drops of ginger, 8 drops of sandalwood, 8 drops of chamomile roman, all mixed into 30ml base oil (see page 169 for how to massage). If your child has a sore bottom, try chamomile oinments such as Kamilosan available from good health-food stores and chemists and apply to your child's bottom to reduce soreness and redness.

Eczema

Eczema is rife in my family, so I know it can be a very distressing condition for both parents and their kids – from the young ones who don't understand enough about their skin condition not to scratch (which makes it ten times worse incidentally, so try to do everything possible to stop them!) to the older ones who find their different skin texture and appearance affects their confidence and can even be a source of bullying at school. Of course how much eczema affects kids varies greatly, ranging from the odd patch on their elbows and behind their knees to those who can be literally covered from top to toe, and who need to have bandages on at night to stop them scratching. Eczema is thought to affect up to a fifth of all children and usually appears before they're eighteen months old, but they can also develop it later on, especially if they suffer from hay fever, asthma or any other atopic/allergy type condition. But the good news is that the majority of kids with this skin condition, which is also known as atopic eczema or dermatitis, grow out of it by the time they're fifteen to sixteen.

WHAT CAUSES IT?

Eczema is an inflammatory skin condition, causing dry, itchy skin that can drive kids wild enough to want to scratch and claw away at their bodies, making the skin break and bleed and leading to secondary infections. Immunologically, it's thought to be an allergic condition where the body over-reacts to something and produces too much immunoglobulin G, aka IgG or Immunoglobulin E, IgE antibodies. Genes definitely play a part, as is the case in my family. But there are also environmental and lifestyle factors, as well as diet, that can have a big impact on whether your child suffers from eczema.

Incidentally, the mother's diet during pregnancy is also a factor in whether their child suffers from eczema. If you eat a diet rich in vitamin E you are less likely to give birth to a child with an allergy – also if you avoid the most common food allergens, namely cow's milk, eggs, citrus fruits, chocolate, food colourings, peanuts and peanut oil, especially if you have a strong history of eczema or allergic conditions that have reacted badly to any of the

afore-mentioned foods. Preliminary studies have also shown that it could be worth taking a probiotic supplement of lactobacillus while pregnant, as this could reduce the chance of your child suffering from eczema.

And of course there is also some evidence that breast-feeding helps prevent allergic disease. One reason for this is that it delays the introduction of foods (such as cow's milk or cow's-milk formula) that may trigger the allergic process. However, it is also thought that specific agents in the breast milk may have protective potential. For instance, vitamin C causes known anti-allergic actions in the body, and low intakes of this nutrient are associated with increased risk of allergic disease. In a study published this month in the European Journal of Clinical Nutrition, Finnish researchers assessed the relationship between the intake of vitamin C by breast-feeding mothers and the health of their babies. Higher concentrations of vitamin C in breast milk were associated with a 70% reduction in risk of eczema. Researchers also found that higher vitamin C intakes from the diet, and not from supplements, translated into higher vitamin C concentration in breast milk. This study suggests that eating foods rich in vitamin C (citrus fruits, berries and green leafy vegetables) during breast-feeding may prevent allergic diseases such as eczema in children.

WHAT TO DO IF YOUR CHILD HAS ECZEMA

The first thing is to target oily fish and other foods rich in omega-3 fatty acids, because these foods can really help to take the edge and the bite off the inflammatory aspects of the condition (see omega oils, page 110). However, since most kids aren't that great at eating sardines, mackerel, herrings,

etc., I would also give your child an omega oil supplement containing 1,000mg of omega-3 fatty acids and 300mg of gammalinoleic acid (GLA). You need to be patient, as it can take several weeks for the skin to calm down, and once their skin has improved they need to keep taking the supplement.

Make sure their diet is generally high in plenty of fresh fruits (apart from citrus fruits, especially oranges) and vegetables, lots of foods rich in vitamin C, in other words, and that they also tend to eat vegetable fats such as olive and hemp, flax or linseed oil instead of butter and animal fats – not only do saturated animal fats adversely affect the way the magic omega oils work, but also vegetable oils are rich in vitamin E, which is great for troubled skin.

LOOK AT THE ISSUE OF FOOD ALLERGENS

When kids with eczema avoid the offending food allergen, their skin can return virtually to normal – it can literally be life-changing. It takes a lot of patience and determination to put your child on a food-restricted diet (see page 190 for how to do this), and it's important to explain to them that you're trying to make their skin better, so they can at least try to understand why you're saying no to what can sometimes be their favourite foods. You could have some sort of incentive chart, so that if they go each day without eating the suspected food allergen, they get a treat at the end of the week. Try as best you can to make the rest of the family's foods similar, so that you're not dangling forbidden fruits under their nose. Nowadays there are so many great alternative foods – for instance, if you have to cut out cow's milk, all the supermarkets stock goat's and sheep's milk and cheese, which can be used in cooking in the same way. The more normal you make children's diet appear, the more likely they will stick to it and you'll be able to see if it makes a difference. Of course you need to weigh up the benefits – for just the odd patch of eczema behind their knee you might decide that other than trying to make their diet well-balanced, with some omega oil supplementation thrown in for good measure, it's just not worth trying to get them to exclude foods. But for more serious eczema cases, changing their diet and avoiding the offending foods can be the only way to make life bearable. I would strongly recommend seeking professional advice from a paediatric dietician if your child has severe eczema and you suspect that food allergy may be aggravating it.

The most common food allergens
* Milk – usually cow's milk, but could be sheep's or goat's (see page 189)
* Eggs
* Citrus fruits (usually oranges are the no-no)
* Seeds
* Nuts, especially peanuts
* Shellfish
* Wheat (see page 192)
* Tomatoes
* Soya (yes, soya can be a problem too, in which case you might have to use rice or oat milk)

Food additives
Colouring and preservatives are frequent culprits, particularly the azo dyes and benzoate preservatives (see page 72).

Eliminating food allergies in kids with eczema can have life-changing results.

THE LIBRARY
NORTH WEST KENT COLLEGE
DERING WAY GRAVESEND

Non-food allergens that should be suspected in cases of eczema

* Irritants – this is really important to look at, as frequently irritants have a much bigger role to play in eczema than foods.
* Detergents – enzymes used in biological washing powders can be a nightmare. Sometimes nowadays washing powders don't use the word enzymes, but generally if a powder is designed to be used at low temperatures, it will usually contain them. For enzyme-free detergents, try the organic ones.
* Soap
* Shampoo
* Household chemicals of all kinds
* Rough clothing, including wool and synthetic fibres – pure cotton is much less irritating and kinder to skin
* Heat
* Scratching – **try to stop them scratching as much as you can**. In severe cases wearing soft cotton gloves and sleep-suits at night can help. But the less they scratch, the better their skin will be.
* Hard water – think about getting a water softener installed if you live in a hard water area
* House dust
* Moulds
* Pets
* Wool

PROBIOTICS

See page 77 on probiotics (good bacteria), as research is suggesting that improving your child's balance of good versus bad bacteria in the gut could improve the way that their gut tends to let in unwanted eczema-aggravating allergens.

A NOTE ON CHINESE MEDICINE

Chinese medicine has shown some really good results in kids with severe eczema, but because of the risk of potential liver toxicity from the herbs, and sometimes from contaminants such as heavy metals, I would definitely only recommend using Chinese herbs if a specific well-trained practitioner has prescribed them for your child. Don't take risks with any self-help measures, they could backfire.

Food allergies and intolerances

As a society, we seem to be becoming more and more food-allergic – schoolteachers seldom came across a child with a peanut allergy twenty years ago, whereas now, schools and all sorts of places where children are being looked after, as well as food manufacturers, are having to take the whole issue of food allergies very seriously. Children are far more likely to have a food allergy than adults, for numerous reasons, including the fact that their immune systems take time to develop so they can over-react to foods if they're given too early – which is why we are careful about which foods we suggest you wean your child on and also what to eat as a mother if you're pregnant and have a history of allergies in your family. Luckily many children grow out of food allergies (apart from, it seems, peanut allergies, which seem to be lifelong), meaning that only 1–2% of adults have a food allergy, as opposed to 5% of children under the age of four.

WHAT IS A FOOD ALLERGY?

True food allergy is an adverse and often immediate reaction to a food or drink, caused by an over-reaction of the body's immune system to something in that particular item. Typical food allergy reactions are swollen lips, an itchy mouth, vomiting, diarrhoea, hives, eczema, coughing, runny nose, wheezing and a headache – although people seldom have all of them. The most common foods to produce an allergic reaction in children are cow's milk, peanuts, other nuts, eggs, soya milk and soya products, wheat, chocolate, sesame seeds, fish and shellfish, although virtually any food or even food additive can potentially cause an allergic reaction in your child's body. Kids may be able to tolerate a food when it's cooked, but not in its raw state.

If you suspect that your child has a food allergy, you need to see your doctor, who can refer them to a paediatrician who specializes in this area. Skin-prick tests and blood tests (RAST or cap assay) will probably be organized in order to work out what your child is allergic to. It's important to get professional help with kids who have food allergies, as not only can their reaction to the foods be very severe (see anaphylaxis, below), but also with a growing body you need to ensure that the child's diet is nutritionally balanced after having cut out the offending food or foods. It's also by speaking to an authority on allergies that you learn about alternative products that your child will be able to eat so that if possible they don't end up being isolated on a very strict diet – the more normal you can make their whole eating experience, the less likely it is that they will start to use foods as a control/power thing.

ANAPHYLAXIS

Anaphylaxis is a severe and life-threatening allergic reaction to a food or drink (or indeed to anything such as a drug or insect bite). It usually occurs after you've eaten the offending food, but it can also come from just touching it and can hit within seconds, or hours. In anaphylaxis the body produces massive amounts of histamines and other chemicals, which then cause the blood vessels to swell and the blood pressure to drop. Body-wise, your child's lips can swell, and so can the throat, which can cause problems with breathing and talking. The heart can start racing, hives and rashes can appear, so can big red wheals, and the child can start wheezing. The lowering of blood pressure can make them feel weak and even collapse. The situation is incredibly serious and frightening for everyone, and you need to immediately give them a pre–loaded junior adrenaline injection – kits are available on prescription. But usually as soon as you give them the injection they return to normal, if slightly exhausted and a little shaken by the experience.

How do you know if your child is at risk from anaphylaxis?
If your child has suffered a bad allergic reaction to any food in the past – whatever the cause – then any future reaction is also likely to be severe. If they have suffered a significant reaction to a tiny dose, or have reacted on skin contact, this might also be a sign that a larger dose may trigger a severe reaction. If they have asthma as well as allergies, a referral to a pediatrician is particularly important because asthma can put them into a higher risk category. Where foods such as nuts, seeds, shellfish and fish are concerned, even mild symptoms should not be ignored because future reactions may be severe.

How to avoid problems with your child's food allergy
Although it sounds all very scary, as an anaphylactic shock sufferer I can tell you that you soon get used to living with it – it just takes time and determination to decrease the risks of being exposed to the allergen. Above all you need to take great care: be vigilant, read labels and look for the 'hidden' allergen. If you have a peanut allergy, for instance, you can easily recognize a packet of peanuts but may miss the word 'groundnuts' in tiny print on the side of a tin of curry sauce, or the Latin word *arachis*, used to signify the presence of peanut in pharmaceutical products.

One of the hardest things I find is conveying to people with whom I come into contact (other than friends and family) how serious the food allergy is – we're not talking a little bit of bloating from eating too much pasta, we're talking a life-threatening situation if I'm exposed to the allergen. So I find myself having to be very assertive in restaurants, where proprietors are under no obligation to list ingredients. Question staff very directly and bear in mind that despite their desire to assure you that your allergens may not be present in the foods you're eating, you always have to be ready to deal with anaphylaxis – they might have been unaware of a food being put in by mistake.

Be alert to all symptoms and take them seriously. Reach for the adrenaline (epinephrine) if you think your child is beginning to show signs of a severe reaction – don't wait until you are sure. Even if adrenaline is administered, you will still need to get them to hospital as soon as possible. Make sure others in your family, friends, nursery, school, etc. know how to administer the adrenaline kit – and when. Do not be frightened of adrenaline, the dose you will give your child has very few side-effects and these will pass quickly – it literally saves their life.

The only way to avoid suffering an allergic reaction to the specific food is to avoid being in contact with it all together.

NUT ALLERGIES

Peanut allergy is the most common nut allergy and is thought to affect around one in 200 people, while other estimates put it at nearer one in 100. Very interestingly, in a recent lecture the eminent allergy consultant Dr Gideon Lac reported that in cultures where children are given peanut products from a very young age, such as Thailand, virtually no peanut allergies are reported, whereas in our society, where by comparison we are late in weaning, we seem to have a lot more allergies and serious reactions to foods. Indeed, in my practice I see mums who leave weaning until late on – nine months plus – then give a very limited range of foods, and the children can develop all sorts of allergies. While this is interesting, I am not of course advocating early weaning (the current recommendation is not before six months), and with the issue of peanuts, the Department of Health states that they should not be introduced into your child's diet before the age of three years if there is a history of atopy in your family – i.e. asthma, eczema, hay fever, food allergies. Whole nuts should not be given to children under the age of five because of the risk of choking.

The peanut is actually a member of the bean family. Tree nuts, such as pecans, walnuts and hazelnuts, and seeds, particularly sesame seeds, and kernels such as pine nuts can also cause reactions. Coconut is not a nut and therefore does not have to be avoided by those who are nut-allergic. Only those allergic to coconut need to avoid products containing it.

* Common foods that can include nuts or sesame seeds include: cakes, desserts, chocolates, sweets, fruit yoghurts, biscuits, salads, salad dressings, dips, curries, pre-made Asian sauces, chillies, stuffings and breakfast cereals.
* Other foods include pesto (pine nuts or walnuts), satay sauces (peanuts), marzipan (almonds), nougat (almonds), halva (sesame), hummus (sesame) and tahini (sesame).
* Peanuts and peanut oil (also called groundnut oil) find their way into many processed foods, such as biscuits, cakes, breakfast cereals, savoury foods, Asian foods, breads and confectionery. A reaction to refined peanut oil (found mainly in processed foods) is unlikely, but unrefined peanut oil (mainly bottled oil and found in ethnic foods) carries a higher risk.

Be aware that foods labelled as containing almonds, for example, may also contain peanuts, which are not labelled. Many products are now labelled 'may contain nuts', and because manufacturers are aware of the dangers of cross-contamination, some are opening segregated production lines.

IS FOOD INTOLERANCE THE SAME AS AN ALLERGY?

The whole area of food intolerance is pretty controversial, as some doctors completely dismiss the concept and consider that unless a child has a true clinical allergy, anything else is purely coincidence or something bordering on the child or the mum being overly obsessive about eating habits. This attitude doesn't get anyone anywhere, and I've certainly successfully treated many children for food intolerances who were really quite poorly– anything from digestive problems to rashes and headaches and unexplained fatigue. As soon as you take the food out of the equation, they can become perfectly normal healthy growing kids.

Of course there are extremes, and some overly restrictive parents, but this isn't the norm, so I think it's a good idea for parents of kids with unexplained symptoms to see whether changing their diet and removing different foods, while swapping them for something equally nutritious, can get rid of symptoms. But I would warn against being told by pseudo-nutritionists and other alternative practitioners to cut foods out of your child's diet without checking their symptoms out with your doctor, as there may be something medical going on that needs help. And you need to be so careful with changing kids' diets, to avoid them becoming deficient in essential nutrients.

Immunologically food intolerance is very different to a food allergy and it's not as serious – but I know it can cause a lot of distress for kids and their parents, although the symptoms tend to be milder. An intolerance is usually down to the body not being able to deal with a certain food as well as we'd like it to. For instance, one well-known intolerance in kids is lactose intolerance, where your child lacks enough of a special enzyme called lactase to break down the lactose, a sugar present in milk. This means that when they drink milk and take in milk products they can become bloated, have diarrhoea, feel sick, and actually be sick as their body tries to get rid of the lactose since it can't cope with it. Sometimes children like my daughter, Maya, who can't take a glass of normal cow's milk otherwise she gets awful bloating, tummy-ache and diarrhoea, are actually able to take goat's and sheep's milk. Although these still contain lactose, in Maya's case they don't seem to upset her as much – she can also tolerate cow's

milk cheese and yoghurt – but all kids vary, and some just can't take any lactose-containing foods. Lactose intolerance can be temporary, too: it can occur if your child is unwell, say with a stomach bug or a bad cold – for some reason the body just decides to take a dislike to lactose, but a few weeks later gets back to being able to tolerate it.

Here are some of the most commonly asked questions with food intolerances.

MILK INTOLERANCE

You only need to look at the supermarket shelves to know that many parents are choosing to avoid cow's milk in their child's diet, either turning to goat's or sheep's milk, or skipping animal milks altogether and drinking soya (the most popular), rice, almond or oat milk. Of course everyone has a right to feed their child whatever they like, but I'd like to discuss a few of the reasons for doing this and some of the myths around.

Numerous symptoms are blamed on cow's milk, from an overly snotty nose to bloating, constipation, eczema, migraine and diarrhoea. Before going any further, I'd like to clear up a little technical stuff. There are usually a couple of reasons why your child might feel better avoiding cow's milk – it could be they have a problem with cow's milk protein, or they may have an issue with lactose, the sugar in milk, in which case it's down to a lack of lactase, the enzyme that breaks down lactose, as I mentioned above. If it's cow's milk protein they have an intolerance to, they should still be able to tolerate other sorts of dairy milk, such as goat's and sheep's, but if it's milk sugar that's their enemy you need to go for cereal-based milks such as soya, oat, almond and rice milk.

How do I know?

Usually it's a case of avoiding all dairy milk, i.e. animal milks and their products – cheese, yoghurt, butter, cream and foods made with milk, which in the case of packaged foods will be described as lactose, milk, skimmed milk powder, cow's milk protein, casein, whey (both derivatives of milk), etc. If something is labelled lactose-free it should be fine. However, before you start cutting anything out of your little one's diet, keep a food diary for a couple of weeks, recording everything they eat and drink (with approximate quantities), and noting their symptoms alongside (see page 122). One thing you need to bear in mind throughout your food intolerance investigation is whether your child's diet was healthy and in balance before you removed the dairy from it, because so often the symptoms parents put down to dairy intolerance, such as tiredness or bloating, can in fact be due to an imbalance in diet (for example, too much fatty food, or not enough water or fruits and vegetables). Just removing a suspected offending item, in this case lactose or cow's milk protein, could mean they start eating more healthily and it's this that cures their symptoms rather than any avoidance of a specific substance. So before you start excluding lactose or cow's milk protein, check that their diet is well-balanced (see Chapter 1). Some kids can tolerate skimmed milk but not full cream, so try this change too.

If when you look at their food diary you still think dairy might be an issue, cut it out completely for a couple of weeks. This means avoiding all the aforementioned foods – milk, skimmed milk, yoghurt, cream, butter, cheese, etc.

Does my child need to take supplements?

Ideally when you take one group of foods out of your child's diet you should make sure you include another source of the key nutrients this food usually provides. With milk this means calcium, so you need to look to non-dairy sources such as fortified soya milks, green leafy vegetables, pulses, seeds such as sesame, small-boned fish such as sardines. You shouldn't need to give a calcium supplement, as a couple of weeks without dairy while the intolerance is being investigated shouldn't cause their bones any harm – but after a couple of weeks, see your doctor or dietician to discuss whether a supplement is necessary.

Probiotics and prebiotics

Probiotics are live good bacteria, such as lactobacilli, which if taken as tablets, drinks, in yoghurts, etc., improve the balance of good versus bad bacteria in your child's gut. (See page 77.)

What do I substitute?

You have a choice. If you think it's cow's milk protein that upsets your child, you could try goat's or sheep's cheese products – as well as the milks, there are delicious cheeses and yoghurts in most supermarkets. You can also buy butters from some delis, or use one of the dairy-free margarines to cook with. Olive oil spreads can sometimes be dairy-free (check the labels, but you also need to check that they don't contain hydrogenated fats or trans fatty acids, as these are bad for the heart). Incorporating sheep's and goat's milk products into the child's diet for at least two to three weeks, within a well-balanced eating plan, may relieve all their symptoms – in which case it's likely they've just got an issue with cow's milk.

What do I need to avoid? What about soya?

If they don't get any better, you need to look at going dairy-free altogether, which is more difficult and potentially damaging for kids, if you don't take care.

> ## Avoid foods labelled as containing any of these ingredients
>
> * casein
> * cow's milk protein
> * lactose
> * milk
> * skimmed milk powder
> * whey

* You need to avoid all cow's, goat's and sheep's milk products, and foods containing the ingredients listed in the box.
* You may want to try soya, rice, almond or oat milk, either to glean some calcium or as an alternative to add to drinks, cereals, etc. These taste different (one way of putting it), and may not suit your child's tastebuds, but you can disguise them by adding honey or using them in cooking.

I do have some reservations about including lots of soya in your child's diet – so much so that I use only a little soya milk at home. Soya milk and soya yogurt are implicated in the fact that in Great Britain we have declining sperm counts and a host of fertility problems, as new research into soya's impact on western diets reveals. A team led by Sheena Lewis, Professor of Reproductive Medicine at Queen's University, Belfast, has conducted studies linking soya to reduced male fertility. Scientists believe chemicals in the soya bean mimic the female hormone oestrogen. Other research has linked the hormonal chemicals in soya to certain cancers, brain disease and developmental abnormalities in infants. Professor Lewis says: 'Chemicals found in soya can lower sperm count . . . The results do give us concerns and there need to be further studies on a much larger scale.'

One of the team, Dr Lorraine Anderson, says: 'If you alter the oestrogen that a man is exposed to, you can not only affect their sperm quality but you can get an increase in structural abnormalities like undescended testes.' She believes this could lead to other problems later in life, such as testicular cancer. The study also warns that babies should not be given infant formula milk made from soya. The Soya Protein Association, which represents food makers, says: 'We have seen no convincing evidence that soya causes any harm.'

However, I prefer to use oat milk (which strangely enough seems to help my daughter sleep at night), almond and rice milk as milk substitutes. You should be aware that intolerance and allergy to soya are becoming increasingly common in kids, and you need to keep a detailed food diary (see page 122) when you make your nutritional changes, so that you can track how their body is responding.

If after a few weeks off dairy you find that your child starts to feel much better, you could explore whether it's possible for them to take in a little lactose, say some sheep's cheese or yoghurt, every couple of days without triggering any symptoms. It may be that they were just eating too much dairy before.

WHEAT ALLERGIES AND INTOLERANCES

I'm seeing an increase in the number of parents who want to take their child off wheat, because they believe that they have an intolerance. The first thing to point out is that if you notice your child having any of the following symptoms after eating wheat, you need to take them to the doctor before you start changing their diet, as they might well have a condition called coeliac disease (see page 156).

* Weight loss or failure to gain weight
* Stomach pains and rectal bleeding
* Very pale, floating stools that have an unpleasant smell
* Pale skin and tiredness, which is due to lack of energy because they're anaemic

If after seeing the doctor you get the all-clear medically, and you still want to look at the whole issue of wheat intolerance because you notice that your child feels lousy after eating wheat and almost miraculously better if they avoid it, as with any suspected food intolerance, see food diaries (page 122). If it's apparent that their body just doesn't feel right after eating wheat – obvious sources are bread, pasta, cakes, pastries, sauces and any food containing flour – it can be worth setting time aside to investigate whether they have an intolerance. It can be relatively easy to take obvious wheat foods out of their diet for a couple of weeks and see how their body feels. Kids who have an intolerance to wheat that isn't diagnosed

as coeliac disease will generally notice that their symptoms disappear or at least lessen significantly if they just avoid obvious sources of wheat – it's not usually necessary to start scrutinizing labels for gluten and other ingredients like wheat starch, because commonly their body can cope with small amounts without showing any symptoms. But if you want to know the fine details of completely wheat-free and gluten-free products, contact the Coeliac Society, www.coeliac.co.uk.

Is there any other cereal or starch my child can eat?

Yes – there are delicious rye and spelt breads, oat biscuits, rice and corn pasta (even chickpea and buckwheat pasta), and starches such as potato, rice, barley couscous (made with barley, not the traditional wheat), quinoa that can be added to soups. You can buy delicious wheat-free breakfast cereals – Rice Crispies, cornflakes – and wheat-free mueslis and porridge. Take a look at www.sharphamparkshop.co.uk for their yummy spelt cereals. It's important to include these non-wheat starches so that children have enough energy and fibre in their diet and don't lose too much weight.

When will I notice an improvement?

Everyone's different – some parents notice within a day or two that their child's symptoms have gone, others find it's more gradual, over a month or so. If you notice a gradual change, you may find that they can in fact digest some wheat – pasta twice weekly may be OK, but beyond this amount their symptoms surface. Perhaps it's just that they've been eating too much wheat up to now – easily done when they start the day with toast, have a sandwich for lunch and then round off the day with pasta. Just cutting down can mean they feel better. And if this is the case, it might be a good idea to let them have the usual wheat-containing foods when they're in social situations, say at friends' parties, or when they're out at a pizza restaurant with friends, so that they can feel normal and not have to be different, a really important point if you decide to cut some food out of your child's diet or have to for medical reasons. For instance, try to have lots of snacks and treats that all kids will love and that your child can eat, so that they don't have to have something different, or go without.

Are there any nutrients they might miss?
If you replace wheat with other cereals and starches, like rye bread and rice, you shouldn't normally need supplements, but ask a dietician if you're worried. Remember – you need to ensure their diet has enough starch and fibre.

If you suspect that your child has a wheat intolerance, make sure tht they see a doctor to check for the more serious coeliac disease.

HERBAL MEDICINE

Herbal remedies are prepared from the leaves, flowers and other parts of plants and are traditionally used to treat tummy-aches, eczema, asthma, mood swings, sleeplessness and other children's complaints. I think they can have their place in treating many problems. I use chamomile flowers to make a soothing, sedating tea for Maya if she's wound up, upset or having difficulty sleeping, but I wouldn't recommend that you start giving tablets or tinctures (extracts) to your child unless either they're prescribed by a medicinal herbalist, or you know that the herbs are completely safe for kids (having bought them from a very reputable supplier and only ones that are specifically packaged for children). You need to check out any unusual herbal teas with your doctor or pharmacist – the usual mint, chamomile, fennel, lemon verbena are fine, but anything more out of the ordinary needs checking.

YUMMY OILS

With tablets and tinctures, kids between four and six generally need a quarter of the recommended adult dose, with children between seven and twelve needing half the recommended adult dose. But you must check with your doctor or pharmacist if your child is taking any other medication, as they could interact.

MY FAVOURITE ESSENTIAL OIL FIRST AID KIT FOR KIDS

To help them sleep

With children from one to five, I use a single shot of chamomile roman, lavender palmarosa or mandarin – and use one drop for each year of their age up to a maximum of three. Another lovely blend is 10 drops palmarosa, 7 drops chamomile roman, 5 drops mandarin - use one drop of the blend per year of their age, up to a max of three.

With kids over five you can use single oils as above, but also choose from geranium, clary sage and nutmeg, using 3 drops until seven years old and 4 drops between seven and ten. For a blend, try 10 drops chamomile roman, 8 drops geranium and 4 drops nutmeg.

Use in the bath, or try a little massage (using 10 drops of essential oil to 30ml base vegetable oil) - be careful not to use more than the recommended dose, as that sometimes turns them into stimulant oils!

Bronchitis and chest infections

To make an inhalation remedy for children up to five years old, make a blend of 8 drops tea tree, 7 drops chamomile roman and 10 drops eucalyptus. Over five, the blend could be 8 drops tea tree, 10 drops red thyme, 7 drops chamomile roman. Use 3 drops of the blend in a diffuser, or use the simple water-bowl method, three times a day.

Constipation

Use a blend of 4 drops geranium, 6 drops patchouli and 15 drops mandarin, diluted in 30ml vegetable base oil. Gentle clockwise massage around the whole abdomen can help stimulate the intestines to move and the bowels to open.

Diarrhoea
Use a blend of 5 drops ginger, 8 drops sandalwood, 8 drops chamomile roman, diluted in 30ml vegetable base oil. Gently rub the child's tummy.

Toothache, sore mouth
Choose from myrrh, lavender, calendula, chamomile roman. Take 1 drop, place in a tumbler of water and get the child to rinse around their mouth, but don't let them swallow. Do this once a day until they start to get better.

Tummy-ache
Make up a massage oil using 15 drops of one of the following essential oils in 30ml vegetable base oil: peppermint, dill, eucalyptus, coriander, geranium, rosemary, lavender. Massage the child's tummy gently in a clockwise direction around the tummy button – you can also massage their back gently too. Another yummy blend is 9 drops dill and 6 drops geranium, diluted in 30ml vegetable base oil.

Herbal teas and remedies can be useful for treating kids' upsets and infections.

CHAPTER FIVE

The Yummy Parent

I know it's a bit of a cliché, but I see so often that a bad parent is one who doesn't look after herself or himself – we all know we should, but boy, it's hard to put it into practice at times. So often we're bottom on the looking-after list – we're the ones who go without the proper meal, as we struggle to just get something good inside our kids. We're the ones who push our bodies to go without something to eat or drink because there are a million and one things to get done before they get back from school – ending up trying to keep going with a takeaway coffee and a biscuit or three, or a grabbed sandwich which is then wolfed down while driving. I've often found myself just relieved to get to the end of the day, with Maya tucked up in bed, having had a good tea, bath and story having gone to plan, only then past the point of hunger and just gasping for a glass of wine. I am human too!

But what I want to concentrate on in this chapter is how you can take a few tricks of the trade to help you look after yourself and in turn find parenting not as draining on your body, how you can keep in shape while also looking after the kids and how to keep up with them. I've interviewed lots of mums about how they manage this, what pitfalls they come across, how their eating habits have changed since becoming a mum – I would have interviewed dads too, but I ran out of time and missed Maya too much to continue, so dads please forgive – and don't just ignore the chapter, as I'm sure there are things here that can make you feel like a great dad too.

BREAKFAST TIME

This is not only the time when you need to get some nourishment inside your kids, but an opportunity to have a good breakfast yourself, especially if you know that your likelihood of having a proper nutritious mid-morning snack or a good sit-down lunch is low. Several mums, myself included, find it makes a massive difference to how the day pans out – moods, energy levels, ability to cope with demands, not having had enough sleep, calls from schools and moaning parents, etc. etc., can all be handled much better if you have some healthy food and hydration/fluid inside you.

Even if you're not much of a breakfast eater, or you aren't ready to eat when they have theirs, perhaps preferring to wait until they're all sorted, maybe gone to school, when you can sit down in the quiet and relax more, I do think a little something first thing helps. So make yourself a fruit smoothie (ideally with some yoghurt or banana, using milk of any sort in it, as this will give you more sustenance than apple juice – although that's still good too) to sip on while the kids are eating. Ideally, make sure you have enough time in the morning to sit down with them – even if you don't have much of an appetite, it gives the message to your child that eating together is important. It also shows them that you're important too, and if they see you just grabbing little bits to eat while dashing around this can confuse them about what they're meant to do. So many times (and I've had to stop myself doing it) mums can get into the habit of just picking at the leftovers and never getting round to eating a proper meal – you never feel satisfied if you do this, because if you eat while doing something else your body won't recognize that you've eaten and you still feel hungry afterwards – which is why grazing never fills you up. It also means you're far less likely to have a balanced meal later on.

PRE-ARMED ON THE SNACK FRONT

If you can, carry a few snacks around with you, such as rice cakes, bread sticks, crackers, fruit, unsalted nuts, organic fruits, etc. It's good to have something to nibble on if you're flagging or your schedule suddenly changes and the mealtime gets put back.

LUNCHTIME

You need refuelling. If you're with your children, sit down and have a meal with them, making a portion for yourself (it helps if you all eat the same types of food). By preparing something you can all eat, you make sure that you have just as good nourishment as they do. The recipes in this book are all perfect for everyone to eat (see pages 212–259). If you're on your own, sit down with a homemade sandwich, or a simple omelette, a bowl of soup and some wholegrain bread. Have fresh fruit or yoghurt afterwards. If you're a working parent, try not to slip into the mindset of 'if I work through my lunch-break I'll be able to get home earlier for the family' – you'll end up exhausted and in a grump nine times out of ten. Stopping for lunch takes time, but you will feel so rested afterwards, having just taken that ten minutes out for yourself. Turn off the phone, turn away from the computer screen, plug your iPod in, or go outside for ten minutes' fresh air in a nice peaceful spot.

THINK ABOUT WHAT WORKS BEST FOR YOUR BODY

It may be that having your main meal at lunchtime works better for you – you have more energy to put something good together, your child might be less grizzly, and it also takes the pressure off the evening, as you can then have a lighter soup, salad, simple pasta. Finally, it gives your body longer to digest the main meal – I sometimes have to go to bed so soon after eating (I can't stay awake any longer) that to expect my body to cope with a big main meal at this time is too tall an order.

THE MEAL AT THE END OF THE DAY

Asking around, it seems to be more the norm for parents to eat separately from their kids at the end of the day. Extended working days mean that partners are arriving home much later, and unless you're Mediterranean and a late-night-eating family, the kids usually eat together and the parents eat after they're in bed. Sadly, this is my normal pattern during the week, but I always prioritize eating together at the weekends. I think it's important for Maya to see me eating, what I'm eating, and I love sharing food and talking about eating. If you're going to be eating later, try to sit down with them to encourage them to eat at the table – eating in front of the TV or computer as the normal, everyday pattern is not good for them. They can't concentrate on both at the same time, and the food usually gets shovelled in, unnoticed and unappreciated, so that they frequently over-eat, eat too quickly, have stomach-ache or wind. And because they haven't really noticed the food, they'll soon be asking for something else to eat when really their body has eaten enough. TV and computers frequently run food adverts at the key mealtimes, when they know kids will be hungry, to get them to pester you to buy their products – so you may find your child refusing to eat the fresh food you've made and demanding the junk that's advertised instead. What they don't see they don't miss!

While they're at the table, take the few minutes while they're occupied with eating to have a healthy snack yourself – a bowl of soup, a simple salad, fresh or dried fruits, a smoothie, a chai, some unsalted nuts, wholegrain biscuits – these will give you enough energy not only to get through the rest of the day until they go to bed, but also to have enough energy to cook something nutritious for yourself later on. Mums who expect their body to go until 9pm without a late afternoon snack hit a brick wall and find cooking too much effort – that's when the takeaway gets ordered or the bottle of wine with some crisps and dips ends up being your meal, as you feel too shattered to cook anything else.

If you can't wait until your partner comes back from work, think about eating your main meal with your child and perhaps having dessert with your partner later, or a simple salad, so that you don't miss out on your time together. Or if it's just too late to eat, sit with a mug of chamomile tea (or a glass of wine) – I gather from friends that losing out on partner time at the end of the day, especially now it's so easy to get into thinking 'Oh, he'll just throw his own ready meal in the microwave and be OK to eat on his own', can head a relationship down the wrong road.

AND THE DRINK AT THE END OF THE DAY

I once joked with my sister-in-law (who has two young boys) that an alcoholic was someone who hit the bottle at 6pm and didn't have kids! I'm really torn over the alcohol issue, as sometimes when they've gone to bed, the house is quiet, it can be a good moment to have a glass, get our breath back, have an 'adult moment'. To deny ourselves this seems silly – the odd glass of wine in the evening is not only very enjoyable, it de-stresses us and need not be bad for us. But when the odd glass becomes half a bottle or more, or you find yourself pouring the wine out of habit and you're not really bothered about the wine, it's more about sitting down in the quiet with something in your hand that marks the moment, perhaps it's time to look again at your drinking. Drinking alcohol when your body's tired, empty, dehydrated can not only make you feel utterly exhausted, so that you can't be bothered to eat anything nutritious afterwards, but it can also mean you sleep less well. You might be conked out for hours, but you don't feel refreshed in the morning (OK, refreshed in the morning is perhaps too tall an order to aim for as a parent!). Certainly having to wake up during the night for a child when you're sporting a little hangover is utter hell, and the morning afterwards can be torture – even if you don't have a headache you can feel shattered, less able to cope with persistent questions that would normally flow like water off a duck's back, but because you've had alcohol the night before make you feel irritated. And this doesn't necessarily have to mean you've drunk lots – even a large glass of wine on an empty stomach when you're tired can make you really sluggish and moody the morning after.

HOW TO ENJOY THE PLEASURE WITHOUT THE DISADVANTAGES

* Drink plenty of water during the day, or if you've been too rushed off your feet, have a couple of glasses before you drink the alcohol.
* Sip water while drinking alcohol – the more water you drink the less dehydrated you will become (a key component of a hangover)
* The first few sips of any drink are frequently just for refreshment, so try to have the water first and move on to the alcohol when you can taste it and enjoy it.
* Try to save the alcohol until you're sitting down, standing around – it doesn't matter where you drink it, but just try to concentrate on it.
* Buy a good bottle stopper so that you can seal the bottle halfway through and don't fall into the 'oh, I might as well finish it' mentality – save it until another day – if wine's sealed properly it can last for days.
* If you can wait until you're having your meal and therefore have a little nutritious food in your stomach before drinking, this is the ideal. Food keeps the alcohol in the stomach for longer and slows its absorption down – which, like drinking water while drinking, can reduce your chances of feeling shattered afterwards and exhausted the morning after.
* If what you really want is just to sit down and have a glass before you start cooking supper, a dip like hummus, tzatziki, babaganoush (roasted aubergines) with raw vegetables, or some little pieces of lean prosciutto, parmesan or other cheese, rice cakes, oatcakes to nibble on can help cushion the absorption of the alcohol. The

classic nibbles (crisps, salted oily nuts, etc.), delicious as they are, are high in calories and could give you indigestion and make you even more thirsty (therefore tempted to pour another glass). So watch these. Put only a small amount of nibbles out too, so you don't end up eating so much that you don't want a meal afterwards.

If you find that drinking becomes your only way to relax, this could mean you're heading down a route that's not so great. Try to break the pattern by having a non-alcoholic treat instead – in the summer have a long glass of sparkling water with some elderflower cordial in, or a fresh cup of unwinding tea served in your favourite cup. Chamomile tea is a good unwinding, de-stressing tea, as is fresh mint tea: just put a few sprigs of fresh mint in a tea pot of boiling water, leave for a few minutes and pour – utter heaven, and great too for an over-tired gut that feels acidic and not much like eating food. Also think about ways to unwind that don't involve food or drink – have a shower or a bath as soon as the kids have gone to bed, as this can often relax you even more than a drink. (Note that if you have a steaming hot bath and then decide to have a glass of wine, you will need to drink even more water, as you have probably sweated a lot and can get drunk very easily.)

If you've been struggling with tiredness, try cutting out alcohol for a couple of weeks – I can virtually guarantee that you will feel much more energized at the end of your time of abstinence.

Watch out for alcohol's appetite-stimulating effects. The apéritif works big-time on tired parents – a glass can not only make you feel more hungry so you eat a larger portion, but also it can cloud your resolve not to over-eat, and overeating at night can give you a disturbed night and pile on the kilos.

PICK-ME-UPS IN THE MORNING

If you've drunk alcohol, try taking 300mg of milk thistle (available from health-food stores) – it helps to detox the liver. Even though I'm generally not a fan of caffeine (too much of it can make you feel exhausted, believe it or not – it sort of hinders the body's natural ability to energize itself if you OD on it), sometimes you just need a caffeine pick-me-up. I'd opt for tea, but if coffee's your thing, have an espresso – it contains less caffeine than an instant coffee (and tastes better too), and adding milk to make it into a cappuccino, latte or macchiato means the increased volume slows down the absorption of the caffeine. Once you're energized, however, try to stay off the caffeine, as too often mums can lurch from one tea to the next and before you know it they've hit double figures.

Non-caffeine drinks to pick you up

Fresh fruit juices or smoothies – throw fruits in a blender, on their own or maybe with some natural yoghurt (see my recipes, page 222).

WHEN YOU'RE SO OVER-TIRED YOU CAN'T SLEEP (EVERY PARENT'S NIGHTMARE!)

THINK ABOUT YOUR NIGHT-TIME DRINK

I find that a glass of cold milk at bedtime helps me to sleep, perhaps because I associate it with comfort. There is some interesting research into drinking milk, especially Night-time Milk (which some supermarkets stock) which has shown that milk can indeed aid slumber, be it cold or warm. Milk contains magnesium, another sleep-promoter, but if you don't like milk, green vegetables, nuts and whole grains are rich in this nutrient too. Try to ensure your diet has enough of these and the other foods listed on page 29. It's best not to add cocoa powder or chocolate to milk, however (or at least not a lot of it), because the caffeine-like substances that these drinks contain (like the caffeine found in tea, coffee and cola) can all act as a stimulant.

Herbal teas can work very well, particularly chamomile, passionflower, lemon balm and valerian. Add a few drops of clary sage, sandalwood or marjoram essential oils to your bath and sprinkle a little lavender essential oil over your pillow.

THINK ABOUT WHAT YOU EAT

The type of food you eat can have an impact on how you sleep, too. Check that you're not overdoing the very sweet (high glycaemic index) foods, such as biscuits and chocolate (see page 84) – these are best avoided because they can cause your blood sugar levels to rise, making you feel even more wired. Cheese and meat, on the other hand, may give rise to bad dreams, or even nightmares, while an evening meal that consists primarily of protein-rich foods – meat, chicken, fish – may energize you, which is great if you have love in mind because, after all, many people find an orgasm a superb sleep-trigger.

By contrast, the best foods to induce a soporific state are starchy carbohydrates, including potatoes, pasta and rice, which stimulate the brain to produce serotonin. I find a big bowl of pasta one of the best sleep-inducers. If you don't have the time or energy to cook anything fancy, a bowl of milky porridge may have a similar effect. Sometimes if you haven't had a proper meal during the day your body may need something more filling, such as a bowl of cereal, to knock you out.

HELPFUL HERBS

Chamomile, gotu kola, lime, lavender, hops and passionflower (listed in ascending order of strength) are all relaxing herbs. Hops are also helpful when the mind just won't switch off, so try taking an infusion made with 1–2 heaped teaspoons of hops per cup of hot water before going to sleep. Alternatively, mix 10 drops of hop tincture with water at night; although you can take up to 40 drops if necessary, don't take any hop remedies if you're feeling depressed. Health-food stores stock pills containing a mixture of hops, passionflower, valerian and similar sleep-promoting herbs and flowers with which to treat mild sleep problems.

WHAT IF YA MAN SNORES!

Snoring is just what every mum doesn't need. Give him a good kick up the backside if he's overweight, and plead with him to lose the excessive kilos because it's highly likely that the weight around the middle, which is where men tend to pack it, is making the problem ten times worse. I have seen snoring men become virtually silent as soon as they shift the excess weight – it's most definitely worth it. Secondly, drinking too much alcohol can turn a mouse into a bear, so if the snoring is reaching operatic levels night after night, think about cutting out alcohol for the two of you. Some people find that eating dairy products, such as yoghurt, milk and cheese, late at night makes matters worse, but there is no scientific evidence to support this cause and effect.

IF YOU'RE FEELING LOW

Despite knowing and feeling that being a parent is the most fantastic thing in the world, there will be moments when you're feeling low. For me it's usually when I'm over-tired, especially if I've had several very broken nights in a row. When I first got Maya back to England, when she was fifteen months old, I found the change from eight hours' heavy, deep sleep a night to a very broken sleep, never the same type and quantity from one night to the next, a very hard transitional period to break through. Sometimes the sheer discomfort of the latter stages of pregnancy prepares you for having less and different sleep, but since I'd adopted Maya I'd had none of this adaptation process. For

me the sleep deprivation at its worst made me feel blues-ish – I wasn't depressed, just a little low. I know from treating many mums, and from my own experience, that it's easy to slip into not having the motivation to eat properly, but as soon as you start to feel low, just turn to page 196, nibble on some fruit, force yourself to eat something healthy even if you don't have much of an appetite. Tell a close friend how you're feeling – they may cook you something, or drop some provisions off if your hectic routine doesn't leave you time to get to the supermarket. Get on the computer or the phone and get a supermarket delivery.

If I'm finding motherhood tough, just getting out of the house for a walk, seeing the sun, breathing fresh air, will usually help, and also tire me out enough to have a good, physically exhausted as opposed to mentally exhausted, sleep. Try to get some kind of exercise, whether it's walking every day or something more structured like my Thai boxing, which is my life-saver – getting those endorphins flowing always helps re balance me. And get a book, so that you can read about how normal it is to feel like this – I swear by Penelope Leach's classic *Your Baby and Child*, and some fantastic parenting leaflets from the Parent Leadership project at www.parentleadership.org.

Never forget that parenting is a great joy but also hard work at times. If you're losing sight of that truth, it doesn't make you a bad parent, just a perfectly normal one! Forgive yourself for any lapses, whether they be related to food or anything else – we all make them.

Conclusion

I hope that by now I'll have enthused you with enough knowledge and inspiration and confidence to feel you're sort of getting the feeding your child thing right. I say sort of, because if there's one thing I've come to realize since becoming a parent, always trying to achieve ideals is a task that very rarely makes me or Maya happy – if a whole day of shopping, cooking and eating goes well and according to plan, I sit back in amazement, thankful to have been able to achieve such a feat. But mostly, I feel I'm doing well if I have the right foods in the fridge and cupboards, or a few things in our bags if we're out – to me this is 90% of the task, so that whenever I need to I'm able to give Maya the nutritionally best possible thing I can. But I try not to beat myself up if a few things have not gone well or according to other holier-than-thou, which-planet-do-they-live on, textbooks. After all, kids are amazingly resilient.

By setting out what I think are the best things to strive for, I hope *Yummy!* gives you the reassurance that the foundations you've started to lay now will stand your child in good stead nutritionally, whatever the future throws at them. As to what the future indeed throws at our children, I am optimistic that the high-octane campaigns by Jamie Oliver and other great ambassadors such as Gordon Ramsay and Prue Leith will have a genuinely positive, hopefully long-lasting effect on the powers that be who regulate the way food is produced, sold and marketed in this country. The nation seems to have finally cottoned on to the fact that caring about what we're feeding our kids isn't just a middle-class indulgence; every child deserves the chance to grow up and stay healthy, and what we put into their bodies is one of the most important factors affecting their future.

We still have a long way to go. I want to see junk food advertising removed from the TV and from any other area where kids can be brainwashed into believing this is the sort of food they should be eating. I want nutrition to be taught in an inspiring way to all schoolchildren. Traditional home economics lessons need to be compulsory and include more useful things than learning how to make a sponge cake – these are the parents of tomorrow, and teaching them how to cook simple, healthy, good-tasting foods will have far-reaching consequences. If the politicians need any other reason than to help improve our kids' health, they should wise up to the fact that eating well staves off all sorts of diseases that currently cost our economy dearly.

As Jamie's campaign over the last six months has shown, a few shouts in the right ears have meant that kids today do have more of a chance of eating better, now that high-sugar and high-fat drinks and snacks are to be banned from school vending machines. Education minister Ruth Kelly has said that school meals need to contain more nourishment than a plate of chips and a reconstituted meat product, so our kids have a chance of eating something that will help rather than hinder their health. At last we all have a real chance of creating a generation of good-food-loving, healthy happy kids.

Recipes

Breakfast is the most important meal of the day, for children and adults alike. These yummy recipes should give you some great ideas for nourishing ways to kick start the day.

American Buckwheat Blueberry and Prune Pancakes

Makes 6–10 small pancakes

60g buckwheat flour

1/2 teaspoon baking powder

250ml buttermilk

2 eggs, separated

handful of blueberries, slightly squashed

50g chopped prunes

butter for greasing the pan

Sift the flour and baking powder into a mixing bowl. Whisk the buttermilk and egg yolks together in another bowl, then add to the flour and mix. Do not worry about the odd lump, but take care not to over-mix as this will make the pancakes tough.

Whisk the egg whites until they form soft peaks, then fold into the mixture. Add the blueberries and prunes. Just a gentle stir through will make sure they are mixed in without letting out any air.

Heat the butter in a frying pan and spoon in a little of the batter. How much depends on how big you like your pancakes! Cook for 1–2 minutes on each side until they are golden brown. Keep going until all the mixture is used up.

Serve with maple syrup and some fresh fruit of your choice.

NOTES

* You can add a couple of tablespoons of ground seeds to the mixture if you wish.
* The pancakes freeze well.

All-in-one Bread

Makes one approx 850g loaf

Oil for greasing the loaf tin

300ml lukewarm water (you may not need it all)

1 x 7g packet dried yeast

1 teaspoon sugar

500g wholemeal bread flour

generous pinch of salt

4 tablespoons ground seeds

1 tablespoon poppy seeds

2 tablespoons honey

1 tablespoon porridge oats

Grease a 25 x 10cm loaf tin with olive oil or pumpkin seed oil and sprinkle it lightly with flour. Preheat the oven to 160°C.

In a small bowl mix 50ml of the water with the yeast and sugar. Sit the bowl somewhere warm until the contents start to foam.

In a large bowl, mix the flour, salt and seeds. Make a well in the middle and add the yeast mix, honey and a generous splash of water. Start to mix with a firm hand, adding more water every so often. Keep mixing, mixing, mixing until you have a dough with minimal lumps.

Tip on to a floured surface and put all your effort into kneading for 5 minutes until the dough is soft and springy. Then sprinkle a large, clean bowl with flour and sit the dough inside. Cover with clingfilm and leave somewhere warm until it has doubled in size (approx. 20–30 minutes).

At this point punch the dough to knock out the air (you could knock it back by kneading only, but this doesn't feel half as satisfying!), then tip it on to the floured surface and knead for 3–4 minutes. When it's smooth and springy, put it in the loaf tin and sprinkle with the porridge oats. Leave it in a warm place to fill with air again.

When the dough has doubled in size, poke it gently with your finger. If it bounces back just slightly it's ready to go into the oven for 30–35 minutes. The loaf is done when the top is golden and it sounds hollow if you tap it. Allow the loaf to cool in the tin before turning out.

Homemade bread is one of the most satisfying, delicious things you can make.

Eggy Bread with Stewed Fruits

Here's a healthy take on French toast. Vary the fruits by season for maximum taste. This recipe uses summer fruits.

Serves 2 children

2 medium eggs

4 tablespoons milk

½ teaspoon cinnamon

1 nectarine, sliced

1 peach, sliced

small handful of raspberries

1 tablespoon of oil

small knob of butter

4 slices of organic bread (not too thick or they won't cook all the way through)

2 dollops of natural organic yoghurt

In a large, shallow dish whisk together the eggs, milk and cinnamon.

Quickly rinse the fruit and place in a small saucepan, using the water that clings to them for cooking liquid. Leave on a very low heat until the raspberries begin to share their colour and the fruit slices start to soften at the edges. Remove from the heat and set aside.

Add the oil and butter to a frying pan over medium heat. While waiting for the butter to melt, dip the bread into the egg mixture, making sure each side has soaked some up.

Fry the bread for a couple of minutes on each side until golden, then serve with the fruits and a dollop of yoghurt.

Morning Rice Pudding

Serves 2 children

100g short-grain brown rice

500ml milk or soya milk

350ml water

½ vanilla pod with the seeds scraped out and retained

50g raisins

1 tablespoon honey

1 tablespoon apple concentrate (add more apple juice to replace the honey if you prefer)

Give the rice a quick rinse in a sieve under cold running water. Place in a heavy-based pan (deep sides are best to keep in the moisture) along with the milk, water, raisins, vanilla seeds and pod. Allow to simmer for 1 hour, stirring little and often.

Remove the vanilla pod and allow the rice to stand for a minute or so before adding the honey and apple juice for sweetness (you can adjust the amounts as necessary).

NOTE: You could also stir through some ground seeds (see page 248) for a nutritional boost.

The Full English

The Full English, though a real treat, is hardly renowned for its wholesomeness. Here are a few ways to help it along the healthy path!

* go for organic sausages and bacon, grilled and not fried!
* poach or scramble eggs
* cook mushrooms in toasted seed oil
* oven-roasted cherry tomatoes are delicious
* use organic homemade bread with mixed seeds and grains
* make your own baked beans
* make your own tomato ketchup

HOMEMADE BAKED BEANS

Serves 2 children

*1 x 400g tin of white beans (haricot, butter or cannellini), drained and rinsed * 200ml tomato batch sauce (see page 241) * 1 tablespoon honey or maple syrup * salt and freshly ground pepper*

Heat all the ingredients together in a pan.

HOMEMADE TOMATO KETCHUP

*4 very ripe tomatoes * 1 x 400g tin of chopped tomatoes * 1 tablespoon tomato purée * 1 tablespoon white wine vinegar * 1 teaspoon mustard powder * maple syrup or honey, to taste * 2 tablespoon olive oil * 1 tablespoon Good Oil * salt and freshly ground black pepper*

Simmer all the ingredients apart from the oils and seasoning in a pan for 40 minutes, then whiz in processor and sieve. Pour back into the processor and, while it's blitzing, steadily pour the oils into the mixture. This will emulsify and thicken it to a rich, glossy sauce. Leave to cool and then add salt and pepper to taste.

Pick 'n' Mix Porridge

Play around with tastes and textures with three grains and three delicious toppings. This recipe makes one serving for a hungry child.

PORRIDGE

Choose from or mix together: *organic rolled porridge oats* ∗ *organic millet flakes* ∗ *organic brown rice flakes*

In a saucepan mix 1 cup of grain, 1 cup of milk (soya milk is fine) and 1½ cups of water.* Pop on a gentle heat and stir for 5 minutes or so until you have a thick, creamy porridge.

    Dish up and stir in your chosen topping. If you prefer to keep it simple, you could always just add apple concentrate to sweeten and a splash of Good Oil to bump up the nutritional content. A dollop of yoghurt will make the porridge richer and creamier.

*The cup measurement is not specific; just stick to these proportions.

TOPPINGS

Each topping is delicious with any of the grains. Once stirred through, the warmth of the porridge will kick-start the flavours and add natural sweetness to your breakfast.

BANANA, ALMOND AND MAPLE SYRUP

1 small ripe banana ∗ *1 tablespoon almond butter (or ground almonds)* ∗ *1 tablespoon Good Oil* ∗ *1 tablespoon maple syrup*

Using a fork, mash up the banana in a bowl (if your banana is not ripe enough, try microwaving it for 30 seconds). Add all other ingredients and keep mashing until you are left with a sweet paste to stir through the porridge.

BERRIES, APPLE AND GROUND SEEDS

handful of mixed blueberries, blackberries and raspberries ✶ *1 teaspoon apple concentrate mixed with 1 teaspoon water* ✶ *¹/₂ organic apple or pear, grated* ✶ *1 tablespoon ground seeds (see page 248)*

Heat the berries and apple concentrate very gently in a pan until the berries start to soften. Add the grated apple or pear and, after a quick stir, pour on top of the porridge and sprinkle with ground seeds. (You can add the seeds to the berries in the pan if you need to disguise them from young eyes!)

STICKY FRUIT COMPOTE

This is great for batch making and keeping in the fridge for a few days. It's also super in winter, when fresh berries are not in season. You can add it to yoghurts, blend it into smoothies and use it for sweetening puddings.

300g mixed dried fruit (choose from prunes, apricots, peaches, blueberries, figs, raisins, sultanas, dates or any other dried fruit that your child enjoys)

Put the fruit into a pan and add enough boiling water to cover. Leave until the fruits are starting to look plump (30 minutes–1 hour) and then simmer for 20–30 minutes.
   When cooled slightly, pour into a food processor and blitz until smooth.

NOTES
* You could add chopped fresh fruit or nuts to jazz up the dish a little more.
* For fun pink porridge, squash a handful of raspberries in a bowl with a teaspoon of apple juice or honey and then stir through your warm porridge to mix the colour and flavour.

DIY Muesli

There are some great cereals available from supermarkets and health food shops. Look for the ones with the fewest additives and beware of those with extra sugar and salt – (Shredded Wheat is good for not having many additives). Of course, the best cereal is the one you make yourself!

150g rolled oats

100g millet flakes

50g rye flakes

2 tablespoons Good Oil or hemp oil

100ml apple juice

handful of sesame seeds

handful of linseeds

handful of pumpkin seeds

handful of sunflower seeds

handful of finely chopped hazelnuts

handful of finely chopped almonds

50g dried apricots

50g dates

50g sultanas

Preheat the oven to 160ºC/Gas Mark 3.

Put all the ingredients other than the dried fruit in a bowl and stir thoroughly, then tip into a roasting tray. Spread evenly and bake in the oven for 20–30 minutes, stirring a couple of times. Allow to cool.

Meanwhile, chop the dried apricots and dates and dust them in a little flour to stop them sticking together. Add them and the sultanas to the muesli.

This will keep in an airtight container for a month.

A lovely way to add sweetness and more nutrients to your muesli, or indeed any cereal, is by using flavoured milk. Try some of the following combinations or create your own, simply blitzing the ingredients in a blender.

FOR 300ML MILK:

½ banana, 1 tablespoon honey and 1 tablespoon prune juice (this is delicious made with almond-flavoured soya milk)

½ banana, ½ skinned peach and the seeds from 1 passion fruit

1 teaspoon vanilla essence, 1 tablespoon toasted ground almonds, handful of mixed berries and 1 tablespoon ground seeds (see page 248)

½ mango and ½ teaspoon cinnamon

It's easy to turn these flavoured milks into smoothies by adding extra banana, natural yoghurt, homemade ice cream or sorbet (see pages 222 and 254).

Seasonal Smoothies and Juices

Here are some great ideas to help you get the most from delicious British produce when it's in season.

SPRING

Easter Treat Smoothie

Combine 1 frozen banana (see bottom of page), thawed, 1 tablespoon honey (or rice syrup), 1 tablespoon almond butter, 1 tablespoon cocoa powder, generous dollop of yoghurt and 300ml milk.

SUMMER

Combine a small handful each of blackcurrants, raspberries and blueberries, 1 skinned and sliced peach (loosen the skin by dipping the peach in boiling water and peel it off), a scoop of kiwi and pineapple sorbet (see page 255) and a splash of apple juice to make up the volume to a glassful.

AUTUMN

Combine the juice of $1/2$ small fennel bulb, 2 pears, 1 apple and a bunch of fresh mint.

WINTER

Combine a spoonful of fruit compote (see page 220), 1 frozen banana (see below), thawed, a spoonful of hazelnut butter, a pinch of cinnamon, a generous splosh of milk and a dollop of yoghurt.

Bananas freeze wonderfully well. Simply peel them, then pop them in a freezer bag and into the freezer. You need to allow them to thaw for 5 minutes before using, but once they're ready you can add them to smoothies, turn them into ice cream or bake with them – whatever your favourite banana recipe demands.

LUNCH

Lunch is the perfect time to re-fuel. Aim to fill their tummy with something nourishing and delicious that will set them up for the afternoon. And take a break yourself, as well. Lunch is the perfect time to pause and relax for a moment before getting on with things.

Rice Paper Parcels

Serves 2 children + 2 grown-ups

12 rice paper pancakes

Filling 1
glass noodles or thin rice noodles
squeeze of lemon juice
splash of tamari

Filling 2
1 tablespoon tahini
1 tablespoon peanut butter
1 tablespoon sesame oil
1 tablespoon honey or maple syrup
150g cooked prawns or tofu, cubed

Filling 3
1 organic carrot
¼ cucumber
small handful of mint, chopped
small handful of coriander, chopped

These self-assembly kits are a great way to make lunchtime fun, whether you're eating at home or having a packed lunch. Each filling will be enough for four rolls.

Fill a shallow baking tray with hot water and soak the rice papers one at a time for 10–15 seconds. Take them out and keep them in a damp tea towel.

Filling 1: Cook the noodles according to the instructions on the packet. Flavour them with a squeeze of lemon juice and a splash of tamari.

Filling 2: Mix the tahini, peanut butter, oil and honey or maple syrup together until you have a smooth paste and add the prawns or tofu. Stir well to coat them in the sauce.

Filling 3: Cut the carrot and cucumber into long, very thin strips to give you a spiky salad and mix in the mint and coriander.

Put the fillings into their own separate bowls. Assemble the parcels by putting your chosen fillings at one side of the rice paper and rolling it up, pancake-style, folding the sides in first.

Serve with soy or tamari sauce for dipping.

Beetroot and Sweet Potato Soup

For a bright pink fun soup there are not many to beat this!

Serves 4–6 children

olive oil

pumpkin seed oil

1 onion, finely chopped

1 carrot, finely chopped

1 garlic clove, finely chopped

1 celery stick, finely chopped

2 raw beetroots, peeled and chopped

2 orange-flesh sweet potatoes, approx 375g, peeled and chopped

1 litre vegetable stock (organic vegetable bouillon)

Splash a little of each oil in a medium-sized pan and heat. Add the onion, carrot, garlic and celery and fry gently. After 5 minutes or so, when they are soft, add the beetroots, sweet potatoes and vegetable stock. Simmer for 30 minutes.

When all the veg are very soft, remove the pan from the heat and leave the soup to cool for 10 minutes. Then, using a blender/processor or stick blender, blitz until creamy and smooth.

Serve with bread and ground seed butter (see page 248).

Sweet Potato Frittata

Serves 4–6 children

2 sweet potatoes (approx. 375g), peeled and chopped into cubes

1 litre vegetable stock (organic vegetable bouillon)

knob of butter

splash of Good Oil (hemp oil)

1 garlic clove, finely chopped

1 small red onion, finely chopped

2 red peppers, deseeded and finely chopped

large handful of washed rocket, chopped

3 medium eggs

2 tablespoons organic whole milk

Grease a 20cm round cake tin and, if it is non-stick, line the base with greaseproof paper.

Boil the sweet potatoes in the vegetable stock for 10 minutes until soft, then drain and roughly mash with a fork.

In a non-stick frying pan heat the butter and oil. Add the garlic, onion and peppers. When the onions are soft, add the mashed sweet potatoes and rocket. Remove from the heat.

Whisk together the eggs and milk, then add the potato mixture and pour into the cake tin. Bake in the oven for 15 minutes, then take it out and gently but firmly pat down the mixture to help make it solid. Put it back in the oven for another 15 minutes. It may well rise in the centre from time to time, but don't worry – it will sink down when it cools.

Cut into wedges to serve. It's delicious hot or cold and is a great addition to lunchboxes!

Pasta with Tomato Sauce and Parmesan

Serves 2 children

couple of handfuls of pasta

splash of avocado oil

1 small courgette, grated

1 small carrot, grated

200ml tomato batch sauce (see page 241)

2 tablespoons of freshly grated Parmesan

Different sorts of pasta for those with special dietary requirements – rice, corn and spelt, for example – are easy to get hold of these days and are perfect for this recipe.

Cook the pasta in a pan of boiling, slightly salted water, following instructions on the packet. Drain.

Heat the avocado oil in a pan, add the courgette and carrot and cook for 3–4 minutes until soft. Add the tomato sauce and Parmesan and heat through. Stir in the pasta and simply dish up!

Maya absolutely loves pasta, as do most kids, and it presents a really quick and easy way to get a nutritious meal inside them.

Butternut Squashed with Mushrooms

This can be made in advance and kept in the fridge once the squash is skinned and squished. Just make sure you warm it through before serving.

Serves 2 children

1 small butternut squash

splash of olive oil and knob of butter

100g baby button mushrooms, halved

2 slices bread for toasting

Preheat the oven to 220°C/Gas Mark 7.

Cut the butternut squash in half, scrape out the seeds, splash with olive oil and wrap in tin foil. Pop in the oven for 30 minutes until soft and golden around the edges. Scrape out the flesh and squash with a fork to make a paste.

After the squash has been baking for 20 minutes, heat a splash of olive oil in a frying pan with the butter. When sizzling, add the mushrooms and cook for 10 minutes until golden.

Spread your toast with the squashed butternut and spoon the mushrooms on top. Serve with a crunchy salad.

Use ground seed butter to fry the mushrooms (see page 248) for a nutritional kick.

Sushi

Makes 24

3 sheets of nori (dried seaweed, available from most supermarkets)

For the rice

125g Japanese sushi rice

1 tablespoon rice vinegar

2 teaspoons honey

pinch of salt

Filling 1

1/2 avocado

1/2 red peper

1/2 yellow pepper

1/2 cucumber

lime juice

Filling 2

2 hard-boiled eggs

2 tablespoons crème fraîche

chopped rocket

1 teaspoon poppy seeds

pinch of salt

Filling 3

4 tablespoons natural yoghurt

2 teaspoons honey

juice of 1/2 lemon

salt and freshly ground black pepper

cooked organic chicken breast, cut into strips

mango, cut into strips

Put the rice into a saucepan with 300ml water and bring to the boil on a high heat. Turn the heat down to a simmer, cover and cook for 12–15 minutes until the water has been absorbed. Stir in the rice vinegar, honey and salt and leave it to sit with the lid on until it is cool.

Filling 1: Cut the vegetables into thin strips and squeeze lime juice over them.

Filling 2: Mash all the ingredients together.

Filling 3: Mix the yoghurt, honey, lemon juice and seasoning together, then stir over the chicken and mango strips.

Have a bowl of water ready so you can keep your fingers wet. Place your sheet of nori on a rolling mat or piece of clingfilm and spread a small handful of rice over the sheet, leaving a 1cm border free of rice.

Line your filling along the side nearest to you – you don't need too much – and then roll up the nori like a Swiss roll, using the clingfilm or rolling mat for support.

When you have used all the rice and fillings, leave the rolls in the fridge for 30 minutes or more so the nori can absorb some moisture from the rice and soften a little.

Using a sharp knife, slice each roll into eight pieces and serve with a bowl of soy sauce. You may want to water down the soy so it is not too strong!

Sandwich Swirls

Tasty, quick and good fun, these are basically savoury Swiss rolls without the baking. Of course, you can use all your old favourite sandwich fillings, but here are a few new ones to try.

Choose your bread: Mediterranean flatbreads ✳ soft flour tortilla wraps ✳ chapattis
Choose your fillings, (as a guide to quantities, each filling recipe will make enough for 4–6 flatbreads):

CREAM CHEESE AND AVOCADO

Whiz 1 ripe avocado with a squeeze of lime in a processor until smooth and then add 200g cream cheese. Blitz until well blended. To add crunch, stir through a handful of grated carrot and 2 teaspoons poppy seeds.

MEXICAN BEAN FILLING

Mix together 1 finely chopped yellow pepper, 1 400g tin of mixed beans (drained and rinsed), 2 sliced spring onions, 1 teaspoon Dijon mustard and 250ml of tomato batch sauce (see page 241). Spoon on to the bread with a dollop of soured cream.

If you want to serve hot, heat the filling in a pan, make up the rolls and pop them in the oven to warm the bread through.

To make vegan soured cream, add a squeeze of lemon juice and a pinch of salt to soya yoghurt or for meat-eaters, try this with strips of cooked chicken breast.

HUMMUS AND CHOP CHOP SALAD

Finely chop $^1/_2$ cucumber, 3 deseeded tomatoes, 50g black olives and a small bunch of coriander. Mix everything together with a squeeze of lemon juice, a splash of oil and 1 teaspoon soy sauce. Spread your bread with hummus (see page 256) then add salad.

SMOKED MACKEREL PÂTÉ

Put 200g smoked mackerel fillets with their skins removed, 200g ricotta and a squeeze of lemon in a processor and blitz to a paste.

Heat the flatbreads through in the oven for 2–3 minutes. When warm, spread with the filling of your choice, add some salad leaves for colour and crunch if necessary, and roll them up. Slice to make a swirl!

Falafel Burgers

Serves 6 children

1 x 400g tin of chickpeas, drained and rinsed

½ small onion, finely chopped

1 garlic clove, finely chopped

small handful of chopped flat-leaf parsley

small handful of chopped coriander

1 teaspoon ground cumin

1 teaspoon ground coriander

½ teaspoon cinnamon

2 tablespoons wholemeal flour + extra for dusting

200ml sunflower oil for frying

Put the chickpeas, onion, garlic, herbs, spices and flour in a food processor and whiz until smooth. Flour your hands and shape the mixture into 10 patties.

Heat the oil in a frying pan until it is nice and hot. Fry the falafels on both sides for 2–3 minutes until golden brown and crispy. Leave them on a sheet of kitchen towel to drain.

Serve in a bun or pitta with lettuce, tomato and a dollop of hummus or home-made ketchup (see page 217).

Kids love these delicious burgers. They're a brilliant healthy replacement for beef burgers.

Fish Fingers with Oat and Rye Crust

Serves 4 children

350g haddock or any firm white fish fillet, skinned

25g oat flakes

25g rye breadcrumbs

salt and freshly ground pepper

1 medium egg

generous splash of olive oil

splash of pumpkin seed oil

Preheat the oven to 160°C/Gas Mark 3.

Cut the fish into strips a similar size to the well-known originals. Mix the oat flakes and breadcrumbs in a bowl, then season lightly. Beat the egg in a wide bowl.

Dip the fish fingers in the egg and then roll in the oats and crumbs until completely coated. Heat the oils in a pan and gently fry the fish fingers on each side until the coating turns golden. Transfer to a baking tray and place in the oven for 10 minutes or so, until cooked through.

These are delicious with mashed potato and steamed mixed greens.

Here's a healthy way to eat an old favourite. Try with mash and lots of salad or green vegetables, rather than chips.

DINNER

Wind down, tuck in, rest well – here are some perfect end-of-the-day meals. Try to get into the habit of eating together, at a table rather than in front of the TV. Food is a pleasure and great for socialising. If you instill that belief in them early, they'll have it for ever!

Bright Green Pea Soup

Serves 4 children

splash of olive oil

1 small leek, finely chopped

1 carrot, finely chopped

1 stick of celery, finely chopped

1 small potato, peeled and chopped

1 litre vegetable stock (organic vegetable bouillon is best)

large handful of washed spinach

250g frozen peas

For the croutons

wholemeal, rye or all-in-one bread (see page 215), torn into small chunks

1 teaspoon sesame seeds

1 teaspoon ground seed mix (see page 248)

splash of olive or nut oil

Preheat the oven to 180°C/Gas Mark 4.

Set a medium-sized pan over a good heat and add your oil, leek, carrot and celery and gently fry until soft. Add the potato and stock and simmer for 10 minutes. Finally, add the spinach and peas and simmer until the peas are cooked but still bright green (approx. 5 minutes).

While you are waiting for the soup to cook through, put all the crouton ingredients in a bowl and mix together. Tip everything on to a baking tray and place in the oven for 10 minutes until golden and crispy.

When the soup is ready, blitz until smooth and then serve with the croutons floating on top.

NOTES

* If you fancy, you could add a sprinkle of ground seeds (see page 248) when you serve the soup.
* For non-vegetarians, it's also delicious to add shredded ham at the end.

Butternut Squash Risotto with Homemade Pesto

Serves 2 children + 2 grown-ups

For the risotto

1 tablespoon olive oil

1 small onion or a couple of shallots, finely chopped

1 celery stick, finely chopped

1 carrot, finely chopped

1 garlic clove, finely chopped

250g risotto rice

50ml grape juice diluted with 50ml water

1 litre vegetable stock (organic vegetable bouillon)

1 small butternut squash, chopped into small cubes

For the pesto

2 large handfuls of basil leaves

1 garlic clove (crush before adding if using a food processor)

pinch of sea salt

large handful of toasted pine nuts

juice of 1/2 lemon

100ml olive oil

The nicest way to make the pesto is in a pestle and mortar. First grind the basil and garlic with the salt (salt acts as an abrasive and makes the job a little easier). When you have a paste, add the pine nuts and do the same. Finally, mix in the lemon juice and then the olive oil. If you would rather use a food processor, throw in all the ingredients and blitz. This will give you a chunkier texture.

To make the risotto, heat the oil in a heavy-based saucepan with high sides and gently fry the onion, celery, carrot and garlic. When these are soft, turn up the heat and add the rice, stirring for 4–5 minutes until it's coated in oil.

Add the grape juice and water, which should sizzle when you pour it into the pan, and allow it to be soaked up. When the pan is almost dry, start to add 300ml of the stock and the butternut squash. Add another splash when the liquid has almost been soaked up. Stir steadily and fairly constantly until you have used all the stock or the risotto rice is cooked and the mixture is nice and loose.

Take the pan off the heat and allow the risotto to rest for a couple of minutes before dishing it up with a little pesto spooned over the top, to be stirred through at the table.

Pumpkin Curry

Serves 2 children + 2 grown-ups

1 medium-sized pumpkin (approx. 1.2–1.8kg)

olive oil

pumpkin seed oil

2 teaspoons garam masala

1 teaspoon mustard seeds

1 teaspoon cumin seeds

1 small onion, sliced

1 green chilli, deseeded and finely chopped

1 garlic clove, finely chopped

450ml vegetable stock

500ml tomato batch sauce (see page 241)

2 medium-sized potatoes, peeled and cubed

1 large sweet potato, peeled and cubed

1 carrot, peeled and sliced

1 x 200g can of chickpeas, drained and rinsed

Preheat the oven to 180°C/Gas Mark 4.

Tear off a long strip of tin foil and fold it in half, then in half again and again, to give you a thick base on which to sit your pumpkin. This will stop the base from overcooking and collapsing.

Use your hands to cover the skin of the pumpkin in olive or sunflower oil and then sit it on the tin foil. Place on a baking sheet and put in the oven for 15–20 minutes. When it has softened, allow the pumpkin to cool slightly to make handling easier. Cut off the top and retain it to be used later as a lid. Scoop out the seeds and discard (or you can dry these out in the oven for later use if you fancy). Start to cut away some of the flesh from the inside of the pumpkin, making sure you leave enough on the sides to keep it rigid. This flesh is to be added to the curry.

In a roomy pan, add a splash of olive oil and a splash of pumpkin seed oil and fry the garam masala and the seeds until they start to pop. Throw in the onion, green chilli and garlic and cook until soft. Pour in the stock and tomato sauce, the remaining vegetables, chickpeas and pumpkin flesh. Simmer for 30 minutes.

When cooked, ladle the curry into the hollow pumpkin, pop on the lid and take to the table ready to dish up.

Serve with rice – brown is best!

Tomato Batch Sauce

Makes approx. 1.6 litres

600g very ripe organic tomatoes

1 small butternut squash, chopped into big pieces and deseeded

olive oil to splash

500ml vegetable stock

1/2 onion, chopped

2 sticks of celery

1 garlic clove, finely chopped

2 carrots, peeled and chopped into small pieces

1 courgette, chopped into small pieces

2 x 400g tins of plum tomatoes

Preheat the oven to 220ºC/Gas Mark 7.

Put the tomatoes and butternut squash into a deep roasting tray, splash on some oil and pop into the oven for 30 minutes until the tomatoes and squash are very soft. Scrape the flesh from the squash and put this and the tomatoes into a blender. Add 250ml stock and blitz. Pass through a sieve to remove the seeds and tomato skin (this is much quicker than peeling your tomatoes beforehand).

In a large saucepan heat a splash of oil, then add the onion, celery, garlic, carrots and courgette and cook until the veg are soft. Add the tins of tomatoes and the remaining stock and simmer for 15 minutes. Allow to cool a little.

Pour both mixtures into a processor or use a stick blender to whiz until smooth. This can now be used as the base for any number of recipes, adding several vegetables to a dish in one easy go.

Layered Vegetable Lasagne

Serves 2 children + 2 grown-ups

olive oil

1 small red onion

2 garlic cloves

150g button mushrooms, chopped

1 x 400g tin of lentils, drained and rinsed

500ml tomato batch sauce (see above) + extra for the topping

small handful of chopped thyme leaves

1 aubergine

2 large courgettes

2 large carrots

3 large tomatoes, sliced

Preheat the oven to 180ºC/Gas Mark 4.

Heat the oil in a pan and fry the onion, garlic and mushrooms until soft. Add the lentils and tomato sauce and simmer for 10 minutes. Stir in the thyme.

Slice the aubergine, courgettes and carrots thinly lengthways (a great way to this with the carrots and courgettes is to use a speed peeler).

In a large pan of boiling water, add the sliced vegetables and cook for 3–4 minutes until they start to soften, being very careful to keep them intact. Lay them on some kitchen towel to drain.

Grease an ovenproof dish large enough to hold all of the ingredients (a 2.5 litre dish should do it) and begin to assemble the lasagna. Start with a layer of carrot slices, topped with a layer of lentils. Next add a layer of aubergine slices, then lentils, then courgette slices and a final layer of lentils with tomato sauce to top it all off.

Spread the sliced tomatoes over the tomato sauce and bake in the oven for 25 minutes.

Baked Giant Bean Crumble

Serves 2 children + 2 grown-ups

4 organic, best-quality pork sausages

olive oil

1 small onion, sliced

2 garlic cloves, crushed

2 x 400g tins butter beans, drained and rinsed

500ml tomato batch sauce (see page 241)

1 teaspoon mustard powder

1 teaspoon tamari/soy sauce

400g cauliflower, separated into florets

salt and freshly ground black pepper

150g breadcrumbs (wholemeal, sourdough or rye)

handful of cornflakes

small bunch of flat-leaf parsley, chopped

Preheat the oven to 180°C/Gas Mark 4.

Grill the sausages until they are cooked through and then cut into bite-sized pieces.

Meanwhile, heat some olive oil in a large pan and add the onion and half the garlic. When softened, add the butter beans, tomato, mustard powder and tamari. Cook through for 15 minutes.

At the same time, cook the cauliflower in boiling water for 10–15 minutes until soft. Mash with a little olive oil and some seasoning and set aside for the topping.

Stir the sausage pieces through the bean mixture and tip into a large ovenproof dish. Spoon the cauliflower on top.

Heat some olive oil into a frying pan and add the rest of the garlic. After a couple of minutes stir in the breadcrumbs and fry until they start to take on a little colour. Remove from the heat and add the cornflakes and parsley.

Sprinkle this crumble mixture over the cauliflower topping and bake in the oven for 20 minutes until the golden and crunchy.

NOTE: Simply leave out the sausages to make the dish vegetarian.

This is a brilliant, hearty dish for winter suppers.

Roast Vegetable and Chicken Couscous

This is a great meal for multi-taskers! Simply throw everything into the oven and get on with other jobs.

Serves 2 children + 2 grown-ups

1 small organic free-range chicken

½ lemon

1 raw beetroot, peeled

1 red onion, sliced into wedges

1 sweet potato, peeled and chopped into chunky pieces

1 small aubergine, chopped into chunky pieces

1 courgette, chopped into chunky pieces

1 garlic clove, finely chopped

olive oil

150g couscous (cooked according to instructions on the packet)

For the dressing

200ml organic natural yoghurt

juice of ½ lemon

1 tablespoon sesame oil

small handful of chopped flat-leaf parsley

pinch of salt and pepper

Preheat the oven to 190ºC/Gas Mark 5 (170ºC for a fan-assisted oven). Put the lemon into the chicken cavity and roast the chicken for 45 minutes per kg, turn the oven up to 220ºC/Gas Mark 7 for the final 15 minutes. Calculate the total cooking time: the vegetables will need to go in the oven for the last 30 minutes.

Put all the vegetables in a roasting tray, mix through the garlic and a generous splash of olive oil and place in the oven.

Mix all the dressing ingredients together and stir well.

Check that the chicken is cooked by using a skewer to pierce deep into the leg. The juices that flow out should be clear.

Portion the chicken and mix together the couscous and roasted vegetables. Serve with a green salad and a dollop of dressing.

NOTES
* If you give the couscous a hearty stir when the vegetables are mixed in, the beetroot will turn the grains pink – perfect to make your meal fun!
* Any leftovers can be used for lunchboxes.

Fish Pie

Serves 4

2 floury potatoes, peeled and cubed

100g broccoli

2 small knobs of butter or splashes of olive oil

small handful of finely shredded leek

1 garlic clove, finely chopped or crushed

400g mixed white fish fillets, skinned and cut into small pieces

100g small cooked prawns

small handful of spinach, washed and finely chopped

3 tablespoons crème fraîche (for a dairy-free dish, substitute tomato batch sauce, see page 241)

1 tsp mustard powder

salt and freshly ground pepper

Preheat the oven to 180°C/Gas Mark 4.

Start to cook the potato cubes in a pan of boiling water. After 8 minutes add the broccoli and cook for 3–4 minutes, making sure you don't overcook it (it should stay bright green). When the potatoes and broccoli are done, drain, add a small knob of butter or a splash of olive oil and mash together.

In a large pan heat the other knob of butter or oil and add the leeks, garlic and mustard powder. When they have softened, add the fish, prawns and spinach and cook on a medium heat for 3–4 minutes. Reduce the heat and add the crème fraîche, mustard powder and seasoning. Stir through, then remove from the heat and divide between four small pie dishes.

Top each pie with the mash and bake for 15 minutes until golden.

Be warned: this is so delicious that adults and kids alike usually want seconds.

Baked Fish with Tomato and Salsa Rice

You could use almost any fish for this dish: mackerel, trout, haddock, cod, brill, plaice, tuna, salmon… My particular favourite is sea bass, which is a delicious firm white-fleshed fish. Allow enough fillets per person to make up a portion. If you are using a small fish such as mackerel, you may need two fillets per grown-up.

Serves 4 (ish)

4 fish fillets, skinned

12 halved cherry tomatoes (different-coloured ones look great)

small handful of chopped rosemary

2 tbsp olive oil

salt and freshly ground black pepper

175g (uncooked quantity) cooked rice

½ red onion finely chopped

1 red pepper, finely chopped

small handful of cooked peas or baby broad beans

2 tablespoons toasted pine nuts (omit for allergy sufferers)

juice of ½ lemon

1 tablespoon avocado oil

1 tablespoon honey

1 tablespoon rice vinegar

small handful of chopped basil

Preheat the oven to 160ºC/Gas Mark 3.

Put the fish fillets on a greased baking sheet. Mix together the tomatoes, rosemary, olive oil and a little seasoning and spoon on top of the fillets. Bake in the oven for 10–12 minutes.

Heat a splash of olive oil in a pan, add the onion and pepper and fry for a couple of minutes. Stir in the rice, peas or beans and pine nuts and allow them to warm through, then remove the pan off the heat.

Mix together the lemon juice, avocado oil, honey and vinegar. Pour over the rice and add the chopped basil. Stir to combine.

Spoon the rice on to four plates and sit the fish fillets on top. Serve with steamed green vegetables and tuck in!

SNACKS, PUDDINGS AND PARTY FOOD

I am a great believer in puddings and cakes, as long as they're not an everyday occurrence and are full of good things. Party food should be about indulgence, too. Try the dips and pizzas – they are the definition of yummy but good food!

Power Pack Cereal Bars

Makes 24

175g unsalted butter
150g honey
75g pear and apricot spread or prune spread
175g raw demerara sugar
250g organic jumbo oats
75g pecan nut halves
75g sultanas
75g dried dates
75g dried apricots
30g pumpkin seeds
25g sunflower seeds
25g pistachios
25g Good Seed
25g linseeds
50g ground almonds

Preheat the oven to 190°C/Gas Mark 5 and line a 23cm square baking tin with greased baking parchment.

In a large saucepan melt the butter, then add the honey, spread and sugar and stir until they are all dissolved. Bring the mixture to the boil for 1–2 minutes. This will make the sugar caramelise to form a really sticky sauce.

Add all the other ingredients, mix really well and pour into your cake tin. Pat everything down so it is nice and firm, then place in the oven for 20 minutes until the edges go golden.

Leave to cool, tip it out and slice into bars.

Apple and Plum Crumble with Oat and Seed Topping

Serves 2 children + 2 adults

For the filling

400g cooking apples, peeled and sliced

6 ripe red plums, stoned and sliced

2 tablespoons apple concentrate

pinch of cinnamon

pinch of mixed spice

For the topping

50g rolled oats

2 handfuls of cornflakes

30g malthouse flour

2 tablespoons ground nuts (see right)

1 tablespoon linseeds

2 tablespoons maple syrup

2 tablespoons apple concentrate

2 tablespoon olive oil or Good Oil

Preheat the oven to 200°C/Gas Mark 6.

In a large pan stew the apples and plums in the concentrate with a splash of water. When the apples begin to soften, add the cinnamon and mixed spice. Pour into an ovenproof dish.

Mix the topping ingredients together and sprinkle generously over the filling. Bake for 20 minutes.

GROUND NUTS MIX

*25g brazil nuts * 25g blanched almonds * 25g walnuts * 25g macadamia nuts * 25g pecans*

Roughly chop all the nuts (this can be done by hand or in a processor). Put them on a baking tray and roast in a hot oven (180°C/Gas Mark 4) for 10 minutes. Allow them to cool and then grind to a powder in a spice grinder or using a pestle and mortar. Store in an airtight jar.

GROUND SEED MIX

*2 tablespoons sesame seeds * 2 tablespoons pumpkin seeds * 2 tablespoons sunflower seeds * 2 tablespoons linseeds * 2 teaspoons hemp seeds*

Heat all the seeds in a large frying pan until you hear them start to pop. Allow to cool, then pour into a grinder or pestle and mortar and grind to a coarse powder.

Store in an airtight jar. The mix will keep for a week.

Muffins

Makes 18 small muffins

30g very soft unsalted butter

4 tablespoons honey

3 eggs

40ml sunflower oil

1 tablespoon Good Oil (optional)

50ml milk

480g wholemeal flour

2 teaspoons baking powder

large handful of crunched cornflakes

2 teaspoons ground mixed spice

1 apple, grated

zest of $\frac{1}{2}$ lemon

100g blueberries

100g raspberries

2 ripe bananas, squashed

Preheat the oven to 180°C/Gas Mark 4.

In a large bowl mix together the butter and honey. Add the eggs and beat till smooth, then add the oils.

Put all the remaining ingredients apart from the fruit in another bowl in the order in which they are listed, mixing a little in between additions.

Gradually add the dry mixture to the wet, combining all the time but lightly as possible. The less you beat the flour, the fluffier your muffins will be! Finally, add the fruit and stir through.

Spoon the mixture into paper cups in a muffin tin and bake for 20 minutes until golden brown.

Carrot Cake

300g wholemeal flour

2 teaspoons baking powder

2 teaspoons ground cinnamon

1 teaspoon mixed spice

175ml olive oil

150ml apple concentrate

2 medium eggs, lightly beaten

2 tablespoons maple syrup

175g grated carrot

1 apple, grated

handful of sultanas

For the topping

250g mascarpone cheese

2 tablespoons natural yoghurt

2 tablespoons maple syrup

2 teaspoons vanilla essence

zest of 1 orange and a squeeze of the juice

Preheat the oven to 180°C/Gas Mark 4.

Grease a round baking tin 20cm in diameter and line the base with baking paper.

Mix the flour, baking powder and spices together in a large mixing bowl. Mix the olive oil, apple concentrate, eggs and maple syrup together in a jug and pour over the dry ingredients. Stir well. Add the grated carrot, apple and sultanas to the mixture, gently stir through and pour into the tin.

Bake for 1 hour 15 minutes until you can sink a skewer into the centre and it comes out clean. Remove the cake from the tin and allow to cool. Mix all the topping ingredients together and cover the cake.

NOTES

This recipe is perfect for a birthday cake and a great excuse to go to town on the decoration. If you want a bigger cake, bake two and sandwich them together with extra topping before covering the outside.

Chocolate sprinkles: Use a large bar of dark chocolate or, if it's a birthday treat, white chocolate. Place in the fridge and, when it's chilled, use a peeler to shave off curls and sprinkle all over the topping.

Edible flowers: If you ask your greengrocer there is a good chance he will be able to get hold of edible flowers for you. Use roses, primroses, violets or certain pansies. In a small bowl whisk up an egg white until it is frothy and cover a small plate with caster sugar. Very gently dip the flowers into the egg white and then the sugar until they are lightly coated in crystals. Leave to set for an hour and then arrange on the crown of the cake. These can be made in advance as they will keep for up to a week in a cool, dark place.

Fruits, nuts and herbs: The cake also looks beautiful when decorated with peach slices, redcurrants, blueberries, raspberries and mint. Or if you'd rather use nuts, toast a large handful of whole nuts in the oven with 2 tablespoons of honey. A mix of pecans, walnuts and macadamia will be delicious. When they are cool, pulse them in the processor or chop finely by hand, then sprinkle them all over the creamy topping.

Bread and Butter Pudding

Serves 2 children + 2 grown-ups

6 thin slices of wholemeal bread with crusts cut off

butter or vegan butter for spreading on the bread

sugar-free raspberry jam

150g fresh raspberries

2 eggs or egg replacer

2 tablespoons fruit compote (see page 220) or pear and apricot sugar-free spread (available from health food shops)

300ml milk or soya milk

1 teaspoon vanilla essence

2 teaspoons mixed all spice

Preheat the oven to 200°C/Gas Mark 6.

Make three rounds of jam and squashed raspberry sandwiches, being generous with the butter. Cut the sandwiches into quarters and then pack them tightly into a 2 litre capacity ovenproof dish to line it.

Whisk the egg and compote vigorously in a jug until there are no lumps. Add the milk, vanilla and all spice, then pour over the sandwiches and leave it to be soaked up for 20 minutes or so. (You may need to pour it in batches if it won't all fit at once.)

Bake for 30–35 minutes until it's golden brown, then serve immediately with raspberry or banana ice cream (see page 254).

Fruit Fondue

Serves 6 children

For the fondue

200ml natural yoghurt or soya yoghurt

50g dark chocolate, roughly chopped

2 tablespoons cocoa

3 teaspoons maple syrup

1 teaspoon vanilla essence

For dipping

banana slices

raspberries

peach slices

mango slices

papaya slices

pineapple chunks

Very slowly and gently warm the yoghurt in a small pan, taking care not to heat too quickly as this can cause the yoghurt to separate. Add the chocolate and stir until it has melted and blended in, then add the cocoa, maple syrup and vanilla essence. Mix until silky smooth.

Serve with a fruit platter and cocktail sticks for dipping.

Frozen Yoghurts and Sorbets

Plastic or metal food-storage containers are great for making frozen desserts in. Even better but not necessary is an ice-cream maker.

RASPBERRY RIPPLE

Serves 4

400ml organic natural yoghurt ∗ *4 tablespoons double cream* ∗ *1 teaspoon vanilla essence* ∗ *2 tablespoons apple concentrate* ∗ *100g raspberries*

Mix the yoghurt with the cream, vanilla essence and half the apple concentrate. Place in the freezer to chill for 30 minutes.

Meanwhile, whiz the raspberries in a blender to make a purée and add the remaining apple concentrate.

Remove the yoghurt from the freezer and stir well (this breaks down the ice crystals and will make the frozen yoghurt smoother and lighter). Return it to the freezer for another 30 minutes, then take it out again and stir well. Add the raspberry purée and stir it through to give a rippled effect. Back it goes into the freezer for 3 hours to chill.

Before you serve the yoghurt, allow it to soften at room temperature for a few minutes.

INSTANT BANANA ICE CREAM

This is the quickest and simplest ice cream ever. Allow one banana per person.

2 frozen bananas (see page 222) ∗ *400ml natural yoghurt or soya yoghurt*

Allow the bananas to thaw for 5 minutes at room temperature, then put them in a liquidiser, blender or jug if you are using a stick blender. Pour the yoghurt over the top and blitz until smooth-ish (there will be the odd lump, but this is part of the pleasure). Indulge immediately.

KIWI AND PINEAPPLE SORBET

250g grape juice ✳ 1 small pineapple, skinned, cored and chopped ✳ 4 kiwifruits, peeled and chopped ✳ 2 tablespoons Good Oil (optional)

Purée the ingredients in a blender and place in the freezer. Stir briskly every 30 minutes for 2 hours (this breaks down the ice crystals and will make the sorbet lighter and smoother).

Pink Lemonade

Makes 1 litre

1 lemon

200g raspberries

50ml water

1 litre sparkling water

4 tablespoons apple or pear concentrate

Put the lemon, raspberries and water into a liquidiser and blitz. Mix the sparkling water and concentrate in a jug. Pour the lemon juice and raspberries through a sieve straight into the jug and stir.

Pineapple Zinger

1 litre apple juice

1cm root ginger, peeled

1 pineapple, peeled and chopped with the core removed

juice of 1 lime

Blitz the apple juice and ginger in a liquidiser, then pour through a sieve to remove the ginger fibres. Return the liquid to the liquidiser and add the pineapple and lime. Blitz until smooth, then chill briefly before serving.

Spreadable Delights

Flavoured butters and spreads are a great way to add a bit of goodness to the much-loved slice of toast and humble sandwich.

BERRY BUTTER

*50g softened unsalted butter * small handful of mixed berries*

Squash the ingredients together with a fork or blitz to a purée, then leave to set in the fridge for 10 minutes.

GROUND SEED BUTTER

*50g softened unsalted butter * 4 tablespoons ground seeds (see page 248)*

Squash the ingredients together with a fork and leave to set in the fridge for 10 minutes.

NUT BUTTER

*50g softened unsalted butter * 4 tablespoons toasted and finely ground mixed nuts (see page 248)*

Squash the ingredients together with a fork and leave to set in the fridge for 10 minutes.

CHOCOLATE AND HAZELNUT SPREAD

*4 tablespoons hazelnut or almond butter (available from health food shops) * 1 teaspoon honey, maple syrup or rice syrup * 1 tablespoon cocoa powder*

Mix all the ingredients together until you have a smooth spread.

LEMON CHEESE SPREAD

*250g ricotta * seeds from 1/2 vanilla pod * 1 teaspoon honey or maple syrup * juice and zest of 1/2 lemon*

Mix all the ingredients together until you have a smooth spread.

Party Dips

These are all delicious served with toasted pitta bread and vegetable batons. All these quantities will serve 6-8 children.

HUMMUS

1 x 400g tin of chickpeas, drained and rinsed (see Note below) ∗ *2 garlic cloves* ∗ *squeeze of lemon juice* ∗ *3 tablespoons tahini* ∗ *a pinch of salt* ∗ *3 tablespoons natural yoghurt or soya yoghurt*

Whiz the chickpeas, garlic, lemon juice, tahini and salt in a processor until smooth, then add the yoghurt until you have a light, smooth consistency.

NOTE: If you don't like yoghurt, you can use the liquid from the chickpeas to loosen the mixture.

SMASHED BROAD BEANS

250g broad beans ∗ *350ml vegetable stock* ∗ *3 tablespoons of crème fraîche* ∗ *1 teaspoon of lemon juice* ∗ *2 tablespoons of finely chopped mint* ∗ *salt and freshly ground pepper*

Cook the broad beans in the stock for 15 minutes, by which time only a fraction of the liquid should be left in the pan. Put them into a processor with the other ingredients and pulse until smooth.

CARROT, HONEY AND SESAME

2 tablespoons honey ∗ *1 tablespoon sesame oil* ∗ *1 tablespoon olive oil* ∗ *1 tablespoon sesame seeds* ∗ *1 tablespoon poppy seeds* ∗ *4 large carrots, peeled and cut in half lengthways*

Preheat the oven to 220°C/Gas Mark 7.
    In a large bowl mix together the honey, oils and seeds.
    Parboil the carrots for 5 minutes, then drain and add to the bowl. Stir to make sure they are coated, then tip everything on to a baking tray and roast in the oven for 20 minutes.
    When soft and sticky, mash and serve.

Party Pizzas

This recipe is for the classic pizza topping, but there are endless variations – just be creative!

Makes approx. 8

For the pizza base

300ml lukewarm water (you may not need it all)

1 x 7g packet dried yeast

1 teaspoon sugar

500g wholemeal bread flour

generous pinch of salt

For the topping

2 tablespoons tomato batch sauce per pizza(see page 241)

1/4 large ball of mozzarella per pizza

1 tablespoon basil pesto per pizza (see page 237)

First, make the bases. In a small bowl mix 50ml of the water with the yeast and sugar. Sit the bowl somewhere warm until the contents start to foam.

Add the flour to a large bowl and make a well in the centre. Pour in the yeast mixture and a generous splash of water. Start to mix with a firm hand, adding more water every so often. Keep mixing until you have a dough with minimal lumps.

Tip on to a floured surface and put all your effort into kneading for 5 minutes until the dough is soft and springy. Then sprinkle a large, clean bowl with flour and sit the dough inside. Cover with clingfilm and leave somewhere warm until it has doubled in size (approx. 20–30 minutes).

At this point punch the dough to knock out the air, then tip it on to the floured surface and knead for 3–4 minutes. Back it goes into the bowl again, with another sprinkling of flour. Leave it to swell in a warm place.

Preheat the oven to 220°C/Gas Mark 7.

After 15 minutes, divide the dough into handful-sized pieces. Squash, push and pull them into flat bases (think pitta bread), then place them on a floured baking sheet, ready for their topping.

Spread the tomato sauce over the pizzas, then tear the mozzarella and dot it on top. Finally, spoon over the pesto. Your pizzas are now ready to go into the oven for 20 minutes.

Index

Main references are indicated in **bold** type.

fast foods **93–6**, 134
  vegetarian 118
fats 8, 10, **18–19**, 21, 36, 38, 66, **75–6**,
      83, 93, 95
  animal 117, 182
  good 76
  hydrogenated 75, 76, 118
  intelligent 125
  polyunsaturated 75
  saturated 75
  trans 20, 75, 76, 93, 118
  vegetable 117–18, 182
Feed Me Better campaign 64, 66
fibre 10, 12, **14**, 20, 38, **114**, 124,
      137
fish 10, 18, 36, 95, 112, 186
  oily 19, 20, 110, 151, 155, 175
  organic 70, 71
flavourings 92
flaxseed 170
flour 10, 12, 157, 165
folic acid *see* vitamin B9
food allergens 182–3
food allergies and intolerances **185–6**,
      188–93
food diary 122, 190
food intolerances 155
food pyramid 10, 20
food rejection 4
food-poisoning 46, 96, **178–9**
'friendly bacteria' 77, 87
friends and relatives 66
fromage frais 40, 87, 89
frozen foods 74, 102–3, 108
fructose 144
fruits 10, **14–16**, 20–21, 38, 39, 177
  citrus 182, 183
  dried 15, 40, 42, 49, **52**, 110, 145,
      146, 177–8
  drinks 100–101
  five portions of fruit and veg a day 14,
      15
  fresh 40, 42, 49, 146, 182
  frozen 102
  fruit bars 40
  laxative 169
  nutrients 107–8
  organic 69
  peeling 15, 42
  portion of 14–15
  scrubbing 108
frying 108, 144
fussy eaters 130, 132–3

gammalinoleic acid (GLA) 182
garlic 162, 164
genetically modified (GM) food 66–7, 69
glucose 171
gluten 137, 156–7, 159–61
glycaemic index (GI) **38**, 54, **83–4**, 125,
      137, 154, 173, 208
GMOs (genetically modified organisms)
      66
grains 10, 14, 18

ham 42, 43
heart disease 1, 3, 45, 75, 90, 146, 173
herbal medicine 194
herbs 208
high blood pressure 58, 90
HKD (Hyperkinetic Disorder) 153
honey 86, 164
hormones 69
hummus 146, 165
hunger 134
hyperglycaemia 172, 173, 175
hypoglycaemia 172, 173

ice cream 16
ice lollies 16
immune system 8, 14, 69, 77, 105, 117,
      162, 164
insulin 83, 171, 172, 175
inulin 81
iron 12, 14, **27**, 29, 117, 127, 135, 156
irritable bowel 77

Japanese food 96
juices 14, 15, 20, 39, 82, **97**, **100–101**,
      108, 138

labelling 74, 75, **84–5**, 92, 105–6, 122,
      157, 159, 188, 191
lactase 189
Lactobacilli 77, 80, 128, 182
lactose intolerance 77, 79–80, **189–92**
laxatives 169, 170
lazy eaters 130, 132–3
LDL (low-density lipoprotein) 75
legumes 18, **115**, 177
lentils 10, 14, 18, 36, 92, 177
listeria 178
lunch recipes 223–35

magnesium 19, **27**, 29, 79, 117, 151,
      208
margarines 76, 190

massage 169, 180
mayonnaise 45, 46
meat 10, 18, 36, 42, 70, 71, 112
melatonin 54, 101
messy eaters 106
milk 18, 19, 40, 53, **54**, **57**, 117, 144,
      183, 208
  drinks 101, 138, 208
  intolerance 87, **189–91**
  puddings 110
millet 10
minerals 10, 12, 21, **27**, 127, 145
  vegetarian children 117
  vitamin and mineral chart 28–9
monosodium glutamate (MSG) 95
MorDHA-mini 111
MorEPA 111
mueslis 10, 49, 110, 124, 133, 192

nausea 128
niacin *see* vitamin B3
noodles, buckwheat 10
nurseries 64, 66
nutrients 10, 14, 15, 20, 25, 28, 36, 38,
      102, **107–8**, 119, 135, 137
nuts 10, 18, 42, 45, 49, **115**, 146, 175,
      183, 186, 208
  allergies 188

oats 10, 14, 58, **159**
obesity/overweight 1, 12, 14, 18, 21, 97,
      135, **139–42**, **144–7**, 171
oestrogen 191
oils
  essential *see* essential oils
  flax (linseed) 19, 110, 182
  hemp 19, 20, 110, 118, 175, 182
  hydrogenated 75
  olive 75, 76, 110, 118, 144, 182
  omega 19, 110, 111, 175
  sunflower 75, 76
  vegetable 75, 144, 175
  walnut 19, 110
omega-3 fatty acids 110, 111, 125, 155,
      182
omega-6 fatty acids 110
omega-rich foods 19, 20, 110
organic food 69–71, 102, 106, 108
overall nutrition package (ONP) 40

packed lunches 40–43
parents' meals 199–207
pasta 20, 54, **58**, 138, 144–5, 157, 192

Acknowledgements

Huge thanks to all who have helped and encouraged, supporting me in endless ways. To everyone at Fresh Partners, especially Lisa Sullivan, Tessa Graham and Esther Philip-Clunis – you are the best and I couldn't have written this without you! For exceptional recipe testing and food styling, a big thank you to Sarah Tildesley and also to Sarah Schenker, you wise person. Huge thanks to Jools Oliver for her kind words.

Enormous thanks to Annie Lee and Lesley Levene for their editing and to Louise Plank for believing in *Yummy!* Thanks to everyone at Hodder. Thanks to Véronique and darling Cat for such gorgeous photos and Kate Halfpenny for rescuing me from appearing all in black. Thanks to Katy Limmer for hiding my 'bags'!

To my unbelievably supportive and loving friends for standing by me through thick and thin over the last tough year, especially Lesja and John, Caroline and David, Matt and Joan, Marcela, Nadine and William, Angelika, Katingo and Anthony, Martin and Cat. Thanks to Toby Doupe, Florence Richards, Harry Munro, William Perry-Parks, Sylvia and Dominic Richards, Yvan and Jéanri Burger, William and Daisy Tod and Zack Foroozan.

Finally, to my family – I love you loads – and to my Maya – we were meant to find each other, to love each other, you are my treasure, my smile.